Shine On! 2

Teacher's Book 2

Dear Teacher,

Thank you for choosing *Shine On!* Lucy, Jack, Megabyte, and I are happy to welcome you to our wonderful world. We're going to have so much fun learning English together. We give you everything you'll need to make your English class a fun and interesting place to be.

Together, we're going to sing songs, read stories, watch videos, do crafts, and even act and dance! It'll be fun for all your students and for you too.

Everyone can join in and have the chance to shine!

Let's get started!

From,

Uncle Alex

D1740496

Great Clarendon Street, Oxford, OX2 6DP, United Kingdom

Oxford University Press is a department of the University of Oxford. It furthers the University's objective of excellence in research, scholarship, and education by publishing worldwide. Oxford is a registered trade mark of Oxford University Press in the UK and in certain other countries

ISBN: 978 0 19 403374 9   Teacher's Book
ISBN: 978 0 19 400135 9   Class Audio
ISBN: 978 0 19 403373 2   Pack

Printed in China

This book is printed on paper from certified and well-managed sources

ACKNOWLEDGEMENTS

Back cover photograph: Oxford University Press building/David Fisher

Cover illustration and character artwork by: Linda Cavallini/Advocate Art.

Song actions illustrations by: Mark Ruffle.

Teacher's Resource Pack flashcards 2
Illustrations by: Linda Cavallini/Advocate Art; Giovanni Abielle/The Organisation; Alida Massari/Advocate Art; Daniela Dogliani/Beehive Illustration; Gail Armstrong/Illustrationweb; Luke Flowers/Bright Agency; Daniel Limon/Beehive Illustration; Fiona Rose; Andy Elkerton/Sylvie Poggio.

Teacher's Resource Pack posters 1–3
Illustrations by: Gergana Hristova/Beehive Illustration (My Body, Numbers/ Colors); Rob McClurkan/The Bright Agency (The Alphabet).

Photos from: Oxford University Press RF (My Body/In the Classroom).

The publishers advise that project work involving cutting and sticking should be carried out under the supervision of an adult.

Contents

Scope and sequence

Unit	Vocabulary	Grammar	CLIL	Value
Starter Unit Welcome Back!	one, two, three, four, five, six, seven, eight, nine, ten, book, backpack, toys, family members, the alphabet; Is it D? Hello, I'm ...	I'm (sad/happy). Look! New neighbors. Welcome! Nice to meet you! And you! Who's that?	–	–
1 Happy Birthday!	balloon, clown, candles, present, card, cake, robot, basketball, puzzle, car, sides, the same, different; How old are you? I'm eight. Me, too! Look!	There's a (present)! There are (five) cards.	Math	We make new friends.
2 What Weather!	stormy, snowy, windy, cloudy, rainy, sunny, wet, dry, cold, hot, today; I don't understand! Let's check.	What's the weather like (today)? It's (rainy).	Geography	We share our things.
Culture 1 Birthday Parties	decorations, party games, pool, sing, party items			
3 My Clothes!	jacket, socks, hat, pants, boots, shoes, T-shirt, sweater, shorts, skirt, wool, cotton, sheep, plant; How about a sweater? Thank you. I'm (hot/cold).	Take off your (jacket)! Put on your (hat)! It's (hot)!	Science	We take care of our clothes.

Unit	Vocabulary	Grammar	CLIL	Value
4 Home, Sweet Home	bedroom, bathroom, living room, dining room, kitchen, yard, bed, sofa, bathtub, table, old, new; I'm scared! Don't worry.	Where's (Uncle Alex)? (He)'s in the (yard). (She)'s in the kitchen.	History	We clean up after craft.
Culture 2 Vacation!	hotel, boat, motor home, tent, clothes			
5 At the Beach	swim, dive, sing, climb, cook, run, dance, jump, fly, catch, safe, dangerous, lifeguard, sign, flag; Oh no! Quick!	I can (swim)! I can't (cook).	Social studies	We follow the rules.
6 Animal Fun!	horse, cow, goat, pig, chicken, duck, bat, squirrel, frog, fox, night time, day time, awake, asleep; What's your favorite animal? A horse!	(A duck) can swim. Can (a cow) swim? Yes, it can. Can it fly? No, it can't!	Science	We are good losers.
Culture 3 Visitors In My Yard	snail, rabbit, chipmunk, butterfly			

Unit	Vocabulary	Grammar	CLIL	Value
7 Picnic Time!	chicken, rice, pasta, milk, salad, cheese, ice cream, fries, water, candy, grass, store; What's wrong? I feel sick!	I like (salad)! I don't like (cheese).	Science	We choose healthy food.
8 Numbers Everywhere!	eleven, twelve, thirteen, fourteen, fifteen, sixteen, seventeen, eighteen, nineteen, twenty, trampoline, hula hoop, jump rope, skateboard, block, graph, students; You can do it!	I have (eleven) (shoes)! I don't have (eleven) (shoes). How many … ?	Math	We work together.
Culture 4 Lunch at School	school lunch, banana, sandwich, packed lunch			
Mother's Day	hug, cookies, flowers, breakfast			
Halloween	skeleton, ghost, mask, pumpkin			

For more information about planning your classes, go to the *Shine On!* Teacher's website:

www.oup.com/elt/teacher/shineon

About *Shine On!*

Welcome to **Shine On!** – a great new six-level course for elementary students in grades 1–6.

This bright, attractive course will make all your students look forward to their English class! With lots of funny stories, catchy songs, bright, colorful artwork, and interesting activities, **Shine On!** makes English class lots of fun!

The course has a clear and simple unit structure and lots of support, making it easy for you to teach from. Students have a bright, full-color *Student Book*, which contains everything they learn in class as well as *Extra Practice* pages—making it easy and fun for them to learn from!

Each unit gives students key building blocks of vocabulary and grammar, clearly presented and practiced through a variety of fun activities, including a unit story.

Students will love to watch the animated versions of the stories (levels 1–3) and songs. The animations are an enjoyable way for them to engage with English without even realizing it! They will make English lessons fun and entertaining.

Alongside lively stories and songs, **Shine On!** provides fascinating culture and holiday lessons and clear, positive values tasks. Regular *CLIL* lessons in each unit bring other subjects into the English classroom, so English lessons are always varied and interesting.

Flexibility

Each level of **Shine On!** is designed to be completed in one school year for teachers teaching between 1–3 lessons of English a week.

In addition to the *Student Book*, **Shine On!** provides a flexible package of teaching materials to make the course thoroughly adaptable to your classroom and your needs.

Student Book lessons can be supplemented in homework time, or additional classroom sessions with *worksheets*, creative craft projects, and varied practice exercises to suit different groups and learners.

The teacher's notes provide ideas for extending or shortening activities, and lots of great suggestions for lively activities and games to make the lessons as flexible and fun

as possible. The *Teacher's Resource Pack* has flashcards and posters to use in class and for playing games.

In addition to the *Teacher's Resource Pack*, the course is supported with extensive digital resources, such as practice activities on the student's website, plus animated stories (levels 1–3), songs, and games to keep the students' motivation high.

Mixed ability and SEN

Shine On! is an inclusive course that recognizes that no two classes or students are the same, and that every student should have a chance to shine.

Notes in the *Teacher's Books* provide lots of helpful suggestions for mixed-ability classes.

Extra *worksheets* at three different levels mean that every student can be given extra practice at a level that allows him or her to progress and learn confidently at his or her own pace.

The tests are supplied at two levels to make sure all students can be assessed and achieve at an appropriate level.

Culture

Learning about the culture of another country is an important part of modern language learning. Culture topics can be fun and quirky, helping students to realize that variety and difference are a key part of international citizenship. They can also show the everyday life of children in the USA, helping students to see that we are not that different after all!

Shine On! has bright, lively culture lessons with lots of photos and activities after every two units in the *Student Book*, and each level features two fun holiday lessons for use at different times of the year.

Values

Values are an important part of **Shine On!** Values help students to work together and interact in a positive way in the classroom. By paying attention to their values lessons, students learn important social skills that are useful in the English classroom and beyond.

Values link to the themes and ideas of the Citizenship curriculum and help students to see how they can contribute in all aspects of their school life.

In levels 1–3, they appear in different places in the unit, always linked to the classroom activities that students are doing. They are clear and demonstrable, allowing students to think about and adapt their behavior, and see a positive result. Students are rewarded with attractive, colorful stickers, which they can stick in their books to show their achievement.

In levels 4–6, values are broadened to help students see themselves as a positive part of the wider community. The values activities encourage them to take responsibility for their actions and think about how their behavior may affect the world around them.

The teacher's notes help teachers to establish a positive values routine and make the most of this important part of students' learning and development.

21st Century Skills

Shine On! has 21st Century Skills integrated at all levels, so students will cover all of the skills appropriate at elementary level. 21st Century Skills are present in a variety of activity types throughout the course. Students are encouraged to think critically and to problem-solve with puzzle-style activity types. Creativity and communication are at the heart of the craft activities provided in every unit.

CLIL

Shine On! has a fully supported *CLIL* syllabus running throughout the course, bringing topics from other subject areas into the English classroom.

There is a fascinating *CLIL* lesson in every unit with full procedural notes in the *Teacher's Book* offering support and extra activities to get the most out of this rich, diverse material.

CLIL worksheets on the teacher's website provide interactive follow-up activities to the *CLIL* lesson in the *Student Book*, to make sure students understand the topic and can practice talking about it in English with their friends.

Stories

The course is presented by a group of fun, friendly characters who accompany your students through their lessons.

There is a lively cartoon story in every unit, featuring a funny new adventure for the course characters.

The stories are an important motivational part of the course. They're bright and lively and give students a chance to practice English with confidence while having lots of fun.

Students can listen to the stories while they read with the fun sound effects that bring the stories to life on the *Class Audio CDs*. There are also dynamic animated versions of the stories for levels 1–3. These can be used for review,

for consolidation, or simply for entertainment in class or at home!

Students will enjoy acting out the stories and bringing them to life themselves in the classroom.

Songs

Each unit has a catchy new song for students to sing and enjoy. The songs are modern and lively and will appeal to 21st century students whose taste in music is increasingly sophisticated.

There are colorful animated versions of the songs, too. These animations bring the songs to life and encourage the students to sing along. All the songs have fun actions to get them up and moving and excited about learning English.

Songs are a great way of reinforcing language, and students will love to sing them and do the actions. They will be developing their confidence and fluency while having lots of fun.

The actions are illustrated for your reference in the back of the *Teacher's Book* and there are ideas for using the songs in the classroom in the teacher's notes.

Supported writing

Writing in **Shine On!** is fully supported and always practiced through fun and engaging activities. Students are introduced to independent writing gradually throughout the course, building up from letter and word level in the lower levels to supported text production by the end of Level 6.

As the levels progress, students are encouraged to write more, but always in a fun, motivating context with plenty of support.

Levels 4–6 provide students with the opportunity to write a variety of text types, giving them plenty of chances to express their ideas. Developing writing in this way forms a good foundation for more challenging material that they will encounter in high school.

Evaluation

With fun artwork and clear mixed-ability support, **Shine On!** tests are another positive, motivating part of students' learning. The tests are provided at two levels for use in mixed-ability classes. Students can feel good about testing because the tests at two levels allow every student to take a test that is suitable to their own learning stage.

Shine On! tests allow you to evaluate the students' overall progress, but also help them to see how much they have learned. The tests follow the **Shine On!** controlled reading and writing progression, so that students are always being tested at the appropriate level, and the level of challenge progresses appropriately through the year.

All the unit and end-of-year tests are also supplied at two levels. The yellow tests are for students who are achieving at the expected level for their age and class. The blue tests have been pitched at a slightly lower level for students who are not yet at the required level. The *Teacher's Resource CD-ROM* contains full answer keys as well as notes and guidance for administering the tests.

Levels 1 to 3 context and characters

Lucy and Jack are friends and neighbors who are accompanied on their adventures by Megabyte, Lucy's pet robotic dog. Megabyte was invented and created by Lucy's Uncle Alex, who is a very clever scientist. At the beginning of Level 1, we see Lucy and Jack meet for the first time and then they meet Megabyte. In each unit story in levels 1–3, the children have a fresh adventure, meet new friends and learn something new. In levels 2 and 3 they make new friends who have moved into their neighborhood called Ellie and Sam.

Megabyte guides Lucy, Jack, and the children using *Shine On!* in their learning. He presents new vocabulary and is the main protagonist in the unit stories, where he is often involved in comic mishaps. Each unit has a different theme, which is explored in the story and consolidated in the real-world context of the *CLIL* lesson.

Lucy, Jack, and their friends are a diverse and creative group who reflect the diverse interests and skills of real children, so there is something for every student to relate to and join in with.

Listening and speaking

Every level of *Shine On!* is fully supported with audio material on *Class Audio CDs* and in the *Oxford CPT* (*Classroom Presentation Tool*) package. Listening is a key part of the course for language presentation and for students' confidence with the spoken language.

The creative craft projects allow an opportunity for speaking practice in a fun, communicative context. Bright, attractive craft projects can be used as classroom displays, or kept as part of a portfolio of students' achievements.

Reading and writing

Reading and writing expectations build up gradually throughout the course, allowing students to advance at a pace that matches their abilities and confidence.

As the course progresses, students will be exposed to a range of exciting text types and stories suitable to their age and interests. Independent reading increases gradually throughout the levels and is always supported by vocabulary preparation, audio support and bright, colorful artwork, and photographs.

The unit stories are fun cartoon stories with friendly, familiar characters whose adventures students will follow throughout the year.

The *CLIL* lessons allow for a more factual style of reading text, bringing other interesting areas of the curriculum into the English classroom, and allow students to draw on their existing knowledge.

In Levels 4–6, the flexible and motivating context of the story setting allows for a wide variety of interesting text types to be explored and enjoyed.

Students also start to build towards more independent writing, as a foundation for tasks they will encounter in high school. Development is still carefully staged and controlled however, so that students will feel supported and confident, as well as challenged to improve.

Lucy

Jack

Megabyte

Component overview

Student Book & Extra Practice

Teacher's Book

Workbook

Class Audio CDs

Teacher's Resource Pack

Megabyte Puppet

Posters

Student Book & Extra Practice

- A Starter Unit with the first episode of the cartoon story, introducing the level characters and bringing students into their world.
- Eight themed units to present and practice the core syllabus, including stories, songs, and cross-curricular content.
- Two *Extra Practice* pages to extend the main unit content.
- Four *Culture* topics
- Two *Holidays* lessons with songs and a craft
- Classroom language reference
- Picture Dictionary

Workbook

- 64 pages of fun practice material
- Consolidation of your students' grammatical understanding
- Constant recycling of vocabulary throughout
- Regular review sections
- *Holidays* and *Culture* pages

Teacher's Book

- Introduction with overview of the course and methodology
- Tour of a unit
- *How to …* section with support notes for managing the English class
- *SEN* section with practical tips and ideas for creating an inclusive classroom
- Tips for using *Graded Readers*
- Ideas Bank with suggestions for flashcard games and optional activities
- Carefully staged procedural notes with additional activities and mixed-ability notes
- Audio transcripts
- Reproduced *Student Book* pages with full answer keys
- Illustrated actions for the **Shine On!** song
- Wordlist
- Photocopiable self-evaluation tables for each unit

Class Audio CDs

- Recordings for all listening activities, stories, songs, and tests
- Audio support for all new language

Teacher's Resource Pack

Megabyte Puppet

Flashcards

- Flashcard for each new vocabulary item

Storycards – Level 1 only

- Each story is presented on a series of storycards.
- Each card contains questions for the teacher to engage students with the story artwork.
- Full audio transcript on the reverse

Posters

The Alphabet, Numbers, Colors, My Body

Digital Resources

Shine On! Student Website

www.oup.com/elt/shineon

- **Shine On!** Online Play games for practicing the language learned in class
- Class Audio files
- Interactive Picture Dictionary
- Song animations
- Story animations (levels 1–3)
- Downloadable activities to do at home
- Section for parents

Oxford Classroom Presentation Tool (CPT)

Presentation and practice material for interactive whiteboards and projectors. Including:

- Song animations
- Story animations
- Class audio

Teacher's Resource CD-ROM

- Tests at two levels for each unit with teacher's notes, answer keys, and audio
- *Worksheets for Student Book* lessons
  - *Vocabulary and Grammar worksheets* at three levels: *Reinforcement*, *Practice*, and *Extension*
  - *Story worksheets*
  - *CLIL worksheets* to follow up cross-curricular lessons
  - *Craft worksheets* for Student Book craft projects

Shine On! Teacher's Website

www.oup.com/elt/teacher/shineon

- Syllabus planning documents
- *Classroom language* support with audio
- Teacher training videos

Shine On! Levels 4–6

- *Student Book & Extra Practice*
  - Eight units
  - Four *Culture* lessons
  - Two *Holidays* lessons
  - Two *Extra Practice* pages per unit
  - Wordlist
  - A grammar reference
  - Classroom language reference
  - *Our Values* page
  - Mystery code page
- *Teacher's Resource Pack*
  - Flashcards
  - Nine posters: one map of English-speaking countries and eight *CLIL* posters
- Teacher's Book with Class Audio
- Classroom Presentation Tool (CPT) with song animations
- Student website
- Teacher's website

Digital Resources

Oxford Classroom
Presentation Tool (CPT)

Teacher's Resource CD-ROM

Student Website

Tour of a unit

Lesson 1

Each unit opens with a bright, colorful artwork that presents the main vocabulary set and sets up the unit theme. New vocabulary is shown in the dynamic context of an artwork scene that has been projected from Megabyte's collar (Units 1 to 8). The style of artwork changes in each unit, to keep each unit opener fresh and engaging, and grab students' attention.

Six new words. New vocabulary presentation with clear audio support.

Sticker activity for students to engage with the new vocabulary.

A chant gets students to practice the new vocabulary in a fun and lively way.

Students listen and find the items in the artwork scene.

In each unit, Lucy or Jack show an item of vocabulary from a previous unit that students have to find in the main illustration.

Student Book

- *Lesson 1* presents the first vocabulary set. *Teacher's Book* lesson notes provide ideas for an interactive lead-in to the lesson using the Megabyte puppet, featuring flashcard presentation and practice games.
- Language presentation is thoroughly supported with audio on the *CPT* or on the *Class Audio CDs*.
- Different learning styles are catered for through a variety of activity types

- The *Teacher's Book* lesson notes provide alternative procedure and differentiated tasks to accommodate different groups of learners, including mixed ability and *SEN*.

Extra

- Vocabulary worksheets for additional practice of the new vocabulary are available at three levels of difficulty.

Lesson 2

The characters Jack and Lucy present the grammar structure for the unit and students are able to practice the new structure in the context of a song. There is a personalization activity so students have the chance to express the new vocabulary for themselves.

> *Jack and Lucy present the new grammar with audio support.*

> *A practice activity with attractive illustrations.*

> *Each unit has a catchy unit song in a modern pop music style. Students will enjoy singing along, while building confidence and fluency. Fun animations are also available.*

> *A craft activity allows students to express themselves creatively while thinking about the new language learned.*

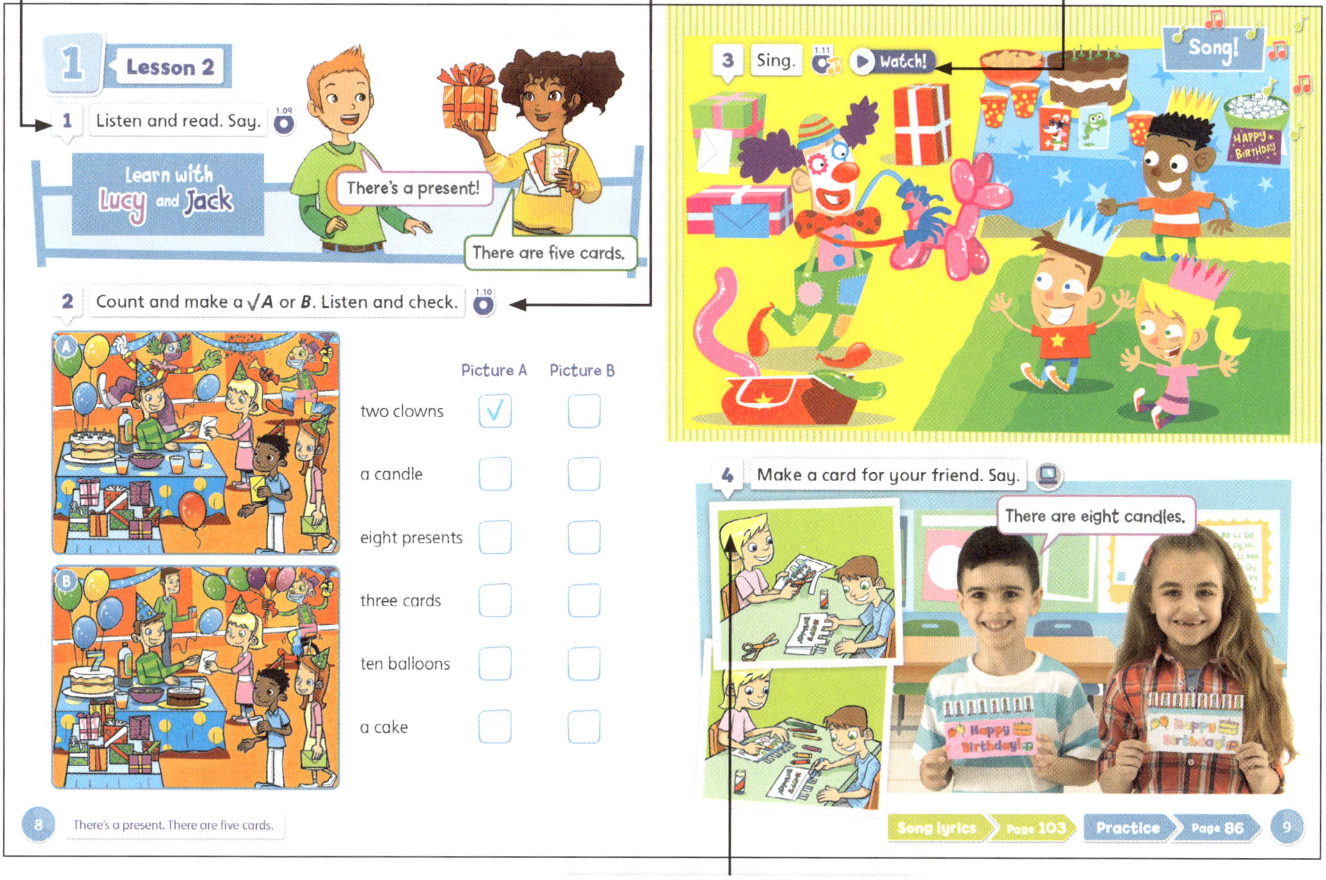

Student Book

- The new grammar structure presentation is supported with audio either on the *CPT* or *Class Audio CDs*.

- The new grammar structure is practiced with review vocabulary from *Lesson 1*. Regular recycling of known language consolidates students' learning and boosts their confidence.

- The unit songs feature the grammar and vocabulary and consolidate the new language. The *Teacher's Book* has suggestions for song actions.

- The songs are also a great way to end lessons throughout the course.

- See the *How to …* section on page 26 for lots of ideas about using songs in the classroom.

- Students learn the grammar in the familiar setting of Jack and Lucy's world, but always have opportunities to personalize and link it to their own experience in the craft activity. The craft templates are available on the *Teacher's Resource CD-ROM*.

- See the *How to …* section on page 26 for ideas about how to manage craft activities.

> **Follow-up practice activity in the Extra Practice section.**

Lesson 2 Extra Practice

Extra

- *Extra Practice* page provides controlled practice of the vocabulary and grammar inputs for each unit.

- Songs animations are on the *CPT* and also on the student's website.

Lesson 3

The story features Jack, Lucy, and Megabyte who have adventures and mishaps at home and in their community. The story is supported by fun audio recordings with sound effects, and lively acting.

Values are presented by Jack and Lucy, so that they are friendly and supportive – the students and characters learn and develop together. The Values activity can appear in a different lesson in each unit and picks up on important themes of citizenship, consideration for others and also personal development and self-confidence.

The new vocabulary is clearly presented with illustrations and audio. The students can look back at the story and use the context to support their understanding.

A fun, interactive activity allows students to practice the new vocabulary through a puzzle activity.

Students watch the story animation or listen to the recording.

Students bring the story to life by acting it out!

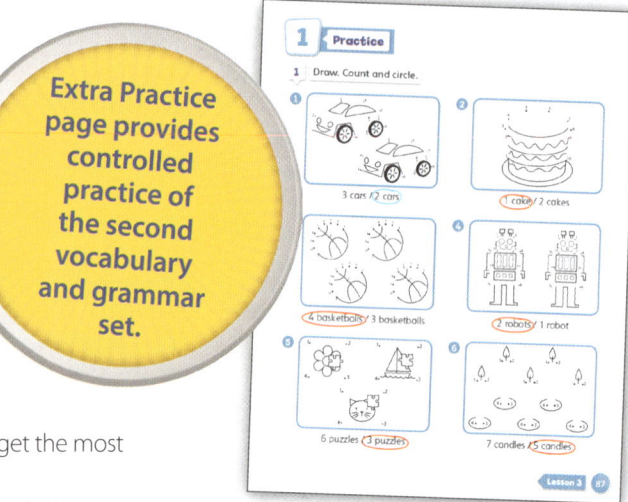

Everyday English phrases are pulled out of the story and supported on the audio for students to practice.

The Values sticker activity (Our Values) encourages students to engage with the value in order to earn the sticker.

Student Book

- The story is supported with a recording on the *Class Audio CDs*.
- Students are exposed to examples of the new vocabulary in the clear context of the story, then they go on to study and practice the form.
- Students are encouraged to act the story out, providing a fun activity for all students regardless of their level of language competence.
- The *Everyday English* phrases are first seen in the context of the story. Students have the opportunity to participate in short dialogs to practice this useful language.
- The *Teacher's Book* lesson notes provide alternative procedure and differentiated tasks to accommodate different groups, including mixed ability and *SEN*.

Extra

- *Story worksheets* allow students to engage with the characters and get the most out of the stories.
- *Vocabulary and Grammar worksheet* provides practice of the new vocabulary together with the unit grammar topic at three levels.

Extra Practice page provides controlled practice of the second vocabulary and grammar set.

Lesson 3 Extra Practice

Lesson 4

The *CLIL* lesson links in with the unit theme, and brings a fascinating real-world dimension to the topic.

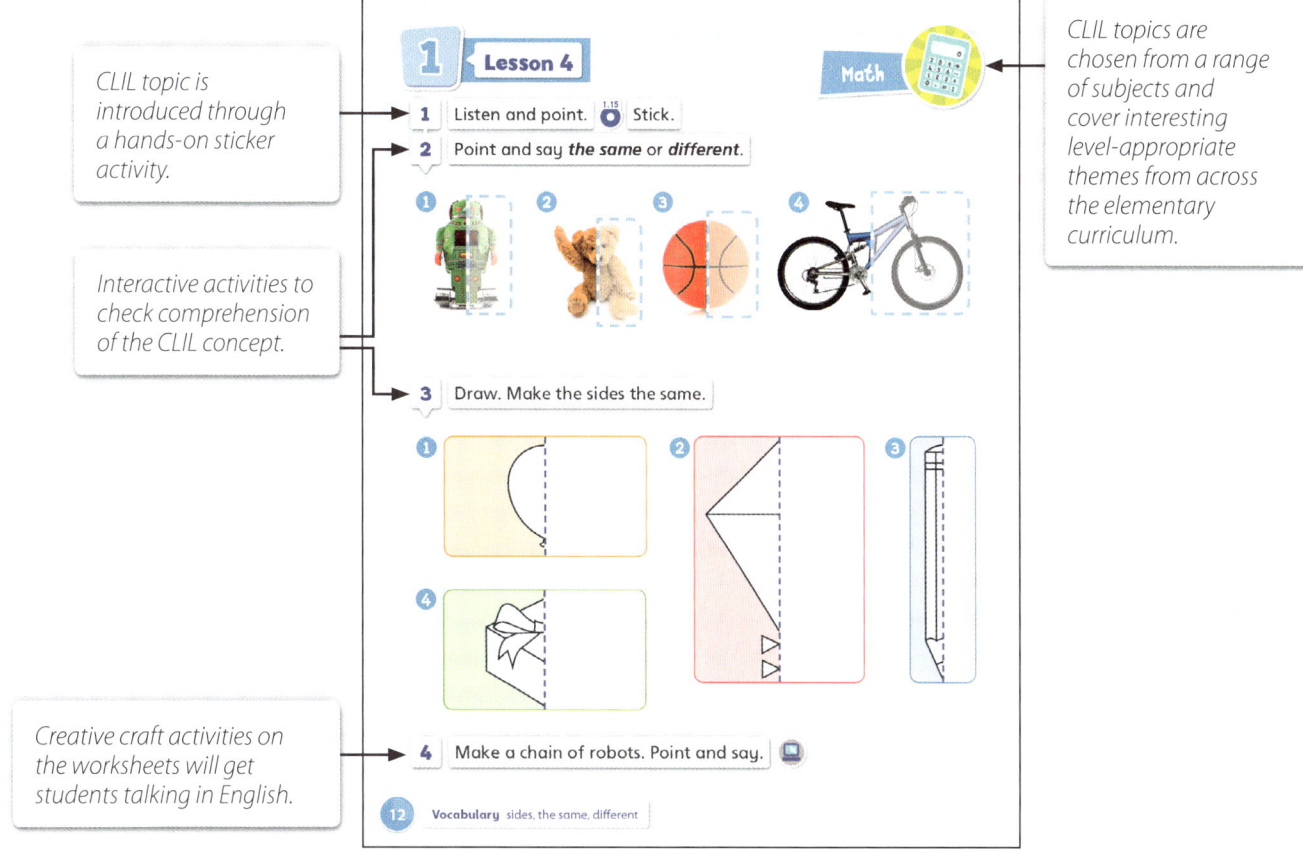

CLIL topic is introduced through a hands-on sticker activity.

Interactive activities to check comprehension of the CLIL concept.

Creative craft activities on the worksheets will get students talking in English.

CLIL topics are chosen from a range of subjects and cover interesting level-appropriate themes from across the elementary curriculum.

Student Book

- The *Teacher's Book* lesson notes provide ideas for an interactive lead-in to the lesson, featuring vocabulary review and practice games.
- Controlled new vocabulary input is clearly supported with artwork and through a sticker activity.
- The *CLIL* activity is supported through audio on *CPT* or the *Class Audio CDs*.
- The fun worksheet provides a supported follow-up activity that allows students to demonstrate their understanding of the *CLIL* concept and use the unit and review language to express or explore it.
- The values syllabus is supported by procedural notes in the *Teacher's Book* lesson notes, helping students to discuss and respond to the ideas and relate them to their own lives.
- The *Teacher's Book* lesson notes provide alternative procedure and differentiated tasks to accommodate different groups of learners, including mixed ability and *SEN*.

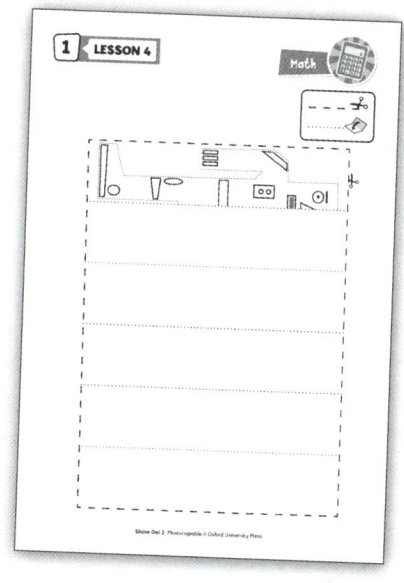

Lesson 4 Worksheet

Extra

- *CLIL worksheets* provide a structured follow-up activity to the *Student Book* lesson, consolidating the *CLIL* concept and building up to a productive outcome.

Review

Each unit ends with a review lesson, giving students the opportunity to bring together the vocabulary and grammar points they have learned in a series of engaging activities.

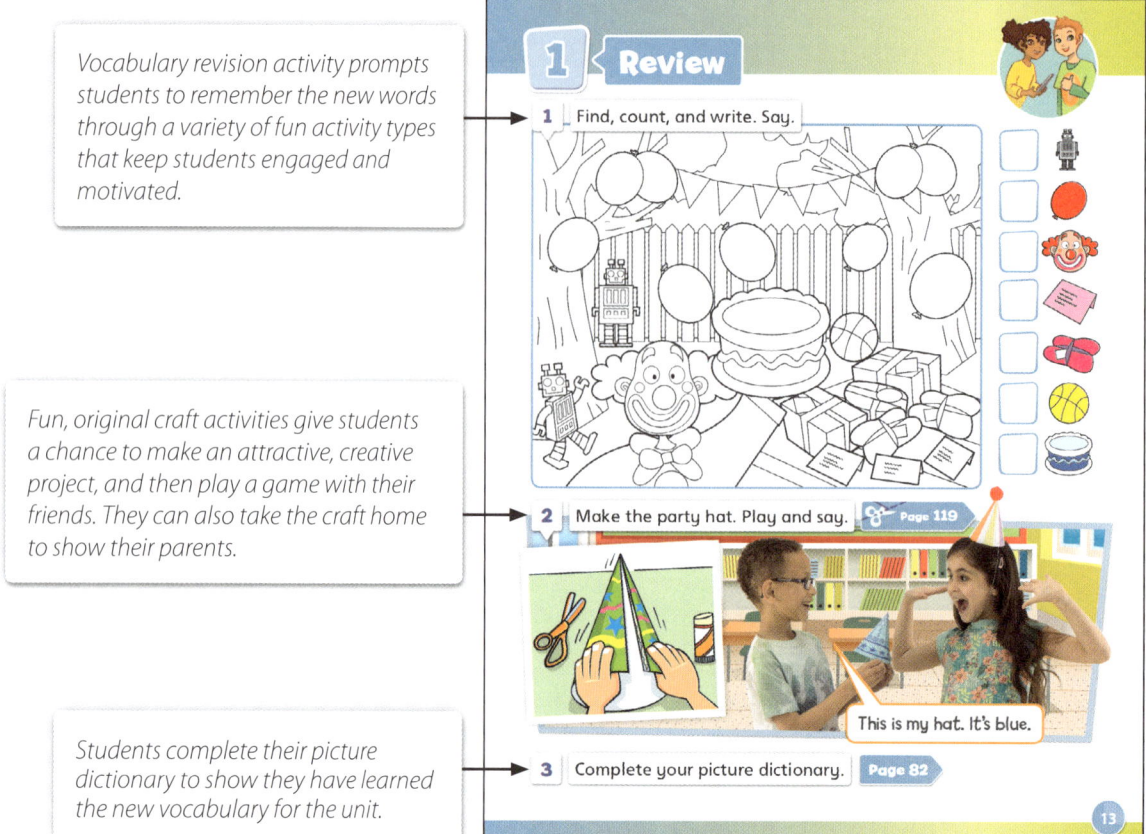

Vocabulary revision activity prompts students to remember the new words through a variety of fun activity types that keep students engaged and motivated.

Fun, original craft activities give students a chance to make an attractive, creative project, and then play a game with their friends. They can also take the craft home to show their parents.

Students complete their picture dictionary to show they have learned the new vocabulary for the unit.

Student Book

- The *Teacher's Book* lesson notes provide ideas for an interactive lead-in to the lesson, featuring vocabulary review and practice games.
- The craft activity leads to a game to promote oral practice of the language learned. The craft templates are available on the *Teacher's Resource CD-ROM*.
- Completion of the Picture Dictionary provides students with the opportunity to acknowledge the new language learned in the course of the unit.
- The *Teacher's Book* lesson notes provide alternative procedures and differentiated tasks to accommodate different groups of learners.

Picture Dictionary

Extra

- *Unit Tests* available on the *Teacher's Resource CD-ROM* at two levels for mixed-ability classes.

Culture

After every two units there is a bright, colorful culture spread presenting an aspect of US culture and life.

New vocabulary presentation supported by audio and photos.

Attractive photos to help students connect to the topic.

Comprehension activities to check students' understanding.

Attractive, fun craft projects promote creativity.

Student Book

- The *Teacher's Book* lesson notes provide ideas for an interactive lead-in to the lesson, featuring vocabulary review activities and fun warmers and fillers.
- All texts are supported by audio and bright, attractive photos.
- Culture notes in the *Teacher's Book* provide further information about the topic in the lesson.
- The project work is supported in the *Teacher's Book* with procedural notes and guidance.

Holidays

Each level has two *Holidays* lessons to use through the year.

New vocabulary presentation supported by audio and photos.

Puzzles and games for a great holiday lesson.

Traditional songs and poems for students to sing and chant.

Attractive photos to help students connect to the topic.

Creative craft projects to take home and share with the family.

Student Book

- All *Holidays* lessons are supported by audio and bright, attractive photos.
- The project work is supported in the *Teacher's Book* with notes.
- The craft templates are available on the *Teacher's Resource CD-ROM*.

Holidays Worksheet

Digital components

 Shine On! **Classroom Presentation Tool**

Deliver heads-up lessons with the Classroom Presentation Tool.

Engage your students in your blended learning classroom with digital features that can be used on your tablet or computer and connected to an interactive whiteboard or projector.

Play audio and video at the touch of a button. Highlight and zoom can be used to focus students' attention. These easy-to-use tools mean lessons run smoothly.

Take your Classroom Presentation Tool with you, and plan your lessons online or offline, across your devices. Save your weblinks and notes directly on the page – all with one account.

Zoom in to focus your students' attention on a single activity.

Play audio and video at the touch of a button.

Speed up or slow down the audio speed to tailor lessons to your students' listening level.

Save your weblinks and other notes for quick access while teaching. Use across devices using one account so that you can plan your lessons wherever you are.

Work on pronunciation in class: record your students speaking, and compare their voices to the course audio.

Websites

For the Teacher

Shine On! teacher's website

www.oup.com/elt/teacher/shineon

The teacher's website contains everything you need to prepare your lessons:

- *Worksheets* for *Student Book* lessons
- Syllabus planning documents
- *Classroom language* support with audio
- Teacher training videos

For the Student

Shine On! student's website

www.oup.com/elt/shineon

The student's website allows students to practice English in a fun and inclusive environment. They will enjoy accessing the material in class or at home with their parents.

The student's website contains:

- **Shine On!** *Online Play* games for practicing the language learned in class.
- *Class Audio CDs* files.
- Interactive *Picture Dictionary*
- Song animations
- Story animations (Levels 1–3)
- Downloadable activities to do at home, e.g. greeting cards, door hangers
- Section for parents

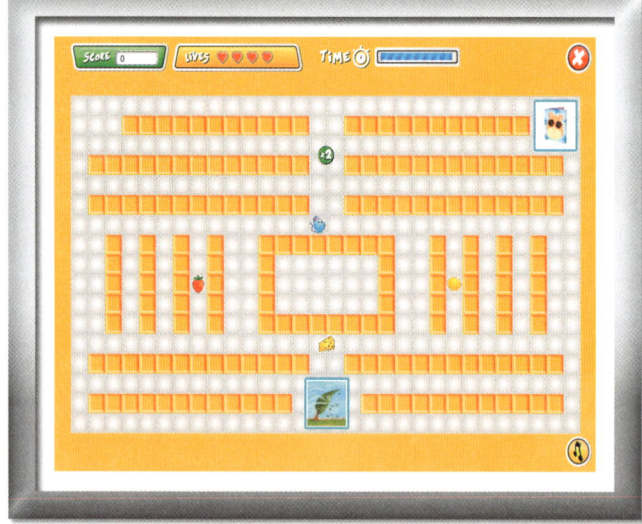

Using Graded Readers with *Shine On!*

Using *Graded Readers* in the Elementary Classroom is an effective way to engage students of all abilities and learning needs. By motivating students to read for pleasure in your English class, you give them the opportunity to learn without the fear of failure. Each student can choose a reader they are interested in and at a level that is appropriate for them. *Graded Readers* are available at a number of different levels and across a broad range of topics, both fiction and non-fiction, so each student will be able to find a book suitable for them.

Classic Tales

Level 1

Level 2

Oxford Read and Imagine

Starter

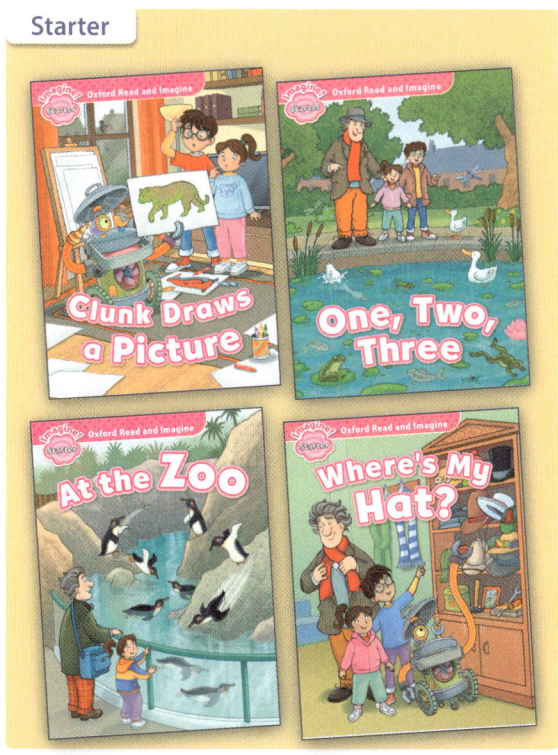

Beginner

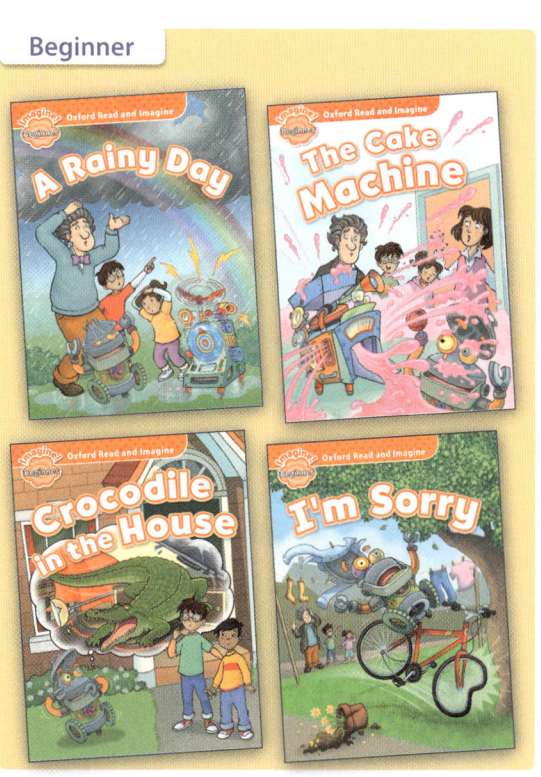

Oxford Read and Discover and CLIL

Oxford Read and Discover provides support for *CLIL* lessons that can be thematically linked to the *Student Book CLIL* lessons or other cross-curricular subjects. Each book contains photos to spark students' interest in the topic and bring the subject matter to life. In addition, there are interesting diagrams, maps, and charts, which encourage critical thinking and support new *CLIL* vocabulary.

Each *Oxford Read and Discover* book contains:

- Audio with the text read in both British and American English
- Language reinforcement activities
- Activities for developing critical thinking skills
- A project activity to complete in class

For a full list of the *Oxford Read and Discover* titles, please visit: www.oup.com/elt

Professional Development

A range of professional development titles to accompany *Shine On!*

Into the Classroom

Short, practical guides to understanding and implementing new developments in teaching. Each guide focuses on a new development in teaching with ideas to help you introduce it into your classroom.

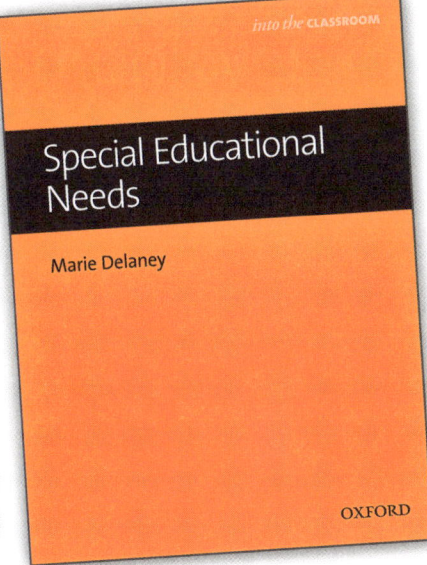

OXFORD TEACHERS' ACADEMY

Teaching English to
young learners
Online professional development

Who is it for?

Teaching English to Young Learners is a course suitable for teachers with an initial teaching qualification and some teaching experience. Non-native speakers are recommended to have a minimum B2 level on the CEFR.

The course aims to enhance the knowledge and skills needed to teach English to young learners. It takes approximately 30 hours to complete and includes input on key concepts and approaches, video, animation and audio clips, discussions, practical tasks, opportunities for reflection, suggestions for further study, and ideas to try out in the classroom.

Session topics and aims

Session 1: How children learn
- To review key learning theories and their application.
- To compare how children of different ages learn.
- To analyse classroom activities and lesson plans in relation to the theories and principles covered in the session.

Session 2: Learning to learn: 21st Century Skills
- To examine the skills children need to be able to learn effectively.
- To identify what the key 21st Century Skills are.
- To explore tools and activities that prepare children for lifelong learning in the 21st century.

Session 3: Classroom management
- To explore ways of managing interaction in the classroom.
- To examine strategies and practical ideas for working with large or mixed-ability classes.
- To identify ways of using the learners' first language (L1) as a resource.

Session 4: Developing listening and speaking skills
- To explore the principles of teaching and learning listening and speaking skills.
- To analyse the sub-skills involved in listening and speaking.
- To evaluate a range of activities, including storytelling, for teaching listening and speaking.

Session 5: Literacy
- To examine the nature and use of literacy in the 21st century.
- To explore how literacy can be taught to younger and older young learners.
- To evaluate a range of practical activities and assess their suitability in helping children to become literate.

Session 6: Grammar and vocabulary
- To review current theories on teaching and learning grammar and vocabulary.
- To identify the aims of a range of grammar and vocabulary activities.
- To examine a range of practical activities and assess their suitability for young learners.

Session 7: Resources evaluation and lesson planning
- To evaluate the suitability of different resources in a specific teaching context.
- To examine the benefits of good practice in lesson planning.
- To consider the range of resources available for a 'teacher's toolbox'.

Session 8: Feedback, evaluation, and assessment
- To examine the importance of assessment in learning.
- To compare different assessment methods.
- To understand how to use appropriate classroom assessment tasks.

Course characteristics

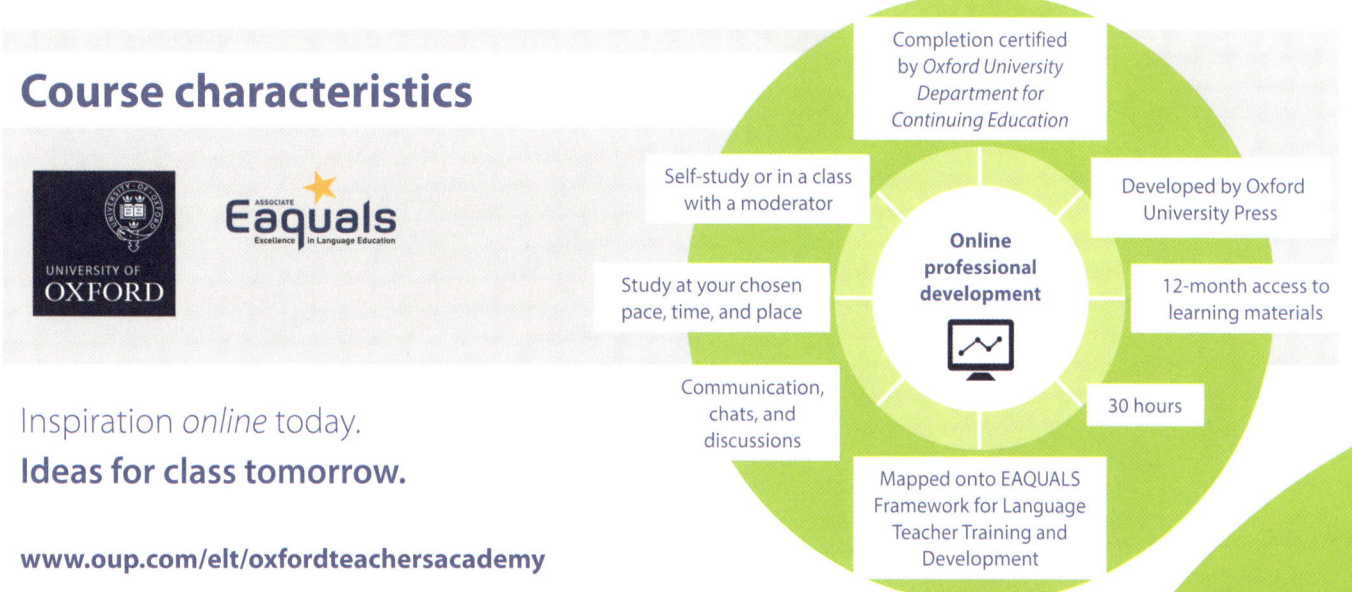

Inspiration *online* today.
Ideas for class tomorrow.

www.oup.com/elt/oxfordteachersacademy

Completion certified by *Oxford University Department for Continuing Education*

Self-study or in a class with a moderator

Developed by Oxford University Press

Study at your chosen pace, time, and place

Online professional development

12-month access to learning materials

Communication, chats, and discussions

30 hours

Mapped onto EAQUALS Framework for Language Teacher Training and Development

How to ...

Teaching young learners English is an incredibly rewarding job. Their youth means they are open to learning and able to learn language at a much quicker rate than older students. Their transformation into English speakers is clear from lesson to lesson, and year to year. In order to engage your class, help them learn effectively and get the most out of your English lessons with **Shine On!**, you might like to incorporate some of the following ideas.

1 Managing your classroom

Organization is key to a free-flowing lesson and well-managed classroom. The following ideas will help you to create a fun, positive and focused learning environment for your students. You will be able to prepare for the class and manage your young learners during it.

1.1 How to organize my classroom and furniture

Consider how you will organize the physical space in your classroom:

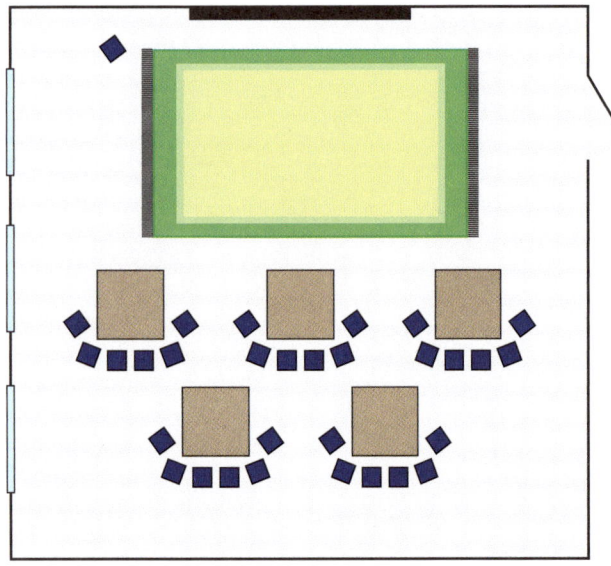

- Young learners work best in pairs and groups. They should be seated at tables where their materials, such as pencils, colored pens, books, paper, paints, etc. can be spread out and reached easily by all the students. If possible, seat the class in groups of four to six students.
- Make sure every student can see the board and that there is space for you to walk around the room between desks and chairs.
- Provide a space where students can sit at the front of the class by the board for activities such as *Flashcard* games and story time.

Think about where you will stand or sit when you do activities:

- Stand directly in the center at the front of the class when you want to focus students' attention on you: to stop, start or explain an activity. This also works well if students start to lose focus on an activity.
- Use the board to set up and explain activities, and stand to the left or right of it when you are showing students what you want them to do. Make sure you don't obscure the board for any of them.
- Walk around the class and kneel next to students to help them when they are completing a task. They will feel more relaxed and able to respond to you from this position rather than you standing above them.
- Sit down when you read stories, so students feel they are on an equal level with you.

If you have a class with a lot of students, but you don't have much space and you aren't able to move the furniture in your classroom, try to make the most of the space you have.

Classroom organization

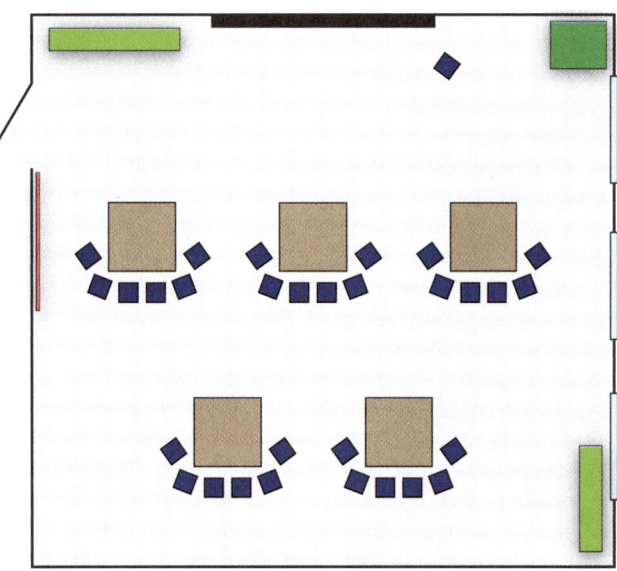

- Ensure students are seated looking at the board for all presentations, stories, and games.
- Ask students to work with the person next to them, sharing colored pens, paper, etc. to enable collaboration.
- Get students to stand at their desks to sing songs, do craft activities, or play vocabulary games with *Flashcards*.
- Provide activities that allow students to stand up, push their chairs in and move around the edges of the room, to make the most of their natural desire to move.

1.2 How to prepare a seating plan

Once you have considered how you will set up your room, think about who will sit where:

- If you know very little about your new class, look at the name list and draw a seating plan making sure you have a mixture of girls and boys seated together, i.e. two boys, two girls, two boys, two girls, etc.

- If you know more about the students, consider who will work well together, who are stronger and more independent, who are more lively, which students may have special educational needs, and which students are shy and reserved. Draw up a seating plan considering these details and tell the students where they will sit. See how it goes for a couple of weeks, and if it isn't working, change it. You are the teacher after all!

- Make sure each group of students you place together has a mixed ability. Put a couple of stronger and weaker students together at the same table. Place a lively student with them, so he/she can be encouraged to work by seeing his/her hardworking peers do well.

- Seat students with special educational needs at the front of the class where you are able to interact with them quickly and one-on-one when they need you. Make sure they are also seated with stronger and weaker students, so they are able to interact with a range of levels.

1.3 How to establish routines

Young learners love the security of a routine. They enjoy repetition and work well in a structured environment. Many routines will give students the opportunity to interact in English, e.g. using classroom language. By putting a few basic routines in place, you will have an easier time managing your class and you will create a more effective learning environment. Once students know the lesson routines, they will understand what is expected of them in class and will be encouraged to use language in a natural and meaningful way.

- When students arrive outside your classroom, ask them to *Line up, please* before they come in to class. Say *Put your bags away,* either on hooks or on the backs of their chairs, so they are out of the way and won't impede movement in classroom activities.

- Say *Sit down (at the front / at your desks). Thank you.* And ask *Who's sitting nicely?* to encourage students to sit up straight with their arms folded.

- Take the register and encourage students to greet you, e.g. *Good morning, Mrs Samuels.*

- Ask students to raise their hands when they want to ask or answer a question in class.

- Have routines throughout the lesson for each stage and activity. For example, to get students to sit at the front for story time, say *It's story time! Stand up, push your chairs in. Sit at the front, please.* Use hand gestures as you say these sentences, e.g. two hands moving up as you say *Stand up.* Two hands pushing an imaginary chair as you say *Push your chairs in*, and point to the front as you say *Sit at the front, please.*

- To set up a *Student Book* activity, show students what they need to do before they open their books. This will keep them focused on you and the board and not on playing with their pencils and books.

- When you want students to focus on their books, say *Take out your books*, and hold up your *Student Book* to help them understand. Say *Open your book to page 4*, showing students the correct page and checking they are all on it to do the activity.

- When an activity ends and you want to move on to something else, or when you want to get students' attention, say a chant, clap a rhythm or count down from five to one. You could silently mime an action and encourage students to silently copy you. Keep going until everyone in the room has joined in and is focused back on you. Set this routine up so students are challenged not to be the last one to join in.

- When the classroom gets noisy, lower your voice rather than raise it. Students will have to be quiet to hear what you are saying.

- Create a place to store art materials so students know where to collect them from and where to return them to. Encourage students to ask for materials politely when they need them, for example, *Paper, please? OK. Thank you.* and to pack away and tidy up after they have used materials.

- Encourage students to place their homework in the same place on your desk or at the front of the class each lesson.

1.4 How to reward the class and give them praise

Students respond brilliantly to praise, and it can really build their self-confidence. They are incredibly eager to please and do well at this young age, so it's a good idea to use it to your advantage.

- When students use English in class, no matter how little or well, praise them. Use a range of positive words and expressions so they quickly learn and understand, for example, *Good job, Anna! Excellent! Amazing! That's brilliant, Carlo!* Accompany these with appropriate gestures such as clapping your hands, a smiley face or, that young learner favorite, a high five! When students see others receiving praise, they will be encouraged to do the same.

- Let students know what you are praising them for, for example, *Good job, Olivia. You finished your picture.* or *That's wonderful, Natalie. You put away your things.*

A **reward system** is a great way of using positive praise to encourage good behavior in the classroom. It helps manage a class of young learners who are naturally competitive.

- If you see your students a few times a week, try a reward chart. Write the students' names in a list, either on an IWB flipchart, on a projector film, or a large piece of paper that you can place on the wall or bring to class each lesson.

- Tell students they will be awarded stars for things they do well. The stars can simply be drawn on with a board marker.

- Establish what students will get stars for: for example, listening to the teacher, following class routines and instructions, working well with their peers, doing their work well, helping the teacher, and showing that they have understood and can use the values they have learned in class.

Reward Chart

Nome	Good job! ★ ★ ★

- When a student, or various students, get ten stars, reward them by giving them a high five and saying *You're the winner*. Then let them stand at the front of the line when they leave class that day, or choose a song to sing, a story to read in the next lesson, or let them have the first turn at using the Megabyte puppet.
- Try to allocate stars fairly, so no one becomes disheartened and students see that reaching ten stars is achievable. Keep a record of who has won ten stars to make sure all of the students reach this milestone and win a prize. Try to time the stars so that they reach them at the end of the week, two weeks, month or term, whichever you feel works best for the class. Start the process again.
- If you see your class only once a week and want to give more immediate praise, simplify the reward chart. For example, tell students their goal is to win five stars by the end of the lesson. Choose achievable targets for them to get stars. For example, saying *Good morning / Good afternoon* when you take the register or sitting up nicely.

Use the *Our Values* stickers and set up a **Values routine**:
- Read the values statement in English and make sure students understand. Give students an example of the value, e.g. *We are friendly.* and explain what it means and why it is important. Use examples from the unit story and your classroom interactions or activities.
- Involve and encourage students to share their ideas about what the value means and how they can apply it or have applied it, both in the classroom and at home.
- Practice and act out situations where students might use these values, e.g. *We take care.* Use the Megabyte puppet, finger puppets or students to model situations.
- Set the class a goal around the specific value. Tell them you'd like them to remember to, e.g. put away their things at the end of each lesson during this week/month.
- At the beginning of the next class, remind students of the value and ask them if they have been friendly / put away their things, etc.
- Incorporate the values into your reward system.

2 Keeping young learners engaged

Keeping young learners engaged in the lesson means creating an active, meaningful, and well-paced lesson. Students of this age are naturally very physical. They are primarily kinaesthetic (learn by doing) and visual (learn by seeing) learners who need to physically interact with each other and the lesson in order to be engaged and motivated.

2.1 How to calm my class down or wake them up

- *Shine On!* provides varied resources to keep young learners engaged and each lesson provides active warmer and finisher activities from the Ideas Bank (see Teacher's Book p140). When you want to motivate, reenergize, or calm and quieten your class, try the following:

How to calm my class down:
- Remove distractors when you're giving instructions. Make sure students' desks are clear of pencils and books when you explain how to do an activity or talk to the class.
- Don't give out art materials for a craft activity until you have shown a model and explained what they need to do.
- Play calm music when students are coloring or making crafts.
- Talk in a calm voice and try not to shout. The louder you get, the louder the students will get. To regain their focus when they are being noisy, raise your hand and ask the rest of the class to copy you silently. The quieter, more focused students will copy you. Once the whole class are raising their hands silently, put down your hand and say *You're too loud. Be quiet, please.*
- Move students and seat them at the front of the class to use the puppets or read a story.
- Do a simple picture dictation. Ask students to listen to your instructions and draw and color a picture. You could practice body parts and colors, or any other vocabulary students know.

How to wake my class up:

- Get students standing up and sing a song or a chant. Play with the pace and sing faster or slower so students really wake up.
- Ask students to stand up, sit down, or clap their hands when they hear a word you've chosen in a story or song.
- If you are teaching your class vocabulary, and they lose focus, place flashcards around the room, and ask the students to walk to the word you say.
- Seat the students at the front of the class when you present new vocabulary and place the flashcards on the board. Ask pairs of students to stand in front of the board and touch, or hit, the correct card when you call it out.
- Use the Megabyte puppet or the finger puppets to move the focus away from you, the teacher.

2.2 How to use puppets

Levels 1–3 of **Shine On!** are accompanied by a lovely cuddly Megabyte puppet. Level 1 also comes with finger puppets for each of the characters, Lucy, Jack, Uncle Alex, and Megabyte. Using puppets creates a fun, non-judgemental, interactive and creative language learning environment. It also takes the focus away from *you*, so students are giving their answers and ideas to a different source that they may feel is on an equal level to them. Students will feel that they can play with the language more and make more mistakes with this puppet character. It will help encourage even the shiest student to speak. It also allows you, the teacher, to change your voice and persona into a fun and cuddly creature. Here are some ways to use the puppets in class:

- Tell students that your puppet is a native English speaker, so they will only speak to students in English and students should try to speak in English to them. For example, when you introduce *Megabyte*, and the other finger puppet characters, remind students that in **Shine On!** all the characters speak English, even Megabyte, the dog! This will motivate students to speak to the puppets in English if they want the puppets to hear them.
- If you can, give your puppet an identity by changing your voice for each character. Use humor to make learning with them fun.

- Use a puppet to present new vocabulary. Seat students together on the floor if possible. Place the flashcards on the floor and use *Megabyte* to say each item. Students repeat the words. *Megabyte* can give well-behaved students the flashcards to hold. Use Megabyte to ask questions, *Where is the pencil, Bella?* then have Megabyte take the card and munch at it like a puppy, *Yum, yum, yum*.
- Review vocabulary with a puppet by placing the flashcards on the floor, or around the room on the walls if you don't have space to sit on the floor. Ask a student to retrieve an item. Encourage interaction in English between students and *Megabyte*, e.g. *Here it is, Megabyte!* and *Megabyte* says *Thank you!*. Encourage more confident students to take the lead and be *Megabyte* and ask other students to find a flashcard.
- Use the Megabyte puppet and the finger puppets of the course characters to retell stories from **Shine On!** Either ask students to tell you what happens next then act it out with the puppets, or with more confident classes, you could give three students a puppet to act out the story, asking the rest of the students to tell them what to say and do next. In a less confident class, give students the chance to be *Megabyte* and use the finger puppets by acting out a sentence from the story.
- Use the finger puppets to help act out the grammar structures and *Everyday English* dialogue. Act out the dialogue with the puppets first. Then ask students to join in with one of the puppets, and then the other. In a more confident class, you could give two students the puppets to act out the complete dialogue.
- Use a puppet to act out feelings. Adapt your voice and the puppet's movements. For example, to show happiness, bounce *Megabyte* around and say *Yay, Yay. I'm happy!* Encourage the class to ask *Why are you happy, Megabyte? It's sunny!* Or to show sadness, hold *Megabyte* still and bend his head down, whimper a bit, and say, *I'm sad.* Encourage the class to ask *Why are you sad, Megabyte? Because I lost my book.* The visual nature of the puppet and your acting will help to give lots of unknown language meaning and context.
- Explain values such as putting things away, taking turns and helping each other using the Megabyte puppet. Award students with their *Our Values* stickers using the Megabyte puppet. For example, *Megabyte* says *Good job! You put away your things.*
- Use a puppet to encourage students to express their thoughts and feelings. For example, at story time, use *Megabyte* to ask students if they liked the story.
- Use a puppet to choose students when you need a helper or a volunteer at the front of the class or you want to form groups. Animate the puppet and use a choosing rhyme to select students around the class.
- Incorporate the puppet as part of your class reward system by allowing students to hold the puppet as a reward.
- You may even ask students to take turns taking the puppet home for the evening, to be returned the next day. This will help them to talk about their English lesson at home and engages parents in your classroom.

2.3 How to use songs and chants

Students love to sing songs because of their musical and physical nature. They also provide a natural way in which to interact with language. Songs work really well in mixed-ability classes, as the whole class works as a group. While stronger and more confident students sing out loud and really get to show off their English, shy and weaker students blend in with the whole class as the music is played. **Shine On!** presents vocabulary through a chant and presents and reviews the vocabulary and grammar structure with an engaging pop song. To make the most of the songs and provide support for the whole class, you could plan your lesson like this:

- Listening 1 – Play the song or chant once for students to listen through fully. They may like to dance or clap along as they listen.
- Listening 2 – Play it again, this time providing a fun kinaesthetic task for students to do as they listen. For example, ask students to point to the correct *Flashcard* when they hear the word (e.g. *pen, book, pencil,* etc.) in a larger class, or run and touch it in a smaller class. Alternatively, give groups of four to six students a flashcard to hold up when they hear that word in the song.
- Listening 3 – Play the song or chant and pause after each line for students to repeat chorally (as a class). Ask them to make up actions for vocabulary in the song. This can be done in groups with students teaching the actions to the rest of the class, or as a whole-class activity.
- Listening 4 – Play the song or chant again for the class to sing all the way through together.
- Play the song or chant in the following lesson to sing through together with actions or *Flashcards* to review the language used in previous lessons.

2.4 How to use stories

Reading stories in young learner classes is a great way to engage students in the lesson and present language in context. Language learning appears secondary to the interesting characters and colorful pictures. Pictures also provide meaning for the language that has been, and will be, taught. To engage the whole class, you could plan your story lessons like this:

- Seat students at the front of the class or where they can all see the board clearly (if using the animations).
- Use the *Storycards* (Level 1 only), holding up each card as the recording plays. In a larger class, or for Levels 2 and 3, use the story animation to engage students. Make sure all students can see the *Storycards* as you hold them up or the interactive whiteboard if you are using the animations.

- Involve students in the story as you tell it. Show the class the first frame of the story and discuss the picture before they listen. Ask questions like *What do you think the story is about? Who is she? How does she feel?* Ask questions to encourage the students to predict what will happen next. Ask *What do you think will happen next*? Allow students time to think and look at the pictures and to predict and hypothesize about the story.
- Pause between each frame or at the end of the story and ask questions about each frame to check students' understanding and to use and elicit the grammar and vocabulary of the story. Use the questions provided on the back of the *Storycards* (Level 1) and in the lesson notes.
- Read the stories a couple of times so students become familiar with the language and story. Encourage them to give their personal response at the end by asking *Did you like the story?*
- Encourage students to join in with the story. You could get them to say the lines along with the recording or use the Megabyte puppet, or the finger puppets (in Level 1). See puppet ideas on page 29. Then allow students to act out the story in small groups. If you prefer not to act out the story, or you don't have space, divide the class into groups by character and play the recording for each group to say the lines for their character.
- Acting out the story is a great way for students to engage with the characters, practise reading and speaking skills and have a fun, motivating lesson.
- Put students in groups and assign a role to each one. Make sure that everyone gets a chance to speak, and larger roles are swapped around and don't always go to the same students! If you know that shy students don't want a big role, encourage them to take a smaller part, but to join in and have fun.
- You can build confidence by rehearsing chorally, by putting all the characters who are playing the same role together and playing the recording for them to speak together.
- Encourage students to listen carefully to the way the characters say their lines, and try to mimic the intonation for dramatic effect.
- Put the groups back together and give them time to rehearse their lines.
- At the end of the lesson ask a few groups to come up and perform for the class. Make sure that a different group performs each time, so that everyone gets a chance to shine!

2.5 How to use the sticker activities

Lesson 1 and Lesson 4 of every unit have colorful and interactive sticker activities to support the vocabulary and *CLIL* lessons in **Shine On!**

With a less confident class, you might want to take a step-by-step approach with students:

• Show students the sticker activity. Say *Let's find the sticker*. Point to the first picture in the *Student Book* and ask *What is it?* The class respond using the vocabulary taught, e.g. *chair!* Say *Good job! Let's find the chair sticker*. Turn to the sticker section as a class and ask students to point to the correct sticker, for example the chair, before they take it out of their books. Check they are pointing to the correct chair sticker. Say *Good job! Let's stick the chair*. Students then take their chair sticker and stick it in the correct space. They then repeat the vocabulary *chair*. Repeat this with the remaining stickers.

With a more confident class, you might want to challenge them a bit more:

• Show students the sticker activity. Ask them to listen carefully. Call out the vocabulary in a random order. For example, say *Find the desk!* Students turn to the sticker section, and point to the *desk* sticker and say *desk*. This enables you to check before they stick and drills the target language. Say *Good job! Let's stick the desk*. Students then stick their sticker and say *It's a desk*. Continue with the remaining vocabulary.

• As students progress through the **Shine On!** course, this could be turned into a race. Say *Find the … desk!* Students quickly race to find the desk, stick it on their finger, and hold it in the air. Who was the winner? They then stick it in their books, say *It's a desk*, and play again. The introduction of this competitive element turns a quiet exercise into a wake-up exercise, which energizes the class.

2.6 How to do craft activities

Craft activities are a great and much loved way for students to interact with English in a kinaesthetic way and use the language they have learned in a natural context. Every unit of **Shine On!** includes two colorful and interactive craft activities. To get the most out of your craft lessons, you could plan your craft lessons like this:

• Prepare a completed example of the craft before class to show students what they will be making. This will engage students and help them to think about what materials they will need. It will also help them understand your instructions better.

• Organize the materials that you will need for groups, e.g. scissors, glue, paint and colored pens, before class. Details about what materials are needed are listed clearly in the materials box in each lesson. As the course progresses, or with more confident classes, encourage students to ask and give out materials when they need them, e.g. *Scissors, please? Here you are. Thank you*.

• Keep your instructions simple and in English so they become part of the learning experience.

• Think about what language you want students to use during the making of the craft, and in the activity after, and model this language as much as you can as you go through the stages.

• If you like, you can get the class to make each craft following your step-by-step instructions. For example, *First, cut out the circle*. Monitor and help students complete this part of the craft. Continue with the next stage when the whole class is ready to move on. Young learners have varied fine motor skill ability, e.g. some are great at using scissors, and some are not, so staging your craft lesson in this way will keep them all at the same pace and provide support to all the students. Once students have finished their craft, ask them to write their name on it, so they don't lose it.

• Allow students to take their crafts home to show and play with their families. This is a great way of involving the parents in their child's learning. Or, you could keep the crafts in class for the next lesson to play with and review the language from the day before. Then, allow students to take them home.

2.7 How to include the animated stories and songs

The stories and songs in **Shine On!** are brought to life through colorful animations, which can be used on your whiteboard. This provides a focal point for you to further engage and focus students when telling stories or singing songs. They also support the needs of a less confident class or less confident students within a mixed-ability class.

• When reading a story to the class for the first time, do so using the story animation. Pause at each frame and ask the class questions, e.g. *Who is he? Where is she? What is that?* Also, ask them prediction questions to help develop their critical thinking skills, e.g. *What do you think will happen next?* Follow this up by reading the story in your *Student Book*, then using the puppets to re-tell a tale.

- Alternatively, after you have a read a story to the class using the *Student Book* and puppets, use the story animations to play some vocabulary revision games. For example, shout out a word and students point to it, e.g. *Desk! There it is! Megabyte! There he is.*

- The song animations provide a visual context to the language used in the songs. They will also help students better understand the actions used in the songs as they can copy what they see on the board.

- Focusing the class on the song animations on the board will also encourage those students who are shier to sing and enjoy the music, as the focus of the class is on the board, and not on individual students.

3 Encouraging and creating an English environment

Surround students in English both visually and aurally so learning is everywhere. As well as using songs, chants and stories in English, build the English environment using some of these ideas:

3.1 How to make English visible

- Bring some English children's books to class. Allow students to look at them when they finish activities quickly or have a spare five minutes, or read them to the class yourself.

- Put the **Shine On!** English language posters on the wall, as well as other English cultural posters you might have.

- Display the students' work on the walls when they create a special piece of work to give them a further sense of achievement.

3.2 How to use classroom language

Shine On! comes with a comprehensive list of functional classroom language to make English the language of your class. The repetition of functional classroom language will be soaked up by your students and their understanding of English will quickly develop.

- Place the *Classroom language* poster on your class wall to refer to easily.

- Use actions or facial expressions and gestures. For example, as you say *Open your book*, use your hands together, opening up like a book. Nod your head and smile as you say *Good job!* Or put your finger to your lips as you say *Quiet, please.* Instructions that are repeated in classroom routines will also quickly be understood, e.g. *Good morning, everyone / sit down, please / put down your pencils / touch the card / Goodbye, see you tomorrow / next week*, etc.

Classroom language for *Shine On!*

The audio version of this language is available on the **Shine On!** Teacher's website.

To start the lesson:

Good morning / Good afternoon.

Hello, everyone.

Are we ready?

Listen.

Sit down, please.

Stand up, please.

Let's sing.

Let's chant.

Let's play a game.

To start an activity:

Open your books. Look at page (four).

Close your books. Look at the board.

Look at the poster.

You need a pencil / your colored pens.

Color the picture.

Draw a picture.

Cut the paper, fold the paper, stick here.

Circle.

Say the word.

Work together.

Move your chairs.

Ready?

During an activity:

Pick up your pencils.

Repeat after me.

Repeat after the CD.

Repeat.

Say it again!

Good job!

Very good!

That's great!

Show me.

Raise your hand!

Can you remember?

Quiet, please!

OK?

General interaction:

Come here!

Give me your book, please.

Touch the flashcard.

Point to the flashcard.

Thank you.

Help me, please.

At the end of a lesson:

OK, stop now.

Put down your pencils.

Close your books.

Right! That's the end for today.

Clean up your books and pencils.

Goodbye, everyone.

See you tomorrow / next week.

4 Engaging with parents

4.1 How to show parents their child's progress

- A quick and easy way to let your students' parents know how their child is doing in class is to mark their work. This can be by awarding them a sticker after they complete each lesson, or simply by drawing a smiley face or a star on their *Student Book*. A brief comment is also great if you have time, such as *Great reading today!* or *Thank you for helping!* Allow time at the end of your lesson to mark each student's work.

- **Shine On!** comes complete with beautiful, easy-to-use crafts as well as comprehensive *Workbook* activities, which help to practice the language of the lessons. Encourage students to show them to their families and tell them what they did in class.

4.2 How to work with the student / parent website

Shine On! comes complete with an interactive website for students and parents to use at home. It is filled with language games and extra English activities that the students can use at home.

- Encourage parents to spend a little time looking at the website and playing the games with their child. Just five minutes of interaction and their interest will encourage students to be interested in learning English. This will also help to motivate them in class.

- Let parents know that it's OK if they don't speak English, as the website is intuitive and students will have covered the language in class. It's just great that they are involved in their children's learning.

- Students and parents can watch the animated stories and sing songs together on the website.

- Encourage parents to ask their children questions about the songs and stories in their own language, to engage the students in learning English.

Oxford Parents is a website where your students' parents can find out how they can help their child with English. They can find lots of activities to do in the home or in everyday life. Even if the parent has little or no English, they can still find ways to help. We have lots of activities and videos to show parents how to do this.

Studies have shown that practicing English outside the classroom can really help students become more confident using the language. If they speak English with their parents, they will see how English can be used in real-life situations and this can increase the students' motivation.

Parents can help by practicing stories, songs and vocabulary that the students have already learned in the classroom. Tell your students' parents to visit www.oup.com/elt/oxfordparents and have fun helping their children with English!

Creating an inclusive classroom

In this section you will get some practical advice and tips on teaching students with special educational needs (*SEN*) in your English classes. These students can learn English, but they may need some extra help and support from you. By following these tips, you will create an inclusive classroom for all of your students.

What are SEN?

Students with *SEN* are students who have a learning difficulty or disability that calls for special educational provision to be made and students who have a significantly greater difficulty in learning than the majority of others of the same age. In schools with a policy of educational inclusion, these students will be in mainstream classes.

What is educational inclusion?

A policy of educational inclusion means that all children have a right to education with other children. Teachers therefore need to ensure that all students feel that they belong in school classes and are accepted for who they are. Differences between students need to be acknowledged, planned for and celebrated.

You can do it!

You might be worried about trying to include students with *SEN* in your class. Perhaps you think that it requires specialist knowledge and too much extra work for the teacher. This does not have to be the case. Students with *SEN* are human beings and as a teacher you are used to dealing with different personalities and abilities in your class. You are probably always adapting to widely differing student needs each day. Students with *SEN* are simply part of this variety and challenge. In addition, the teaching techniques that help to support students with *SEN* are good, practical techniques that will benefit all the students in your class.

Top tips for creating an inclusive classroom

You do not need to be an expert on *SEN* to teach students with *SEN*. You do need to want to work with these students and to be prepared to learn from them.

Tip 1: Be a role model

Students will take their lead from their teacher. It is important to show that you respect and celebrate differences between people. You need to believe that all students are unique and have a right to be taught. If you do not have much experience of interacting with people with *SEN*, you might feel worried about how to approach them. This is understandable, but you need to acknowledge this feeling and be prepared to learn more about *SEN*. For example, you can ask your student to tell you what helps them to learn and what makes learning more difficult for them.

For example, if you notice some students do not want to work with a student, make sure you talk to those students privately about their behavior and give praise and rewards to the students who are working well in teams.

Tip 2: See the person not the label

It is very important to get to know each student as a person and to not label them according to their *SEN*. If you have students who wear glasses in your classes, you do not assume that they have all got the same personality. In the same way, you should not assume every student with *SEN* is the same. Find out their interests and their strengths. Remember also that the range of *SEN* is wide, so take time to find out the level of a student's difficulty. Do not assume, for example, that a visually impaired person cannot see anything, they may have some sight. Do not be scared of talking to the person about their *SEN*.

> **REGISTER GAME**
> Build opportunities to get to know your students into your normal class routines. For example, when you call the register, ask students to answer with their favorite color, food or favorite word from the topic of the week.

Tip 3: Avoid judgements of behavior

Do not label a student as lazy or not trying. Students with *SEN* are often trying really hard and get criticized unfairly by teachers. They might look like they are daydreaming in class, but their brains might be overloaded with information that they cannot process and they need a short brain break. These students also need positive feedback on appropriate behavior, so make sure that you notice when they are behaving appropriately. Many students with *SEN* and behavioral difficulties only get noticed negatively by the teacher.

> **SEPARATE DESCRIPTION FROM JUDGEMENT**
> When you speak to students or their parents/carers, separate out a description of their behavior from your judgement of it. For example, if you say *You're not listening*, this is a judgement and will make the student react defensively. If you say *When you look out of the window, I think you are not listening*, you can have a more positive discussion with the student of the issue.

Tip 4: Celebrate difference and diversity

The classroom and the world would be a boring place if everyone was the same. You can use the differences between students to learn from each other and about each other. For example, if you have students who speak a different L1 to the rest of the class, ask them to teach the class a couple of words in their language and compare these to your own L1 and English. Use the topics in the **Shine On!** Student Book to compare different experiences, such as Level 2, Unit 7 on food.

BOASTER POSTERS SEPARATE DESCRIPTION FROM JUDGEMENT

Display a large sheet of paper prominently in your classroom where you can record all student successes. These successes will often seem to be small steps for students with SEN, but can be very motivating. Focus on something the class or the student is working on. For example, for a student who has problems with social skills, you can note James worked well with Albert today.

Tip 5: Teach in a multi-sensory way

Students all learn in different ways. Some like to see information, some like to hear it and some like to get up, do and touch things. Students with SEN particularly need practice in all the senses because they find it difficult to learn in traditional ways. Use a multi-sensory approach to present and practice information in your lessons.

PRACTICING WORD STRESS

When you are teaching the pronunciation of a word, you can show the stressed part of the word in a visual, auditory or kinaesthetic way as follows:
Visual – write the stressed part of the word in a different color on the board.
Auditory – ask students to hum or sing the stress of the word with louder sounds on the stressed sound.
Kinaesthetic – ask students to step out the stress by taking steps around the room and making longer strides for the stressed part of the word.

3D VOCABULARY

Vocabulary and spelling can be practiced in 3D. For example, use 3D letter shapes to practice keywords or allow students to trace the letters in sand, clay or in the air in front of them.

WORDS FROM BODIES

Ask students to work in teams and to choose a word to review. Tell them to make the word from their bodies. Each student should choose one letter to represent with their body. Each group then stands in a line and shows their word. Other students guess the word.

Tip 6: Plan ways to adapt your lesson plan

You need to sometimes adapt your lesson plans. This is called differentiation. Differentiation means planning and teaching to take account of all students in the class, whatever their level or capability. The students can make progress in their learning wherever they start from. All students should achieve the same main aim, but they may do this in different ways.

DIFFERENTIATE BY TASK

If you think that a student will have a problem with a certain type of task, you can set them a slightly different task. For example, if the Student Book asks students to listen and draw a picture, give some students a partially drawn outline and ask them to fill in the missing detail, give others a blank page and ask them to draw the whole picture. Similarly, some units ask students to listen and circle an item and students with SEN such as dyspraxia may find drawing the circle difficult. Ask these students to simply put a mark next to the correct item.

DIFFERENTIATE BY RESPONSE

You can differentiate by asking students to show their understanding of the lesson by responding in different ways, not always orally. For example, students can hold up a colored card to indicate whether they understand the point of the language presentation.
Red card = I don't understand.
Orange card = I understand some of it.
Green card = I understand all of it.
Individual mini-whiteboards are also useful ways for students to show their answers without having to speak in class. Students can draw or write their answer and hold up the mini-whiteboard. This is helpful for students with speech and language difficulties who do not like speaking in class and also for students who shout out answers inappropriately. If you cannot find mini-whiteboards, you can make them by laminating white A4 paper.

DIFFERENTIATE BY CONTENT

You can sometimes simplify the content of a task, particularly reading texts. Some students receive a simplified text, but all students get the same questions on the text. Preparation for this can be time-consuming so you should only do this if you can use the material again with another class.

DIFFERENTIATE BY RESPONSIBILITY

Students who find it difficult to participate, perhaps because they have communication difficulties, can be included in the class by getting a job from the teacher. Try to match the job with the student's need. For example, students who find it hard to keep quiet or keep on-task, can be given the job of monitoring the noise of the group. They can indicate how the class is behaving with agreed signals: A frowning face card to show the group is too noisy or not speaking English, a neutral face card to show the group is becoming a bit too noisy or not using enough English, a smiley face card for groups who are on track.

DIFFERENTIATION UPWARDS

It is important to think also about differentiation upwards, for those students who need more challenge and stretch. Easy ways to do this include:
Ask them to help another student.
Ask them to make up a test for other students.
Ask them to make up their own examples of the language.

Tip 7: Work on class management

Clear, consistent classroom management is very important for students with *SEN*. They often have problems understanding and following rules and instructions so it is important to think about the best way to do this. It is very important, for example, to think about your seating plan.

> **SEATING PLAN**
>
> Do you have a seating plan for your classes? Some students need to sit near the teacher, some need to sit somewhere where they can see the teacher's face, some need to sit with other students who are positive role models, some, such as students with ADHD, need to sit away from distractions such as window blinds, radiators and projectors, some will need to sit near a door to feel safe. Work with the student to decide where is the best place for them to sit.
> You will find more ideas for classroom management in section 3.

Tip 8: Work cooperatively with adults and students

Teamwork is the best approach to teaching students with *SEN*. It is particularly important to work with parents/carers. Sometimes these parents/carers can seem challenging to the teacher as they often ask for meetings and have many ideas and questions about the teaching. Remember that they have often had to fight for their children's rights. They can be your best ally and source of support if you keep good relationships and communication with them. They know their child best and will often have helpful strategies to suggest.

You will find more ideas for working with parents/carers in section 4.

Other people who can help you include school psychologists, counselors, speech and language therapists, occupational therapists, *SEN* organizations and charities. Try to find out what's available in your local area and keep a list of useful contacts.

Tip 9: Work with students' strengths

Try to find out what your students' strengths and interests are and include these in your teaching. Students who have problems reading can sometimes be good at drawing and acting. Students who find it hard to sit still might be very good at organizing teams and role play. Students who are struggling academically might be very kind and helpful to other students.

> **STUDENT OF THE WEEK**
>
> Introduce a student of the week or month award. Give this to a student who has shown some special skill during the class and choose skills not related to academic achievement. For example, your student of the week could be a student who is the kindest student, the student who showed most empathy with other students or the student who persevered the most.

Section 2: Categories of SEN

Cognition and learning

The category of cognition and learning difficulties includes general learning difficulties and specific learning difficulties. Children with general learning difficulties usually have problems in many subjects. They are usually behind their peers in reading and writing. They can, for example, have problems understanding abstract ideas or making generalizations from examples given to them. They usually have difficulty with basic literacy, numeracy, and general understanding.

Some children have specific learning difficulties. These children have problems with a specific area of learning, but are not behind their peers in general learning.

Some of these specific learning difficulties may impact on a student's ability to learn another language, but do not mean it is impossible for them to learn a language. *SEN* in this category include dyslexia and dyspraxia.

> **USE COLOR**
>
> Students with cognition difficulties benefit from the use of different colors in learning. For example, color code parts of words that have the same sound.
> 'c**at**, b**at**, s**at**, p**at** '

Communication and interaction

The category of communication and interaction difficulties covers a wide range of problems. Children in this category have problems with speech, language, communication or a combination of all three. Their problems can range from mild to severe. This group includes students with autistic spectrum conditions (ASC), such as Asperger syndrome.

Speech and language difficulties can be productive and/or receptive. A student has problems with productive language when he/she has problems making others understand him/her. Students have problems with receptive language when they cannot understand another person's communication. For example, they cannot understand humor or the appropriate language for a social situation.

> **GIVING CHOICES**
>
> Give students with speech and language difficulties closed rather than open choices wherever possible. For example, ask them *Do you want the red or blue pen?* rather than *Which color pen do you want?*

Medical conditions

Some children have medical conditions that need on-going management and treatment. There are many medical conditions and they also range in severity. Your school should have a medical register with information on any medical conditions of your students that has been provided by their parents. All staff need to know where the register is kept and what to do in case of a medical emergency.

Social, emotional and behavioral difficulties (SEBDs)

This category is the most difficult to define and can cause strong differences of opinion between teachers. We know that all children behave badly sometimes, it is a part of growing up. It can be difficult to know if a student's behavior is a sign of a *SEN*. A child is usually considered to have social, emotional and behavioral difficulties when the problem behavior occurs in many different situations, occurs frequently, is severe and not age appropriate. You will need to check with other teachers to find out if the student is behaving badly in all lessons or only in English.

CATCH ME BEING GOOD

Give students with *SEBD*s a card with the title 'Catch me being good'. Tell them to leave this card on their desk. As you walk around the class, put a tick every time you notice that the student is on-task and behaving appropriately. These students need to be noticed positively and not always negatively.

Sensory impairments

This category also covers a wide spectrum of need and ability. Children in this category have hearing, visual or physical impairments. These disabilities might not have an impact on their ability to learn a language. However, the teacher will need to make adjustments to the classroom. For example, it will be important to consider seating arrangements and the layout of furniture.

REFRAME POOR BEHAVIOR

Sometimes a student is misbehaving because they cannot see or hear properly. Check this out before assuming a student is simply being naughty.

Students with different L1

You may have some students in your class who have a different L1. These students might speak one language at home, another at school and English might be their third language to learn. This can affect their thinking and processing time and it can also affect them emotionally, they might feel quite displaced. Try to provide opportunities for them to share their culture and be sensitive when teaching materials such as holidays and traditions, which may cause the student to feel isolated and different. Praise their ability to learn different languages so that it becomes a positive and not a negative.

PLAY WITH PRONUNCIATION

If students are having trouble with English pronunciation, ask them to say the word as they would in their own language, exaggerating the 'wrong' pronunciation. Then ask them to say it in a very English way. Permission to use their own language system often leads to better English pronunciation!

How can a teacher recognize that a student might have a SEN?

Although the teacher should not diagnose *SEN*, you are usually the first person to notice that a student is having problems. If you think these problems are more than you would expect at the student's age and stage of learning, you can use the checklist below to decide if further action needs to be taken. However, remember that all students have some of these problems at times so use the checklist with care.

There are further checklists for specific *SEN*s available on the website.

Student inclusion checklist

Name: ....

- ☐ Am I sitting in the right place? Can I see and hear properly?
- ☐ Have I told the teacher what helps me to learn?
- ☐ Am I sitting next to a helpful friend?
- ☐ What can I do if I don't understand?
- ☐ Have I tried to talk to everyone in my class?
- ☐ Have I worked with any students who are new?
- ☐ Have I taken the time to see if anyone needs extra kindness or help?
- ☐ Do I know what other students are good at?
- ☐ Do I wait patiently if someone needs to speak?

Student inclusion checklist

Name: ....

- ☐ Am I sitting in the right place? Can I see and hear properly?
- ☐ Have I told the teacher what helps me to learn?
- ☐ Am I sitting next to a helpful friend?
- ☐ What can I do if I don't understand?
- ☐ Have I tried to talk to everyone in my class?
- ☐ Have I worked with any students who are new?
- ☐ Have I taken the time to see if anyone needs extra kindness or help?
- ☐ Do I know what other students are good at?
- ☐ Do I wait patiently if someone needs to speak?

Section 3: Teaching tips for including students with SEN

In this section we will look at some more planning and management techniques for including students with *SEN*.

Planning

Physical layout

Consider the layout of the room and how suitable it is for all your students. For example, is it easy for students in a wheelchair to move around? Is there an area that can be used for role play or physical games and is there a quiet area? Some students, such as those with ASC, will need a quiet area away from the group to calm down when they get agitated.

Visual displays

What is the impact of your environment on your students? Is your room stimulating enough, but not over-stimulating for any students with sensory needs?

Have you got displays on the walls? Can you encourage students to make things for the wall? They often remember things that they have touched and constructed much more clearly than pieces of writing.

Sensitive topics

Try to be sensitive to your students' needs and think about the topics in your *Student Book*. If you are introducing family members, for example, some students may live in complex, separated families and start to behave badly when asked to talk about their family. In Unit 7 of **Shine On!** 1, students are asked to draw their family tree. If you think any students will have a problem with this, they can be given the choice of drawing the family of the characters from the book. Each level also introduces some holidays, for example Easter and Christmas. These might not be celebrated by some of your students and it might be an opportunity to ask about their festivals.

Difficult tasks

Craft activities

Be careful if you are using tasks that require the student to make things. Some students, for example those with dyspraxia, have difficulty holding and using scissors. They may need to read the instructions while another student makes the object.

Writing tasks

Students with dyslexia have trouble reading and copying down words from the board. Students with dyspraxia have trouble holding a pen and writing. Try using different colors for different words or parts of words, make sure your own handwriting is clear and give students handouts wherever possible.

Tasks that require focus and sitting still

Some students, such as those with ADHD, will find it hard to sit still and concentrate on longer tasks. These students need short tasks, praise for doing the right things. Let them run around or stretch and give brain breaks. Acting out real situations will also appeal to these students.

Brain breaks

Brain breaks are quiet calming points of your lesson where students can rest their brains. Students with *SEN* can often feel that their brain is overloaded with information and anxiety. Notice how long your class can concentrate and build in brain breaks for this time. Students can give their brain a short break by:

- Standing up and stretching
- Having a drink of water
- Closing their eyes and resting their head on the desk for a couple of minutes
- Spending a couple of minutes doodling
- Massaging their head.

Spelling tasks

Teach students how to visualize words. Ask the student to imagine the word up high, visualizing it rather than sounding it out. They hold the word as a photo in their mind. Write new words on the right of your board, up high. This encourages students to access their visual memory.

Words on the wall

Have a high-frequency word bank on your wall, put the words on Velcro strips or use strips on the board. Students can then borrow a word from the wall when they need a reminder of how to spell it.

Classroom management techniques

Teaching students with *SEN* is not about learning a secret magic formula. Good classroom management can really help them.

Give clear instructions

Clear instructions are essential for all students, but particularly important for those with *SEN*. When you give instructions, use a non-verbal gesture to support the message. For example, point to your ear or show a picture of an ear to indicate *Listen*. Give an example of what you require and then get an example from your students to show they understand.

Use visual reminders

Non-verbal signals are very effective for helping students with *SEN* to understand and remember what to do. Use non-verbal reminders for classroom routines and rules. You could use visual aids such as traffic lights to show when the group is going off-task, for example.

Lesson stages order

Use pictures to show the different stages of your lesson. For example, an ear for listening, a mouth for speaking. Put these pictures on the board at the start of your lesson to show the order of activities.

Use your space

Think about your use of space in the room. Choose a place at the front of the class where you will try to always stand when giving instructions. Choose another place where you will stand when you are reminding about rules.

Think also about the energy you create in the room. If you are running around the room, you will create stress and make hyperactive students very restless, for example.

Create structure

All students need structure and consistency to feel safe in the classroom and this is particularly true of students with *SEN*. Make sure you have clear classroom rules. Remember that it is easier to start with clear rules and expectations than to try to establish them when things are going wrong. Involve your students in making the rules. Even young students can do this. You can use the values in the **Shine On!** *Student Book* to make a class contract.

Class contracts

Create class contracts with your students that focus on rules that will make the class safe and inclusive. Ask students to write down five rules for the class that they think would make learning safe and fun. Ask them to begin each rule with *In this class, we …* Give them some examples from the **Shine On!** *Student Book* values and encourage them to use these words.

Examples of values:

- *Be friendly.*
- *Be careful.*
- *Take turns.*
- *Share things.*
- *Be active.*
- *We pay attention.*
- *We listen carefully.*

Examples of rules:

- *In this class we listen carefully to each other and the teacher.*
- *In this class we are friendly to everyone.*
- *In this class we are helpful to everyone.*

You can then discuss which rules to use in the contract and put it up on your classroom wall. If students break the rules, come back to the class contract and discuss what is not working. Be specific about what you have noticed, without naming students. Say *We have a rule about listening to each other and I have noticed that some students are laughing when some people are speaking. How can we stop that?*

Teacher language

Teacher language greatly influences students. Many students with *SEN* do not understand or remember what they have been told to do. It is vital therefore to use assertive, clear language for instructions, praise and general comments in class.

Say what needs to happen

Tell students what you want them to do, not what you don't want them to do. For example, say *Look at the board* rather than *Don't turn around*.

Do not repeat and rephrase instructions continually. Give them and give students a chance to process them.

Name a positive intention

Find and name a positive intention behind an inappropriate behavior. For example, saying *I know you want to show me you know the answer; I need you to put your hand up and wait* is more positive than saying *Stop calling out all the time and disrupting the class*. If you have a student who is always making jokes about other students, you can say *I know you are very funny; you can be funny without being unkind*.

Name the right thing

Praise students for doing the right thing, rather than always noticing when they do the wrong thing. For example, you can say *Thanks for waiting with your hand up* rather than *Stop interrupting*.

Use inclusive language

Make sure to use the pronoun *we* whenever possible and keep the focus on group learning. For example, you can say *We are not learning well today; how can we all make that better?*

Student involvement

Study buddies

Children often understand each other's needs better than adults. They can help and support students with *SEN* and building relationships will help foster a positive climate for learning. *Study buddies* are students who agree to help another student. It can be done by asking the student with *SEN* who they would like to help them. Or you can give the job to a student who needs to experience responsibility. Emphasize that they will be helping each other at times as well. Sometimes a student with behavioral difficulties likes to help others and sometimes quiet students benefit from being a *study buddy* for someone with *SEN*.

Thank you stars

Each student takes a piece of paper and draws a star on one side. On the other side they write something nice to each student in the class. This can be set up as a routine where students can collect the stars from a place in the class and give them out at any time.

This activity encourages all students to focus on the strengths and positive attributes of each other.

Listening to each other

In general in your class, encourage students to listen to each other by asking them to repeat what a student just said and doing choral repetition of good answers. You can say *So, John told us that …What did John tell us …?* and all the class repeat the answer together.

Section 4: Work with parents/carers

Communication

Open communication channels between home and school ensure that ideas can be shared and situations dealt with as they arise. Discuss with the parent/carer a way of keeping in contact that suits you and them. This might be email or phone calls. It is better to set a regular time and way of communicating rather than only contacting the parent/carer when a problem arises.

Home–school notebook/diary

Use a home–school notebook/diary where parents/carers and the teacher can write important information and feedback on the day.

Meetings with parents/carers

When planning meetings with parents/carers, try to find times that are convenient for them. If they cannot attend, check if another family member is able to represent them. Consider the best place to hold the meeting. If it is in a formal office, it might be intimidating for the parent/carer. Do not sit behind your desk, this will make the parent/carer feel like a child sitting on the other side.

Praise postcards

Parents/carers of students with *SEN* are often only contacted to discuss problems. Make sure you also communicate good news. Create or buy a set of postcards with positive pictures on them. Try to send a positive message to the parents on the postcard throughout the school year. Focus on something specific, such as progress made in speaking or listening.

Acceptance of *SEN*

Some parents, for personal or cultural reasons, find it difficult to accept that their child might have *SEN*. Be respectful of their feelings and remember that teachers should not give diagnoses. Focus on the problems you see the student having in class and ask if they have noticed similar issues at home. Try to frame the interventions as a positive step. You can say *I understand that this is worrying, but I can see John is really trying hard and would like to find ways to support him more.* Use inclusive language and say *How can we work on this together?*

Objections from other parents

Parents of other students in your class might sometimes be concerned that their child is in a class with a student with *SEN*. They may be worried that their own child will not make good progress if the teacher is dealing with the needs of students with *SEN*.

These parents want reassurance from you as the teacher that that their child is not being overlooked. Emphasize that all students benefit from learning in inclusive classrooms because they will learn to value diversity, difference, develop empathy and understanding of others' needs, something that is valuable for all citizens, for a society to flourish.

Checklist for communication with parents / carers

- ☐ Have I got a system for regular communication?

- ☐ Do I send home positive reports regularly?

- ☐ Do I use inclusive language *we* rather than *you*?

- ☐ Do I describe what has happened rather than judge it?

- ☐ Have I acknowledged their feelings and objections?

- ☐ Do I use open questions, *How … Tell me …* rather than closed?

- ☐ Do parents get advance warning of meetings and are they set up to accommodate their timing?

- ☐ Have I suggested the parent can bring a friend / supporter?

- ☐ Does the meeting take place in a friendly place or is the room and set-up intimidating?

Section 5: Exercises to develop empathy and listening skills

Build activities into your lesson planning that encourage all students to develop the skills of listening and understanding each other. In this way you will create an inclusive ethos in your classes. Here are some techniques for doing this that can be adapted for different language points and different levels.

Shadowing and doubling

In role plays, ask two students to share one role. One student stands behind their partner and helps them with language (by whispering in their ear to give encouragement or new language). Alternatively, one student stands behind their partner and taps them on the shoulder when they want to take over.

Answer for me

Ask one student (A) to come to the front of the class. Then ask two other students who know this student to come and stand behind student A. The class should then ask student A questions. Students B and C must answer on behalf of student A. For example, the class could ask *What's your favorite food?* and students B and C must guess what student A would answer. Student A can nod or shake their head to indicate if the answer is correct. This activity means students have to imagine what it is like to be someone else in the class. Language topics can be chosen according to the level of the group.

Think, pair, share

When you ask the class a question: First give students two minutes to think on their own, then one minute to share their answer with another student. Then ask pairs to share their ideas with the group/class. This gives students time to process questions and think of a response.

Collective identity

Encourage the class to make predictions about their classmates. For example:

All of us …

Some of us …

None of us …

When they have agreed on statements, put these statements on the wall and add to them as the year goes on. A student can make a prediction and see if it's correct. If it's correct, put it on the wall.

Checklist for possible further action

Name: ....

- [ ] Is the problem across all classes and all times of day?
- [ ] Is the problem in certain class groupings?
- [ ] Who is the student sitting with? Does this make a difference?
- [ ] Can the student hear and see properly?
- [ ] Does the student remember and follow instructions?
- [ ] Does the student have problems starting and / or finishing tasks?
- [ ] Can the student focus on their own work for longer periods of time?
- [ ] Is the student easily distracted?
- [ ] Can the student wait for their turn in class and in group work?
- [ ] Is the student generally able to interact with other students?
- [ ] What kinds of tasks can the student do?
- [ ] When the student is engaged, what engages them?
- [ ] Is the work too easy or too difficult? How do you know?
- [ ] Is the student able to ask for and accept help from the teacher?
- [ ] Does the work involve a lot of writing? Sitting still? Copying from the board?
- [ ] Does the student find this difficult?
- [ ] Is there a big difference between the student's spoken and written ability?
- [ ] Is the student often in trouble because of poor behavior?
- [ ] Does the student have trouble with remembering information and recently learned facts – Visually? Auditory?

Inclusion checklist for teachers

Class: ....

- [ ] Do I know if any of my students have SEN?
- [ ] Have I checked the medical register?
- [ ] Have I included activities for different learning styles in my lesson?
- [ ] Do I know all my students names and the correct pronunciation?
- [ ] Do I make sure that my instructions are clear and checked in different ways?
- [ ] Are all students able to cope with the assigned tasks and activities or do I need to differentiate?
- [ ] Have I designed my classroom to allow movement and participation of all students?
- [ ] Have I included a quiet area?
- [ ] Are my rules / routines clear and stated positively? Have students been involved in designing them?
- [ ] Do I have a variety of rewards / consequences that are well known to my students?
- [ ] Do I give students an opportunity to work with all their classmates? Do I use a variety of group work and pairwork?
- [ ] Do I promote an ethos of belonging and co-operation?
- [ ] Do I always demonstrate respect for my students and value their contribution? Do I use inclusive and positive language?
- [ ] Have I got students with a different L1? Have I tried to find out about their culture and language?
- [ ] Do I give students opportunities to show their strengths and interests?

Starter Unit
Welcome Back!
Lesson 1 pages 2–3
Classroom Presentation Tool

Objectives
To introduce the main course characters.

To sing a song.

To review numbers 1–10, family members, and toys.

Language and structures
Active: *numbers 1–10; book, backpack, teddy, ball, scooter, bike, mom, dad, grandma, grandpa; Hello, I'm …*

Passive: *sing, listen, point, say, stick, chant*

Materials
Starter Unit flashcards; Class Audio CD 1; Megabyte puppet; stickers section

Warmer
• Say *Hello, I'm (name)* and wave to the class. Ask the class to stand, say hello and their name as they wave to you, e.g. *Hello, I'm (Anna)*.

• Put students into pairs. Ask them to turn and say *Hello, I'm (Adrian)* to their partner. Put students into new pairs and repeat.

1 Sing. 🔘 1·01
• Play the *Shine On!* song once for students to listen.

• Play the song again, modeling actions. (See Teacher's Book page 143 for lyrics and actions.)

• Play the song again for students to sing and do the actions.

Shine On!
Hello! Hello. It's English time!
Hello! Hello! It's time to shine!
Let's be friendly and wave hello!
We can shine, shine on!

Come on everyone! Let's sing our song.
Shine on! Shine on!
It's time to shine! It's time to shine!
Shine, shine on!

Hello! Hello. It's English time!
Hello! Hello! It's time to shine!
Let's work together, you and me.
We can shine, shine on!

(Repeat chorus)

2 Listen and point. Say. 🔘 1·02
• Show students the Megabyte puppet. Say *Hello. I'm Megabyte!* The class says *Hello Megabyte!* Ask if they remember why Megabyte is special.

• Books closed. Review numbers 1–10. Use Megabyte to place the flashcards on the board in a random order. Students say the number that they see. Megabyte says *Good job!* when they are correct. (See *How to …* section on using puppets, Teacher's Book page 29).

• Books open. Play the recording again for students to listen, point to, and repeat the numbers.

Transcript
one, two, three, four, five, six, seven, eight, nine, ten
two, nine, one, eight, six, three, five, four, ten, seven

Extension activity
Use the picture on Student Book pages 2–3 to review vocabulary from Level 1. Point to the main course characters and elicit their names (Lucy, Jack, Uncle Alex, and Megabyte). Call out words from Level 1 and ask students to point to them in the picture (*mom, dad, grandma, grandpa, teddy, ball, scooter, bike, book, chair, backpack, flowers, colors,* etc). With a more confident class, elicit the words from the class.

EXTRA VOCABULARY:

car
grass
helmet
ladder
lawnmower
motorcycle
trash can
tree house

Notes

3 Stick.

4 Chant. 1.03

3 Stick.

- Ask students to turn to the stickers section in the Student Book. Hold up your book and point to the stickers page. Encourage students to say the words. Then say the words for students to point to the correct stickers.

- Students stick the stickers in the correct spaces on page 3. When they have finished, ask students to point to the stickers and say the words.

21ST CENTURY SKILLS:

Communication
Students learn and review vocabulary using visual and audio media.

4 Chant. 1·03

- Play the chant once for students to listen.

- Play the chant again pointing to the flashcards.

- Play the chant once more. Ask students to hold up the correct number of fingers as they say the chant.

Chant

one, one, one
two, two, two
three, three, three
four, four, four
five, five, five
six, six, six
seven, seven, seven
eight, eight, eight
nine, nine, nine
ten, ten, ten

Lesson 2 page 4
Classroom Presentation Tool

Objectives
To review the alphabet.

Language and structures
Active: *the alphabet*
Passive: *write, letters, play*

Materials
Class Audio CD 1; cards with letters of the alphabet written on them

Warmer
- Play the *Shine On!* song from Starter Unit Lesson 1 page 2 🔊 1.01 for students to listen and join in.

1 Listen and point. Say. 🔊 1.04
- Point to the picture and ask students to say the names of the course characters (Lucy and Jack).
- Point to the alphabet poster and read the letters of the alphabet as a class.
- Play the recording for students to listen, then play it again and encourage students to repeat the letters.

Transcript
A, B, C, D, E, F, G, H, I, J, K, L, M, N, O, P, Q, R, S, T, U, V, W, X, Y, Z

2 Chant. 🔊 1.05
- Play the chant once for students to listen and point to the letters in their Student Books.
- Hand out the letter cards to pairs of students. Play the chant again. Students hold up the correct letter card when it is mentioned.

Chant
a, b, c
d, e, f
g, h, i
j, k, l
m, n, o
p, q, r
s, t, u
v, w, x
y, z

3 Write letters. Play and say.
- Put students into pairs. Ask them to stand. Tell students they will take turns writing a letter on their partner's back. Their partner feels what they are writing and guesses which letter it is.
- Do a couple of examples as a class. One student in each pair turns their back to the board. Write a letter, e.g. *H*, on the board for the other child in the pair to see and write on their partner's back. They guess saying, e.g. *Is it D?* Choose

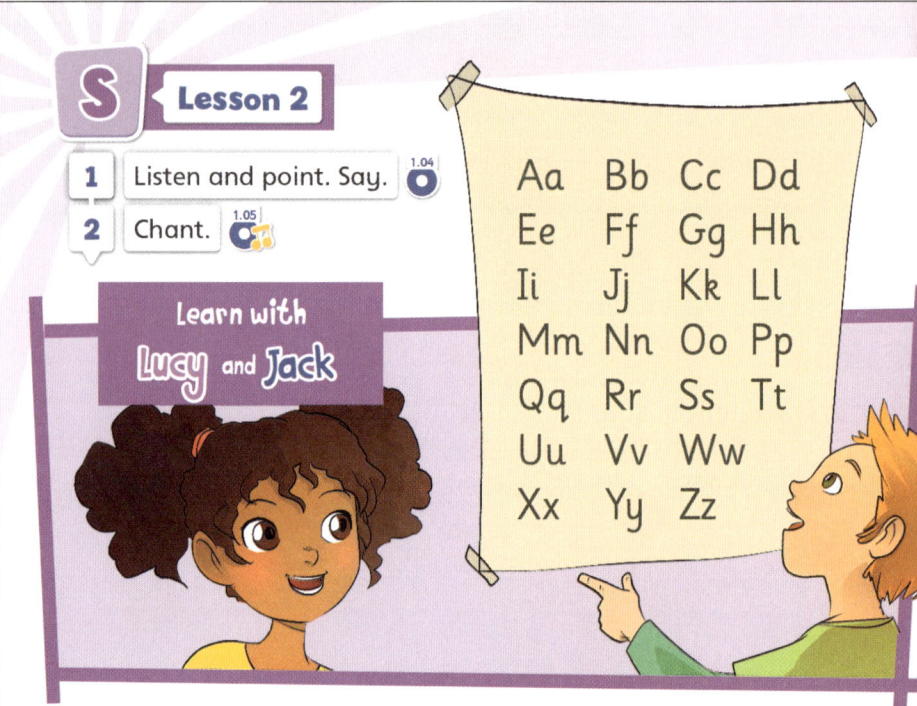

another letter and repeat with the pairs swapping roles.
- Students then choose any letter from the alphabet to write on their partner's back.
- Move around the class monitoring and checking that students are pronouncing the letters correctly and taking turns nicely.

TEACHING TIP

With a less confident class, ask students to write the letters on the palm of their partner's hand. This allows them to see as well as feel the letter being written.

21ˢᵀCENTURY SKILLS:

Collaboration
Students play a game together involving physical movement to consolidate their knowledge of the English alphabet.

Finisher
- Play *Mystery flashcard* using the letter cards. Encourage students to say the letter they wrote each time. See Ideas Bank (Teacher's Book page 140) for instructions.

Further practice
CD-ROM: Vocabulary and Grammar Worksheet Starter Unit Lesson 2

New Neighbors

1 Watch or listen. ▶ Watch! 🔘 1.06 Act it out.

Goodbye!

Goodbye.

2 I'm sad.

Oh, Ellie!

I'm happy!

Jack! Look! New neighbors.

4 I'm sad.

Hello. Welcome!

Hello. I'm Jack.

Nice to meet you, too!

6 Nice to meet you, Jack!

Who's that?

5

Lesson 3 (page 5)
Classroom Presentation Tool

Objectives
To present new vocabulary in the context of the story.

To practice a short role play taken from the story.

Language and structures
Active: *hello, goodbye; I'm (sad/happy). Look! New neighbors. Welcome! Nice to meet you! And you! Who's that?*

Passive: *watch, listen, act it out*

Materials
Starter Unit flashcards; Class Audio CD 1; cards with letters of the alphabet written on them

Warmer
- Play *Bingo!* See Ideas Bank (Teacher's Book page 141) for instructions. Play with letters of the alphabet.

---

1 Watch or listen. 🔘 1.06 Act it out.
- Point to the first frame of the story and ask students who they can see in the picture. Point to known items (*teddy, cat, car*) and ask students to name them.
- Point to the second frame of the story. Tell students *The little girl is Ellie* and that the other people we can see in the picture with her are *Mom and Dad*.
- Play the recording. Encourage students to point to the correct pictures as they listen.
- Play the recording again and ask students questions about each frame.

  Frame 1: *What is Ellie doing? (Saying goodbye to a friend.) Why? (Her family is moving to a new house.)*

  Frame 2: *Where is Ellie now? (At the airport.) How does she feel? (Sad.)*

  Frame 3: *Where are Ellie and her family now? (At their new house.) How does her mom feel? (Happy.)*

  Frame 4: *How does Ellie feel in her new house? (Sad.)*

Frame 5: *Who has come to visit Ellie's family? (Her new neighbors: Jack and Lucy.)*

Frame 6: *Who is looking at Ellie? (Megabyte.)*

- Allow students to talk about the story. Ask if they have ever had the same experience.
- Divide the class into groups to act out the story. Allow students time to practice in their groups. Then invite groups to act out the story for the class.

21ST CENTURY SKILLS:
Information literacy
Students learn new vocabulary in context. They develop their understanding of a story and then act it out.

Extension activity
Ask students to stand and make two lines on either side of the classroom. Pairs of students stand opposite each other. Then pairs move together and greet each other, saying *A: Hello. I'm (Victor). B: Hello. I'm (Alice). A: Nice to meet you! B: And you! A: Goodbye. B: Goodbye.* Move one child from the end of one line to the other end. The students now have a new partner. They greet each other again.

Finisher
- Play *Hit the card!* See Ideas Bank (Teacher's Book page 140) for instructions. Play with number flashcards and letter cards.

Unit 1 Happy Birthday!
Lesson 1 pages 6–7
Classroom Presentation Tool

Objectives
To present and practice six new items of vocabulary.

To review vocabulary from a previous unit.

Language and structures
Active: *balloon, clown, candles, present, card, cake; bike*

Passive: *listen, point, say, stick, stickers, chant, find it, picture dictionary*

Materials
Unit 1 flashcards; Class Audio CD 1; Megabyte puppet; stickers section; colored pens

Warmer
- Play the *Shine On!* song from Starter Unit page 2 🔊 1·01 for students to listen and join in as much as possible.

1 Listen and point. Say. 🔊 1·07
- Books closed. Introduce the new words using the Megabyte puppet and the flashcards. Place the flashcards on the board. Use Megabyte to point to the flashcards and say the words for students to repeat (see *How to …* section on using puppets, Teacher's Book page 29).
- Books open. Play the recording for students to listen and point to the items in the picture. Play the recording again for students to listen, point, and repeat the words.

Extra activity
Ask students who are sitting nicely to take turns coming to the front and holding Megabyte. Say a word. The student touches the correct flashcard with the puppet and says the word. The class repeat the word.

Transcript
balloon, clown, candles, present, card, cake
card, present, balloon, candles, clown, cake

2 Stick.
- Ask students to turn to the stickers section in the Student Book. Hold up your book and point to each of the birthday object stickers in turn. Encourage students to say the words. Then say the words for students to point to the correct stickers.
- Students stick the stickers in the correct spaces on page 7. When they have finished, ask students to point to the stickers and say the words.

1 Happy Birthday!

Lesson 1

1 Listen and point. Say. 1.07

clown

present

card

6 **Vocabulary** balloon, clown, candles, present, card, cake

Fast finishers
Ask fast finishers to count the different birthday objects in the main picture and write the correct number next to them (*cards (3)*, *presents (6)*, *candles (8)*, *balloons (4)*, *clown (1)*, and *cakes (1)*).

3 Chant. 🔊 1·08
- Play the chant for students to listen and point to the birthday objects in their Student Books.
- Place the flashcards on the walls around the room. Play the chant again for students to join in, stand, and point to the correct flashcard when it is mentioned.

Chant
cake, cake, cake
present, present, present
card, card, card
candles, candles, candles
balloon, balloon, balloon
clown, clown, clown

Find it!

- Point to Lucy's tablet and ask students what they can see (*a bike*). Ask students to find a bike in the main picture. (*It's next to the balloons.*)
- Tell students to turn to the Picture Dictionary for Unit 1 (Student Book page 82) and find a bike. Ask students to color the bike in the Picture Dictionary the same colors as the main artwork on Student Book page 7.

21ST CENTURY SKILLS:

Information literacy
Students work with their Picture Dictionary to keep a clear and organized record of new vocabulary.

Finisher

- Play *Mystery flashcard*. See Ideas Bank (Teacher's Book page 140) for instructions.

EXTRA VOCABULARY:

bowling pin
car
cup
doorbell
hose
house
sandbox
table
watering can
window

Further practice

CD-ROM: Vocabulary and Grammar Worksheet Unit 1 Lesson 1
Workbook page 4

Lesson 2 pages 8–9
pages 8–9
Classroom Presentation Tool

Objectives

To present a new grammar structure.

To practice the new grammar structure with the Lesson 1 vocabulary.

To sing a song using the Lesson 1 vocabulary and the new grammar.

To do a personalization activity that involves a simple craft activity.

Language and structures

Active: *birthday objects; There's a (present)! There are (five) (cards).*

Passive: *read, count, check, sing, make, friend; Happy birthday!*

Materials

Unit 1 flashcards; Class Audio CD 1; Craft Worksheet Unit 1 Lesson 2; colored pens, scissors, glue

Warmer

- Play the chant from Unit 1 Lesson 1 page 7 🎵 1·08 for students to listen and join in.
- Place the birthday objects flashcards around the room and ask students to point to the objects as they say the chant.

1 Listen and read. Say. 🎵 1·09

- Point to the picture and ask students to say the names of the course characters.
- Play the recording for students to listen. Then play it again and encourage students to repeat the grammar structure.
- Point to the present in the picture and ask *How many presents?* Encourage students to reply, *One*. Praise students and repeat the structure *Excellent! There's a present.* The students repeat.
- Point to the cards in the picture and ask *How many cards?* Encourage students to count. Praise them and repeat the structure *Excellent! There are five cards.*

2 Count and make a ✓ A or B. Listen and check. 🎵 1.10

- Point to the two pictures. Place the clown flashcard on the board and ask *How many clowns in Picture A?* Encourage students to answer *There are two clowns.* Ask *How many clowns in Picture B?* Elicit *There's a clown.*
- Write *Picture A* and *Picture B* at the top of the board as in the Student Book. Write *two clowns* on the board and say *There are two clowns, Picture A or Picture B?* Students respond, *Picture A.* Draw a check under A on the board and show students the example in the Student Book.

- Work through the remaining objects. Students check the correct boxes in their Student Books.
- Play the recording for students to listen and check their answers. Pause the recording after each sentence and ask students to repeat the structure.

Transcript

1	There are two clowns.	Picture A
2	There's a candle.	Picture B
3	There are eight presents.	Picture A
4	There are three cards.	Picture A
5	There are ten balloons.	Picture B
6	There's a cake.	Picture A

3 Sing. 🎵 1.11 ▶ Watch!

Song!

4 Make a card for your friend. Say. 💻

There are eight candles.

| Song lyrics | Page 103 | Practice | Page 86 | 9 |

- When the class is ready, students stand and say *There are (eight) candles. Happy birthday!* They give their card to their partner. Their partner says, *Thank you.*

Finisher

- Play *Pass the flashcards.* See Ideas Bank (Teacher's Book page 140) for instructions.

Further practice
Extra Practice Student Book page 86
Workbook page 5

Notes

_____

_____

_____

_____

_____

_____

_____

_____

_____

_____

_____

_____

_____

_____

_____

_____

---

3 Sing. 💿 1·11

- Play the *Happy Birthday!* song once for students to listen.
- Play the song again, modeling actions: *clown;* pinch your nose; *cake;* eat a piece of cake; *candle;* put up a finger; *twist* your body; *stamp* your feet; *present;* hold an imaginary present in two hands; *card;* put your hands together and open them; *balloon* use your arms to make a big circle; *Hooray!* jump in the air; *Happy birthday;* clap your hands.
- Play the song once more for students to join in and do the actions.

Happy Birthday!
There's a clown, a clown at the party.
There's a cake, a cake at the party.
There are candles, candles at the party.
Happy birthday! Happy birthday!

Let's twist, let's twist at the party.
Let's stamp, let's stamp at the party.
Everyone shout Hooray!
Happy birthday! Happy birthday!

There are presents, presents at the party.
There are cards, cards at the party.
There are big, big balloons at the party.
Happy birthday! Happy birthday!

Let's twist, let's twist at the party.
Let's stamp, let's stamp at the party.
Everyone shout Hooray!
Happy birthday! Happy birthday!

> **21ST CENTURY SKILLS:**
> **Creativity and innovation**
> Students learn how to express ideas through music.

4 Make a card for your friend. Say.

- Tell students that they are going to cut out and make a birthday card for their partner.
- Put students into pairs. Make sure each student has scissors, glue, and colored pens.
- Students cut out the card and the correct number of candles for their partner's age. They color the card.

Lesson 3 pages 10–11

Classroom Presentation Tool

Objectives

To present new vocabulary in the context of the story.

To practice the new vocabulary using the grammar from Lesson 2.

To practice a short Everyday English role play taken from the story.

To talk about a value.

Language and structures

Active: *robot, basketball, puzzle, car; How old are you? I'm (eight). Me, too!*

Passive: *Look! watch, act it out, write, repeat; We make new friends!*

Materials

Unit 1 flashcards; Class Audio CD 1; Megabyte puppet; Our Values sticker

Warmer

- Play the *Happy Birthday!* song from Unit 1 Lesson 2 page 9 🔊 1.11 for students to listen and join in.

1 Watch or listen. 🔊 1·12 Act it out.

- Point to the first frame of the story and ask students who they can see in the picture (Jack, Lucy, and Megabyte). Point to Ellie in the second frame and ask the class if they can remember who she is. Point to known items (balloons, presents, cake, candle) and ask students to name them.

- Play the recording. Encourage students to point to the correct pictures as they listen.

- Play the recording again and ask students questions about each frame.
  Frame 1: *What can Megabyte see? (A balloon.) What can Lucy and Jack hear? (Music.)*
  Frame 2: *What does Ellie have? (Presents and a cake.) Why? (It's her birthday.)*
  Frame 3: *Where is Megabyte? (He's in the tree.) What is Ellie holding? (A cat.)*
  Frame 4: *What does Megabyte do? (He jumps on the table.)*
  Frame 5: *Why does Jack say sorry? (Because Megabyte frightens Ellie.)*
  Frame 6: *How do the children feel? (They feel happy.)*

- Allow students to talk about the story. Do they think the children will be friends?

- Divide the class into groups to act out the story. Allow students time to practice in their groups. Then invite groups to act out the story for the class.

2 Listen and point. Say. 🔊 1·13

- Hold up the Megabyte puppet and encourage students to say *Hello, Megabyte!* Introduce the new words with Megabyte using the flashcards or bring real toys to class. Hold up or point to the flashcard items and say the words for students to repeat.

- Play the recording for students to listen and point to the correct items in their Student Books. Play the recording again for students to listen, point, and repeat the words.

- Students point to the items in the story and say the words.

Transcript

robot, basketball, puzzle, car
puzzle, robot, car, basketball

3 Find, count, and write. Say.

- Point to the picture in the Student Book and ask students what they can see. Point to the robot at the bottom of the picture. Say *Find the robots.* Ask *How many robots?* Elicit *There's a robot.* Say *Write one.*

- Repeat the process for basketball, puzzle, and car. Students write the number of items in the boxes. With a more confident class, allow students to work independently.

- Check answers by inviting confident students to come up and write the answers on the board next to the relevant flashcard.

2 Listen and point. Say. 1.13

1 robot
2 basketball
3 puzzle
4 car

3 Find, count, and write. Say.

🤖 [1] 🏀 [3] 🧩 [5] 🚗 [8]

Everyday English!

4 Listen and repeat. 1.14

5 Act it out.

Our Values
We make new friends!

How old are you?
Me, too!
I'm eight.

Vocabulary robot, basketball, puzzle, car

Practice ▷ Page 87 11

Notes

---

4 Listen and repeat. 💿 1·14
- Play the recording for students to listen. Then play it again, pausing after each line for students to repeat the phrases.

5 Act it out.
- Model the dialogue a few times with the Megabyte puppet, or with more confident students.
- Ask students to stand. Play some music. Ask students to walk around the room. Pause the music. Students turn to the person next to them and act out the exchange. Repeat.
- Tell students they can use this exchange whenever they make a new friend.

Our Values
- Show the class the space for the *Our Values* sticker. Read out the value (*We make new friends!*) Tell students that it is good to welcome new people when you meet them.

- Tell students they worked well with different classmates today. Congratulate students and award them with the *Our Values* sticker to stick in the space on page 11.

21ST CENTURY SKILLS:

Leadership and responsibility
Students learn the value of welcoming newcomers into a group and the advantages of working well in a team.

Finisher
- Play *Find the flashcards*. See Ideas Bank (Teacher's Book page 140) for instructions.

Further practice
Extra Practice Student Book page 87
CD-ROM: Vocabulary and Grammar Worksheet Unit 1 Lesson 3
Workbook pages 6–7

Lesson 4 page 12

Classroom Presentation Tool

Objectives

To present a CLIL concept (Math).

To practice the unit vocabulary and grammar through a CLIL concept.

Language and structures

Active: *sides, the same, different; robot, teddy bear, basketball, bike, balloon, present, kite, pencil*

Passive: *draw, make a chain*

Materials

Unit 1 and Starter Unit flashcards; Class Audio CD 1; CLIL stickers; CLIL Worksheet Unit 1 Lesson 4; scissors, colored pens, sticky tape, ball (optional)

Warmer

• Play *Little by little*. See Ideas Bank (Teacher's Book page 140) for instructions. Use the flashcards from Unit 1 and the Starter Unit.

1 Listen and point. 🎵 1·15 Stick.

• Point to pictures 1–4 in the Student Book. Play the recording. Pause after each item and ask students to point to the correct pictures on page 12.

• Ask students to turn to the stickers section in the Student Book. Hold up your book and point to each of the CLIL stickers in turn. Encourage students to name the items.

• Play the recording again for students to listen and stick the stickers in the correct spaces on page 12.

Transcript

1 There's a robot. The two sides are the same.

2 There's a teddy bear. The two sides are different.

3 There's a basketball. The two sides are the same.

4 There's a bike. The two sides are different.

2 Point and say *the same* or *different*.

• Explain the meaning of *same* and *different*.

• Ask students to point to the toys that have two sides the same (the robot and the basketball). Elicit *same*. Ask students to point to the two toys that have sides that are different (the teddy bear and the bike). Elicit *different*.

3 Draw. Make the sides the same.

• Draw one half of a present on the board. Ask *What is it?* Say *Draw the sides the same*. Draw the other half of the present.

• Point to the four pictures in the Student Book and elicit the words (*balloon, kite, pencil, present*).

• Say *Draw the sides the same*. Move around the room monitoring and offering help.

• When the class is ready, point to each picture and chant as a class *The two sides are the same*.

4 Make a chain of robots. Point and say.

• Play *Simon Says* to review parts of the body. See Ideas Bank (Teacher's Book page 141) for instructions. Tell students to act like robots, making jerky, robotic movements. Use a robot voice to give instructions.

• Hand out CLIL worksheets. Point to the robot half and ask *What is it? A robot!*

• Go through the instruction pictures together. Check that students understand which lines are fold lines and which lines are cut lines. Demonstrate how to fold the strip along the dotted lines and only cut the robot once. Unfold the paper chain.

• When students have cut out the chain and unfolded it, point to a robot. Hold it up and say *Look at the two sides*. Ask *Same or different? Same!*

• Allow students time to color their robots. Move around the room asking students about their pictures: *What is it? A robot. What is it? The head. What color is it?*

• Make a big chain of robots and display it on the classroom wall. Invite students to come to the front and stick their robots together using tape.

Finisher

• Play *Hit the card!* with the Unit 1 and Starter Unit flashcards. See Ideas Bank (Teacher's Book page 140) for instructions. Use a rolled up piece of paper if you don't have a ball.

| Further practice
Workbook page 8

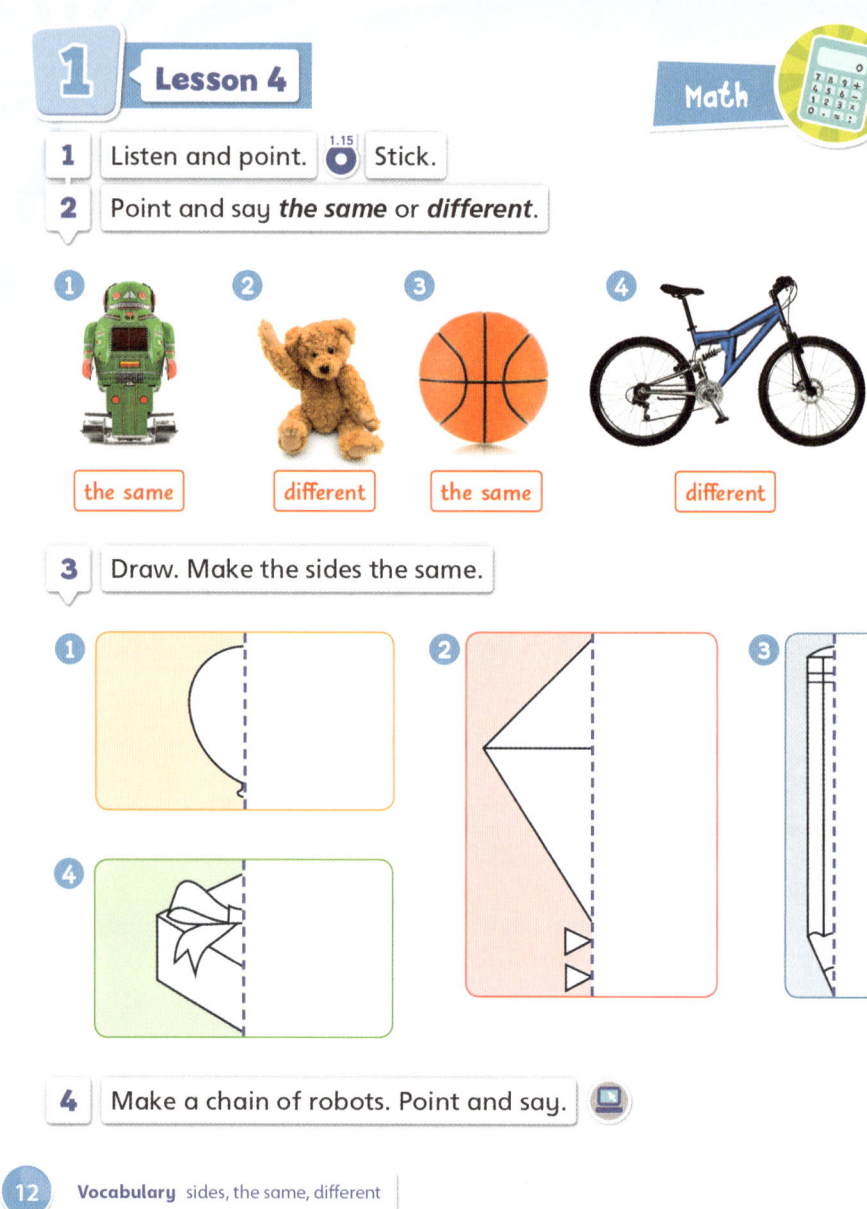

1 Review

1 Find, count, and write. Say.

2 | robot
9 | balloon
1 | clown
3 | card
5 | present
1 | basketball
1 | cake

2 Make the party hat. Play and say. ✂ Page 119

This is my hat. It's blue.

3 Complete your picture dictionary. Page 82

13

21ST CENTURY SKILLS:
Problem solving
Students use visual information to problem solve.

2 Make the party hat. Play and say.

- Tell students they are going to make a party hat. Point to the pictures and ask students what they need to make one (card or paper, scissors, glue, colored pens).
- Tell students to turn to page 119 and cut the Craft cut-out from their Student Books. Model how to make a party hat by coloring it in and cutting out the shape. Then bend it around and stick the sides together.
- Make sure students have all the materials. Move around the class offering help if necessary. Ask students questions about their party hats, e.g. *What is it? What color is it?*
- Students can talk about their party hats in pairs, saying *This is my hat. It's (red and green).*

3 Complete your picture dictionary.

- Tell students to turn to page 82 of their Student Books and look at the Picture Dictionary section for Unit 1.
- Point to each of the pictures and ask students to say the words.
- Students color the items in the Picture Dictionary. Move around the class as they work, asking questions, e.g. *What is it? Is it a (card)? Where's the (robot)?*

Finisher

- Play *Which one is missing?* See Ideas Bank (Teacher's Book page 140) for instructions.

Further practice
Unit 1 Test
Workbook page 9

Review page 13
Classroom Presentation Tool

Objectives
To review the linguistic content of the unit.

Language and structures
Active: *balloon, clown, candles, present, card, cake, robot, basketball, puzzle, car; There is a (cake). There are (nine balloons).*
Passive: *play; Make the party hat. Complete your picture dictionary.*

Materials
Unit 1 flashcards; Craft cut-out Unit 1 Review; card, paper, scissors, glue, colored pens

Warmer
- Play *Memory game.* See Ideas Bank (Teacher's Book page 141) for instructions.

1 Find, count, and write. Say.

- Place the following flashcards vertically on the right of the board: *robot, balloon, clown, card, present, basketball, cake.* Elicit the vocabulary as you go.
- Point to the picture in the Student Book and ask what students can see. Point to the small picture of the robot. Say *Find and count the robots.*
- Point to and count them as a class *1, 2.* Say *Write 2 in the box.* Students write 2 as you write 2 on the board. Say *There are two robots.* Students repeat the structure *There are two robots.*
- Continue the process for the remaining objects. With a more confident class, allow students to work independently. Check answers together as a class, eliciting the structure, e.g. *There are (9) balloons.*

Unit 2 What Weather!
Lesson 1 pages 14–15
Classroom Presentation Tool

Objectives
To present and practice six new items of vocabulary.

To review vocabulary from a previous unit.

Language and structures
Active: *stormy, snowy, windy, cloudy, rainy, sunny; present*

Passive: *weather*

Materials
Unit 1, 2 and Starter Unit flashcards; Class Audio CD 1; Megabyte puppet; stickers section; colored pens

Warmer
• Play *Which one is missing?* See Ideas Bank (Teacher's Book page 140) for instructions. Use 10 flashcards from the Starter Unit and Unit 1 and the alphabet poster to review the alphabet, numbers, and birthday vocabulary.

1 Listen and point. Say. 1•16
• Books closed. Introduce the new words using the Megabyte puppet and the flashcards. Place the flashcards on the board. Use Megabyte to point to the flashcards and say the words for students to repeat.

• Books open. Play the recording for students to listen and point to the items in the picture. Play the recording again for students to listen, point, and repeat the words.

> **TEACHING TIP**
>
> Make weather sounds and use Megabyte to act out the different weather types.

Transcript
stormy, snowy, windy, cloudy, rainy, sunny
rainy, windy, snowy, sunny, stormy, cloudy

> **21ST CENTURY SKILLS:**
>
> **Communication**
> Students learn to describe the weather in oral and written form.

2 Listen and point. Say. 1.16

cloudy · sunny · windy · stormy · rainy

14 Vocabulary stormy, snowy, windy, cloudy, rainy, sunny

2 Stick.
• Ask students to turn to the stickers section in the Student Book. Hold up your book and point to each of the weather stickers in turn. Encourage students to say the words. Then say the words for students to point to the correct stickers.

• Students stick the stickers in the correct spaces on page 15. When they have finished, ask students to point to the stickers and say the words.

> **Extra activity**
>
> With a less confident class, ask students to turn to their sticker page. Call out a weather word, e.g. *sunny*. Students point to the correct sticker and say the word, checking with their partner. They stick the sticker in the correct place in their Student Books and repeat the word, *sunny*. Repeat with the remaining words.

snowy

2 Stick.

3 Chant. 1.17

find it!

15

EXTRA VOCABULARY:
boots
coat
dome
Frisbee
gloves
raincoat
scarf
snowman
stroller
umbrella
wool hat

Further practice
CD-ROM: Vocabulary and Grammar Worksheet
Unit 2 Lesson 1
Workbook page 10

Notes

_____

_____

_____

_____

_____

_____

_____

_____

_____

_____

_____

_____

_____

_____

3 Chant. 1•17
- Play the chant once for students to listen.
- Play the chant again. Point to the flashcards on the board.
- Play the chant once more and encourage students to point to the correct weather symbol in their Student Books.

Extra activity
Hand out the weather flashcards randomly to groups of students. Play the chant again. When the groups hear their word, they hold up the correct flashcard.

Chant
cloudy, cloudy, cloudy
windy, windy, windy
rainy, rainy, rainy
stormy, stormy, stormy
sunny, sunny, sunny
snowy, snowy, snowy

Find it!
- Point to Jack's drawing pad and ask students what they can see (a present). Ask students to find a present in the main picture. (It's below the word *sunny*.)
- Tell students to turn to the Picture Dictionary for Unit 2 (Student Book page 82) and find a present. Ask students to color the present in the Picture Dictionary the same colors as the main artwork on Student Book page 14.

Finisher
- Play *Fast flashcards* using the Unit 1 and 2 flashcards. See Ideas Bank (Teacher's Book page 140) for instructions.

Lesson 2 pages 16–17
Classroom Presentation Tool

Objectives
To present a new grammar structure.

To practice the new grammar structure with the Lesson 1 vocabulary.

To sing a song using the Lesson 1 vocabulary and the new grammar.

To do a personalization activity that involves a simple craft activity.

Language and structures
Active: *What's the weather like? It's (rainy); stormy, snowy, windy, cloudy, sunny*

Passive: *follow, listen again, repeat; Make your weather window.*

Materials
Unit 2 flashcards; Class Audio CD 1; Craft Worksheet Unit 2 Lesson 2; scissors, colored pens

Warmer
- Play the chant from Unit 2 Lesson 1 page 15 🎵 1.17 for students to listen and join in.
- Place the weather flashcards around the room and ask students to point to the correct object as they say the chant.

Extra activity
Encourage students to make up actions for the different weather types as a class. They can do these as they say the chant. For example, wriggle your fingers through the air to show rain falling for *rainy*, etc.

1 Listen and read. Say. 🎵 1·18
- Point to the picture and ask students to say the names of the course characters.
- Play the recording for students to listen. Then play it again and encourage students to repeat the grammar structure.
- Place the weather flashcards on the board and elicit the weather vocabulary as you go. Point to a flashcard and ask *What's the weather like? It's (snowy)*. Repeat with the other weather flashcards.

21ST CENTURY SKILLS:
Communication
Students learn to ask for and give information about the weather.

2 Listen, follow, and make a ✓.
🎵 1·19 Listen again and repeat.
- Tell students to listen to the weather they hear described and follow the

arrows around the maze with their fingers.
- Play the recording. Pause after each sentence to check the class are pointing to the correct picture.
- Ask students to draw a check next to the correct final picture in the maze (picture 2). Ask *What's the weather like?* The class responds *It's stormy.*

Transcript
What's the weather like?	It's sunny.
What's the weather like?	It's windy.
What's the weather like?	It's snowy.
What's the weather like?	It's stormy.
What's the weather like?	It's rainy.

Extension activity
Repeat the activity. This time give the class the instructions yourself. Guide the class through the maze to one of the other destinations (1 or 3). When you reach it, ask *What's the weather like?* The class responds *It's (snowy)!* Repeat with the final destination. With a more confident class, ask pairs of students to guide each other through the maze.

3 Sing. 1.20 ► Watch! **Song!**

4 Make your weather window. Play and say.

What's the weather like?

It's windy!

Song lyrics ▶ Page 103   Practice ▶ Page 88   17

Finisher
• Play *Find the flashcards*. See Ideas Bank (Teacher's Book page 140) for instructions.

Further practice
Extra Practice Student Book page 88
Workbook page 11

Notes

---

3 Sing. 1.20

• Play the *My Weather Machine* song once, modeling actions: *sunny*: open and close your fingers on both hands; *rainy*: wiggle your fingers in the air to show rain falling; *windy*: sway arms from side to side; *snowy*: wrap your arms around your body and shiver; *stormy*: clap (to represent thunder).
• Play the song again for students to join in and do the actions.

My Weather Machine
Clunk, whirrr. My weather machine!
Click, pssh. My weather machine!
What's the weather like today?
It's rainy.
Oh no! It's rainy.
What's the weather like today?
It's cloudy.
Oh no! It's cloudy.
What's the weather like today?
It's windy.
Oh no! It's windy.
What's the weather like today?
It's snowy.

Oh no! It's snowy.
What's the weather like today?
It's stormy.
Oh no! It's stormy.
What's the weather like today?
It's sunny.
Oh yes! It's sunny.
Clunk, whirrr. My weather machine!
Click, pssh. My weather machine!

4 Make your weather window. Play and say.

• Tell students that they are going to cut out and make a weather window.
• Make sure each child has scissors and colored pens. Students cut out their weather window and color it in.
• When the class is ready, students ask and answer about the weather with their partner. They move the weather through the window and ask *What's the weather like?* Their partner answers correctly using the structure, *It's (sunny).*

Lesson 3 (pages 18–19)

Classroom Presentation Tool

Objectives

To present new vocabulary in the context of the story.

To practice the new vocabulary using the grammar from Lesson 2.

To practice a short Everyday English role play taken from the story.

Language and structures

Active: *wet, dry, cold, hot; I don't understand. Let's check.*

Passive: *It's (windy). Sorry! Who is the winner?*

Materials

Unit 2 flashcards; Class Audio CD 1; Megabyte puppet

Warmer

• Play the *My Weather Machine* song from Unit 2 Lesson 2 page 17  1.20 for students to listen and join in if possible.

1 Watch or listen.  1•21 Act it out.

• Point to the first frame of the story and ask students who they can see in the picture (Jack, Lucy, Ellie, and Megabyte). Point to the weather outside and ask *What's the weather like? (It's rainy.)*

• Play the recording. Encourage students to point to the correct pictures as they listen.

• Play the recording again and ask students questions about each frame.

Frame 1: *What are the children doing? (Playing games, reading.)*

Frame 2: *What's the weather like? (Stormy and windy.) Is Megabyte happy? (No.)*

Frame 3: *What's the weather like now? (Snowy.)*

Frame 4: *Why is Lucy confused? (Because it's snowy outside, but sunny on her tablet.)*

Frame 5: *Why is it dry and hot? (Because it's sunny outside.)*

Frame 6: *What was Uncle Alex doing? (Changing the weather with his weather machine.)*

• Divide the class into groups to act out the story. Allow students time to practice in their groups. Then invite groups to act out the story for the class.

2 Listen and point. Say.  1•22

• Introduce the new words with Megabyte using the flashcards. Hold up or point to the flashcards and say the words for students to repeat.

• Play the recording for students to listen and point to the correct items in their Student Books. Play the recording again for students to listen, point, and repeat the words.

Extension activity

Place the flashcards on the walls around the room. Ask students to stand. Say *It's sunny!* Students walk to that flashcard and say *It's sunny.* With a more confident class, ask students to take turns calling out the weather.

Transcript

wet, dry, cold, hot
cold, dry, hot, wet

---

2 Lesson 3 — Rainy Day Surprise

1 Watch or listen. ▶ Watch! 1.21 Act it out.

1. It's rainy!
   Yes. It's wet.

2. Listen! It's stormy!
   It's windy, too!

3. Later
   It's cold. What's the weather like now?
   It's snowy!

4. I don't understand!
   Let's check.

5. It's dry!
   It's hot!

6. Sorry!
   It's you, Uncle Alex!

18

2 Listen and point. Say. 1.22

① wet
② dry
③ cold
④ hot

3 Listen and make a ✓. Who is the winner? 1.23

Everyday English!

I don't understand!

Let's check.

4 Listen and repeat. 1.24

5 Act it out.

Vocabulary wet, dry, cold, hot

Practice > Page 89 19

---

gestures. Line B replies *Let's check*. Play the music again. Repeat swapping roles.

- Tell students they can use this exchange whenever they have a problem in English that they don't understand.

Finisher

- Play *Pass the flashcards*. See Ideas Bank (Teacher's Book page 140) for instructions.

Further practice
Extra Practice Student Book page 89
CD-ROM: Vocabulary and Grammar Worksheet
Unit 2 Lesson 3
Workbook pages 12–13

Notes

---

3 Listen and make a ✓. Who is the winner? 🎧 1·23

- Play the first line of the recording and pause. Ask *What's the weather like?* Students answer *It's snowy*. Show the class the checks in the snowy boxes for both Lucy and Jack.
- Tell students to listen and check the weather words they hear. If Lucy or Jack don't have a picture for the word, they don't put a check.
- Play the recording. Pause after each item for students to check.
- Ask *Who is the winner?* Students count who has the most checks.

Transcript

What's the weather like?	It's snowy!
What's the weather like?	It's stormy.
What's the weather like?	It's dry.
What's the weather like?	It's windy.
What's the weather like?	It's wet.
What's the weather like?	It's cold. Brrrr!

Extension activity

With a less confident class, play *Picture Bingo!* using the weather words. See Ideas Bank (Teacher's book page 141) for instructions.
With a more confident class, use words instead of pictures and ask confident students to call out the weather words.

4 Listen and repeat. 🎧 1·24

- Play the recording for students to listen. Then play it again. Pause after each line for students to repeat the phrases.

5 Act it out.

- Model the dialogue a few times with the Megabyte puppet, or with more confident students.
- Divide the class in half and ask students to line up in two lines facing each other. Play the *My Weather Machine* song from Lesson 2 🎧 1.20. Pause the music. Line A says *I don't understand!* using hand

Lesson 4 page 20
Classroom Presentation Tool

Objectives
To present a CLIL concept (Geography).

To practice the unit vocabulary and grammar through a CLIL concept.

Language and structures
Active: *today, stormy, snowy, windy, cloudy, rainy, sunny, hot, dry, cold, wet; It's (windy).*

Passive: *circle; Make a weather map.*

Materials
Unit 2 flashcards; Class Audio CD 1; CLIL stickers; CLIL Worksheet Unit 2 Lesson 4; scissors, colored pens

Warmer
- Play *Mime the word*. See Ideas Bank (Teacher's Book page 140) for instructions.

1 Listen and point. 🔊 1·25 Stick.
- Point to the two pictures at the top of the page and ask the class what they can see. Say *Listen and point*. Play the recording. Pause after each item for students to point.
- Ask students to turn to the stickers section in the Student Book. Hold up your book and point to each of the CLIL stickers in turn. Encourage students to say the weather.
- Play the recording again for students to listen and stick the stickers in the correct spaces on page 20.

Transcript
1 A: What's the weather like today?
 B: It's rainy and cloudy. It's hot.
2 A: What's the weather like today?
 B: It's snowy and windy. It's cold.

2 Point and say.
- Put students into pairs. Ask them to take turns pointing to the two pictures. They ask their partner *What's the weather like?* Their partner replies *It's (rainy) and (cloudy). It's hot.* etc.

3 Listen and circle the words. 🔊 1·26 Draw.
- Read the words in the word box aloud with the class. Tell students to listen to the weather reports and circle the words they hear.
- Play the recording. Pause after the first item. Ask *What's the weather like?* Allow students to check in pairs before confirming the answers. Repeat with the remainder of the recording.

- Ask students to draw a picture of the weather words in the spaces on the maps.

Transcript
1 Now for today's weather. It is very windy. It's cloudy.
2 Well, what's the weather like today? Today, it's rainy and stormy.

21ST CENTURY SKILLS:

Information literacy
Students learn to understand how weather varies in different regions and in different countries.
---

4 Make a weather map. Point and say.
- Hand out CLIL worksheets. Look at the map together and ask students to tell you some of the major landmarks that they know. Help students to find the approximate location of your town. Tell them to draw a dot and label it.

- Put students into pairs. Ask them to work together to cut out the weather symbols and color their map.
- Students take turns asking and answering about the weather. One student chooses two symbols. Their partner asks *What's the weather like?* and the first student places the symbols on the map and says *It's (cloudy) and (cold)*.
- Bring the class back together, and ask *What's the weather like today?* Elicit suggestions for the current weather, and agree on a report. Students stick today's weather on their maps.
- Ask confident pairs to come to the front and present their weather report to the class.

Finisher
- Play *Musical flashcards*. See Ideas Bank (Teacher's Book page 141) for instructions.

Further practice
Workbook page 14

  **Lesson 4**

 Geography

1 Listen and point. 1·25 Stick.
2 Point and say.

3 Listen and circle the words. 1·26 Draw.

snowy (windy) (cloudy)   sunny (rainy) (stormy)

4 Make a weather map. Point and say.

20   **Vocabulary** today

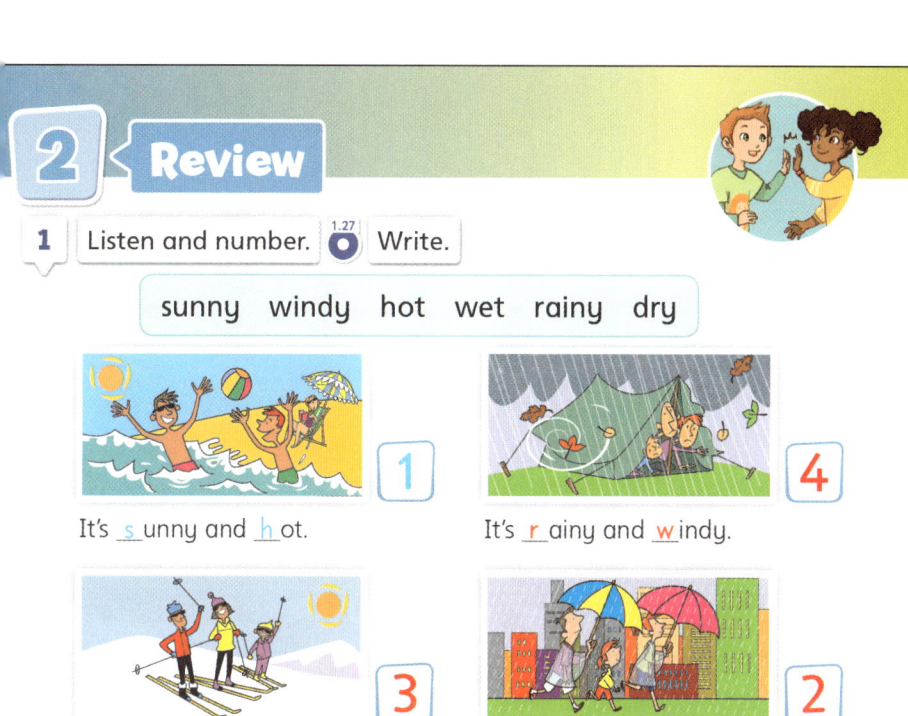

1 Listen and number. 🎧 1.27 Write.

| sunny | windy | hot | wet | rainy | dry |

1

It's _s_ unny and _h_ ot.

3

It's _s_ unny and _d_ ry.

4

It's _r_ ainy and _w_ indy.

2

It's _h_ ot and _w_ et.

2 Make your weather wheel. Play and say. ✂ Page 117

What's the weather like today?

It's stormy and wet.

Our Values
We share our things.

3 Complete your picture dictionary. Page 82

21

Review (page 21)

Classroom Presentation Tool

Objectives

To review the linguistic content of the unit.

To talk about a value.

Language and structures

Active: *stormy, snowy, windy, cloudy, rainy, sunny, hot, dry, cold, wet, today; What's the weather like today? It's (stormy).*

Passive: *weather wheel; We share our things.*

Materials

Unit 2 flashcards; Class Audio CD 1; Craft cut-out Unit 2 Review; scissors, colored pens, craft pin; Our Values sticker

Warmer

- Play *Change places*. See Ideas Bank (Teacher's Book page 141) for instructions.

1 Listen and number. 🎧 1·27 Write.

- Look at the pictures and ask *What's the weather like?* Elicit the weather in each one, e.g. *It's sunny and hot.*
- Play the recording. Pause after the first item. Tell students to point to the correct picture. *(It's sunny and hot.)* Point to the example number 1.
- Play the remainder of the recording. Check students are writing the numbers in the box. They do not write the letters yet.
- Allow students to check their answers in pairs before checking together as a class. Ask *What's the weather like in picture (2)?* and elicit the answers.
- Tell students to read the words in the word box together. Ask *How do you spell sunny/hot?* Elicit the letters. Ask the class to write the correct letters in the spaces provided to complete the words.

Transcript

1 **Boy:** Hi, Grandma!
Grandma: Hello. What's the weather like?
Boy: It's sunny and hot.
2 **Girl:** Hello!
Grandpa: Hello. It's Grandpa. What's the weather like?
Girl: It's hot and wet!
3 **Boy:** Hello, Mom!
Mom: Hello. What's the weather like there?
Boy: It's sunny and dry.
4 **Boy:** Hi, Uncle Tom!
Uncle Tom: Hello! What's the weather like?
Boy: It's rainy and windy today.

2 Make your weather wheel. Play and say.

- Tell students they are going to make a weather wheel. Point to the pictures and ask students what they need (card/paper, scissors, craft pin, colored pens).
- Tell students to turn to page 117 and cut the Craft cut-out from their Student Books. Model how to make a weather wheel by coloring it in, cutting out the shape, then fixing it together with a craft pin.
- Make sure students have all the materials. Move around the class offering help. Ask students questions about their weather wheels, e.g. *What's the weather like? Is it sunny? What color is it?*
- In pairs, students ask and answer about the weather using their weather wheels: *What's the weather like? It's (sunny).*

Our Values

- Show the class the space for the *Our Values* sticker. Read out the value (*We share our things*). Tell students that it is good to share with your classmates.
- Tell students they worked well sharing their weather wheels material today. Congratulate students and award them with the *Our Values* sticker to stick in the space on page 21.

3 Complete your picture dictionary.

- Tell students to turn to page 82 of their Student Books and look at the Picture Dictionary section for Unit 2.
- Point to each of the pictures and ask students to say the words.
- Students color the items. Move around the class as they work, asking questions, e.g. *What's the weather like? Is it (rainy)?*

Finisher

- Play *Yes or No*. See Ideas Bank (Teacher's Book page 141) for instructions.

Further practice
Unit 2 Test
Workbook pages 15–17

Culture 1
Birthday Parties pages 22–23
Classroom Presentation Tool

Objectives
To present and practice four new items of vocabulary.

To think about what happens at birthday parties.

To review the vocabulary from a previous unit.

Language and structures
Active: *decorations, party games, pool, sing; balloon, clown, candles, present, card, cake*

Passive: *birthday party, puzzle; What can you see? Draw your birthday party!*

Materials
Unit 1 flashcards; Class Audio CD 1; Megabyte puppet; colored pens

Warmer
- Play *Little by little* with the Unit 1 flashcards. See Ideas Bank (Teacher's Book page 140) for instructions.
- Ask students *When do we see these things?* Elicit *birthday (party).* Write *birthday party* on the board.
- Tell the class today is Megabyte's birthday. Sing Happy Birthday in English or your country's birthday song to Megabyte as a class.

1 Listen and point. Say. 🔊 1·28
- Read the words aloud and point to each photo. Repeat the words and ask students to listen and point to the correct photo.
- Play the recording for students to listen and point to the photos. Play the recording again for students to listen, point, and repeat the words.
- Say the words again and ask students to point to the correct photo. Start slowly and then get faster and faster.

Transcript
decorations, party games, pool, sing
party games, sing, pool, decorations

2 Listen and number. 🔊 1·29
- Ask students to look at the photos again. Ask them *What can you see?* Elicit the Unit 1 and Culture 1 vocabulary (*balloon, candle, cake, party games, decorations, pool, sing*).
- Tell students to listen and write the numbers 1, 2, 3, and 4 in the correct boxes next to the photos.
- Play the recording, pausing after the first item. Elicit the correct photo

---

Birthday Parties

1 Listen and point. Say. 🔵 1.28
2 Listen and number. 🔵 1.29
3 Number the pictures. Circle the words.
4 Draw your birthday party!

party games **4**

decorations **1**

pool **2**

sing **3**

22 **Vocabulary** decorations, party games, pool, sing

(*decorations*) and tell students to write the number 1 in the box.

- Play the remainder of the recording for students to number the photos. With a less confident class, pause after each item or play the recording twice.

Transcript
1 This is my birthday party! There are decorations, look!
2 There's a pool at my party, too. It's great!
3 Look, there's a cake and candles and my friends sing to me.
4 Look. There are party games for my birthday.

3 Number the pictures. Circle the words.
- Point to the eight pictures around the word search on page 23. Elicit the vocabulary from the class.
- Point to the word box at the top of the page. Ask students to read the words aloud. Point to the example, *card.* Tell students that they need to find the

other words in the word search. They may go across or down.

Fast finishers
Ask fast finishers to draw lines from the words in the word box to the pictures.

21ST CENTURY SKILLS:
Communication
Students use pictures and a word search to help them recall and consolidate their knowledge of new and previously acquired vocabulary.

4 Draw your birthday party!
- Ask the class *What do you like about birthday parties?* Listen to students' ideas and praise them.
- Tell students to draw a picture in the space on page 23 of the things they like doing at a party. It could be from their party or from a party they would like to have.

1 card 2 sing 3 decorations 4 clown
5 party games 6 present 7 candles 8 balloons

This is my birthday party!

23

Extension activity
Ask students to label their picture with the birthday and culture vocabulary.

Finisher
- Play a traditional party game, *Statues*. Ask students to stand, and play some music. Pause the music. Students must stand still like a statue until the music starts again. If anyone moves, they are out and must sit down. Continue to play until you have a winner.

Culture note
Pass the present is a very popular party game in many English-speaking countries. A present is wrapped in lots of layers of paper. Students sit in a circle and pass the present around the circle to music. When the music stops, the student who is holding the present takes the first layer of paper off. The music plays again. The winner is the student who takes off the final layer of paper to reveal the present.

Unit 3 My Clothes!
Lesson 1 pages 24–25
Classroom Presentation Tool

Objectives
To present and practice six new items of vocabulary.

To review vocabulary from a previous unit.

Language and structures
Active: *jacket, socks, hat, pants, boots, shoes; It's sunny.*
Passive: *clothes*

Materials
Unit 2 and 3 flashcards; Class Audio CD 1; Megabyte puppet; stickers section; colored pens

Warmer
• Play *Fast flashcards* with the Unit 2 flashcards to review weather. See Ideas Bank (Teacher's Book page 140) for instructions.

1 Listen and point. Say. 💿 1·30
• Books closed. Introduce the new words using the Megabyte puppet and the flashcards or bring some clothes to class. Place the flashcards on the board or the clothes on the table. Use Megabyte to point to the flashcards or pick up the clothes and say the words for students to repeat.
• Books open. Play the recording for students to listen and point to the items in the picture. Play the recording again for students to listen, point, and repeat the words.

Transcript
jacket, socks, hat, pants, boots, shoes
boots, hat, pants, jacket, shoes, socks

2 Stick.
• Ask students to turn to the stickers section in the Student Book. Hold up your book and point to each of the clothes stickers in turn. Encourage students to say the words. Then say the words for students to point to the correct stickers.
• Students stick the stickers in the correct spaces on page 25. When they have finished, ask students to point to the stickers and say the words.

Fast finishers
Put students into pairs to take turns pointing to the stickers and saying what clothes item it is and what color it is, e.g. *green and brown shoes,* etc.

3 Chant. 💿 1·31
• Play the chant once for students to listen and point to the flashcards on the board.
• Play the chant again and encourage students to point to the correct clothes in their Student Books.
• Play the chant once more. When students hear the words, they point to the item of clothing on themselves or on another person in the class.

Chant
pants, pants, pants
shoes, shoes, shoes
hat, hat, hat
socks, socks, socks
boots, boots, boots
jacket, jacket, jacket

Find it!
• Point to Lucy's tablet and ask students *What's the weather like? (It's sunny.)* Ask students to find the sun in the main picture. (It's at the top of page 25.)

• Tell students to turn to the Picture Dictionary for Unit 3 (Student Book page 83) and find the sun. Ask students to color the sun in the Picture Dictionary the same colors as the main artwork on Student Book page 25.

21ST CENTURY SKILLS:
Information literacy
Students interpret visual and audio media to help learn new vocabulary.

Extension activity
Place the Unit 2 weather flashcards on the board (*rainy, snowy, windy, sunny, stormy, cloudy*). Hand out the clothes flashcards to pairs of students. Ask them to come to the front and place the card under an appropriate weather flashcard. They should explain why they chose that flashcard. (*It's hot/cold/wet/dry/sunny.*)

2 Stick.

3 Chant. 🎵 1.31

① ② ③ ④ ⑤ ⑥

shoes

find it! 25

Finisher

- Play *Mime the word*. See Ideas Bank (Teacher's Book page 140) for instructions.

EXTRA VOCABULARY:

jungle gym
ladder
monkey bars
pirate ship
rings
rope bridge

Further practice
CD-ROM: Vocabulary and Grammar Worksheet
Unit 3 Lesson 1
Workbook page 18

Notes

Lesson 2 pages 26–27

Classroom Presentation Tool

Objectives

To present a new grammar structure.

To practice the new grammar with the Lesson 1 vocabulary.

To sing a song using the Lesson 1 vocabulary and the new grammar.

To do a personalization activity that involves a simple craft activity.

Language and structures

Active: *jacket, socks, hat, pants, boots, shoes; Take off your (jacket)! Put on your (hat)!*

Passive: *Let's play in the park/splash. Dress your bear.*

Materials

Unit 2 and 3 flashcards; Class Audio CD 1; Craft Worksheet Unit 3 Lesson 2; scissors, colored pens

Warmer

- Play the chant from Unit 3 Lesson 1 page 25 1.31 for students to listen and join in.
- Place the clothes flashcards around the room and ask students to point to the correct object as they say the chant.

Extra activity

Play the chant again and ask students to mime putting on the clothes as they say the chant.

1 Listen and read. Say. 1·32

- Point to the picture and ask students to say the names of the course characters (Jack, Lucy, and Ellie). Ask *What's the weather like?*
- Play the recording for students to listen. Then play it again and encourage students to repeat the grammar structure.
- Place the clothes flashcards on the board and elicit the vocabulary as you go. Point to the jacket and say *It's hot*. Elicit *Take off your jacket*. Point to the hat flashcard and say *It's hot!* Elicit *Put on your hat*.
- Repeat using *It's cold*, with *boots and hat* to elicit *Put on your / Take off your* and reinforce the meaning of the structure.

2 Listen and match. 1.33 Listen again and repeat.

- Tell students to look at the pictures and elicit the vocabulary (*rainy, windy, sunny, hot, hat, boots, boots, and hat*).
- Say *Put on your hat* and ask students to point to the correct picture. Repeat

with *Take off your hat. Put on your boots. Take off your boots.*

- Tell students they need to listen and match the weather to the correct clothes picture by drawing a line. Point to the example matching line.
- Play the recording. With a less confident class, play the recording twice or pause after each item.
- Ask students to check their answers in pairs before checking together as a class. Check answers by saying *It's wet* and eliciting, e.g. *Put on your boots.*

Transcript

1 It's wet. Put on your boots!

2 It's windy. Take off your hat!

3 It's sunny. Put on your hat!

4 It's hot. Take off your boots!

3 Sing. 🎵1·34 ▶ Watch!

Song!

4 Dress your bear. Play and say.

It's hot! Take off your boots!

Song lyrics ➤ Page 103   Practice ➤ Page 90   27

---

to numbers 2 and 3. Swap roles so numbers 2 and 3 then give the instructions.

Finisher

• Play *Pass the flashcards* with the Unit 2 and 3 flashcards. See Ideas Bank (Teacher's Book page 140) for instructions. With a more confident class, ask students to use the full structure. *It's hot* or *Put on your boots*.

Further practice
Extra Practice Student Book page 90
Workbook page 19

Notes

_____

_____

_____

_____

_____

_____

_____

_____

_____

_____

_____

_____

_____

_____

_____

_____

_____

_____

---

3 Sing. 💿 1·34

• Play the song once for students to listen.
• Play the song again, modeling actions: mime putting on or taking off the appropriate clothing. Ask students to help you create these actions.
• Play the song once more for students to join in and do the actions.

> **21ST CENTURY SKILLS:**
>
> **Creativity and innovation**
> Students learn how to express ideas through music.

Put On Your Socks!
Put on your socks. Let's play in the park.
Put on your pants. Let's go.
Put on your socks. Let's play in the park.
Put on your pants. Let's go.
Put on your jacket. Let's play in the park.
Oh put on your shoes! Let's go.
Put on your jacket. Let's play in the park.
Let's play in the park. Let's go.
Oh look. It's rainy! Take off your shoes.

Put on your boots. Let's go.
Oh look. It's rainy! Take off your shoes.
Put on your boots. Let's go.
Oh look. It's rainy! Put on your hat.
Put on your hat. Let's go.
Oh look. It's rainy! Put on your hat.
Let's play in the park. Let's go.
Oh look. It's rainy! Hey, let's splash!
Splash, splash, splash with our boots.
Oh look. It's rainy! Hey, let's splash!
Splash, splash, splash with our boots.

4 Dress your bear. Play and say.

• Tell students that they are going to cut out and make a bear. Then students will cut out clothes for the bear.
• Make sure each child has scissors and colored pens. Students cut out their bears and the clothes. Then students can color in the clothes.
• When the class is ready, give instructions to the whole class to dress their bears, e.g. *It's hot. Put on your hat.* Then put students into groups of three and number each child 1, 2, or 3. Ask number 1s to give instructions

Lesson 3 pages 28–29

Classroom Presentation Tool

Objectives

To present new vocabulary in the context of the story.

To practice the new vocabulary using the grammar from Lesson 2.

To practice a short Everyday English role play taken from the story.

Language and structures

Active: *T-shirt, sweater, shorts, skirt; How about (a sweater)? Thank you. I'm (hot/cold). Put on / Take off your (sweater).*

Materials

Unit 1, 2, and 3 flashcards; Class Audio CD 1; Megabyte puppet

Warmer

- Play the *My Weather Machine* song from Unit 2, Lesson 2, page 17 🎵 1.20 for students to listen and join in if possible.
- Encourage students to do the actions as they sing the song.

1 Watch or listen. 🎵 1·35 Act it out.

- Point to the first frame of the story and ask students who they can see in the picture (Jack, Lucy, Ellie, Megabyte, and Uncle Alex).
- Point to Uncle Alex's machine and ask *What do you think this machine is for?* Take ideas from the class.
- Play the recording. Encourage students to point to the correct pictures as they listen. Ask them to tell you what Uncle Alex's machine does. (*The machine makes clothes.*)
- Play the recording again and ask students questions about each frame.

    Frame 1: *How does Ellie feel? (She's cold.)*

    Frame 2: *What does the machine make? (A sweater.)*

    Frame 3: *How does Jack feel? (He's hot.)*

    Frame 4: *What does the machine make? (A T-shirt.)*

    Frame 5: *What is Jack wearing now? (A T-shirt and shorts.)*

    Frame 6: *What does Megabyte put on Uncle Alex? (A jacket.) What does Megabyte put on Lucy? (A skirt.) Do they want to wear them? (No!)*

- Divide the class into groups to act out the story. Allow students time to practice in their groups. Then invite groups to act out the story for the class.

21ST CENTURY SKILLS:

Information literacy
Students learn new vocabulary in the context of a story.

2 Listen and point. Say. 🎵 1·36

- Introduce the new words with Megabyte using the flashcards. Slowly reveal the flashcards from behind a piece of paper and place them on the board. Point to the flashcards and say the words for students to repeat.
- Play the recording for students to listen and point to the correct items in their Student Books. Play the recording again for students to listen, point, and repeat the words.
- Ask students to find the items in the story and say the words.

Transcript

T-shirt, sweater, shorts, skirt

skirt, T-shirt, shorts, sweater

2 Listen and point. Say. 1.36

1. **T-shirt**
2. **sweater**
3. **shorts**
4. **skirt**

3 Read and number.

1. Put on your sweater.
2. Put on your shorts.
3. Take off your skirt.
4. Take off your T-shirt.

A — 2
B — 4
C — 1
D — 3

Everyday English!

How about a sweater?

Thank you.

4 Listen and repeat. 1.37
5 Act it out.

Vocabulary T-shirt, sweater, shorts, skirt

Practice ▸ Page 91   29

Further practice
Extra Practice Student Book page 91
CD-ROM: Vocabulary and Grammar Worksheet
Unit 3 Lesson 3
Workbook pages 20–21

Notes

---

3 Read and number.

- Ask students to look at the four pictures. Ask them *What clothes can you see?* Take all of the students' ideas, praising them as they answer.
- Tell the class to read sentences 1–4. Then students will match them to the pictures and write the numbers in the boxes.
- Allow students to check their answers in pairs before checking together as a class. Ask *Which sentence is A?* With a more confident class, elicit the reasons why.

4 Listen and repeat. 1·37

- Play the recording for students to listen. Then play it again. Pause after each line for students to repeat the phrases.

5 Act it out.

- Model the dialogue a few times with the Megabyte puppet, or with more confident students.
- Place the clothes flashcards face down around the room. Ask students to stand.

Play some music and ask students to move around the room. Pause the music. Ask students to form a small group around the flashcard nearest to them. They turn over the flashcard. One child offers the others the card, saying *How about a (T-shirt)?* The others reply, *Thank you.* Play again.

- Tell students they can use this exchange whenever they want to offer something to someone in English.

Extension activity

Ask students to draw a picture of a person wearing some of the clothes from Unit 3. They keep their picture a secret. Put students into pairs to take turns describing their picture to each other. Their partner listens and draws what they hear.

Finisher

- Play *Odd one out* with the Unit 1, 2, and 3 flashcards. See Ideas Bank (Teacher's Book page 140) for instructions.

Classroom Presentation Tool

Objectives

To present a CLIL concept (Science).

To practice the unit vocabulary and grammar through a CLIL concept.

To talk about a value.

Language and structures

Active: *wool, cotton, sheep, plant; It's a (skirt). It's (wool). It's from a plant/an animal.*

Passive: *We take care of our clothes. Make a poster.*

Materials

Unit 1, 2, and 3 flashcards; Class Audio CD 1; CLIL stickers; items made of wool/cotton (optional); CLIL Worksheet Unit 3 Lesson 4; scissors, colored pens, glue, magazines/paper, catalogues/leaflets; Our Values sticker

Warmer

- Play *Which one is missing?* with the Unit 3 flashcards. See Ideas Bank (Teacher's Book page 140) for instructions.

1 Listen and point. 🔊 1·38 Stick.

- Point to the eight pictures in the Student Book. Ask students to tell you what they can see before you listen. Listen to their ideas and praise them.
- Play the recording. Pause after each item and ask students to point to the correct pictures.
- Ask students to turn to the stickers in the Student Book. Hold up your book and point to each of the CLIL stickers. Encourage students to name the items.
- Play the recording again for students to listen and stick the stickers in the correct spaces on page 30.

Transcript

1 This is a sheep. This is wool. Wool is from sheep. Look at the sweater. It's made of wool. Look at the hat. It's made of wool.

2 This is a cotton plant. This is cotton. Cotton is from a cotton plant. Look at the T-shirt. It's made of cotton. Look at the skirt. It's made of cotton, too.

2 Listen, point, and say *sheep* or *plant*. 🔊 1·39

- Tell students to look at the pictures again. Read out the first line of the recording from the transcript. Students listen and point to the correct picture. They complete the sentence (*It's from a … plant*).
- Play the recording. Pause after each sentence. Ask students to complete the sentences by saying the correct word.

Transcript

It's a skirt. It's cotton. It's from a …
It's a sweater. It's wool. It's from a …
It's a T-shirt. It's cotton. It's from a …
It's a hat. It's wool. It's from a …

3 Look and draw.

- Look at the pictures. Ask the class to point to the *wool*. Elicit *It's wool*. Ask the class to point to the *cotton*. Elicit *It's cotton*.
- Ask *Where does wool come from?* Elicit *A sheep*. Say *Draw a sheep*. Students draw a sheep in the first box on the left. Ask the class *Where does cotton come from?* Elicit *A plant*. Say *Draw a plant*. They draw a cotton plant in the second box on the left.
- Ask the class to draw one piece of wool clothing and one piece of cotton clothing in the boxes on the right.

4 Make a poster. Point and say.

- Hand out CLIL worksheets. Students will use the poster template to make a collage of clothes made of cotton and wool. They can either draw or stick pictures of clothes that are made of wool or cotton.

- While students are drawing and/or sticking, ask about their different posters: *What is it? It's a hat. Is it cotton or wool?*
- Use show-and-tell to give feedback on students' ideas. Ask students to point to something on their poster and say, e.g. *It's a T-shirt. It's cotton. It's from a plant.*

Our Values

- Show the class the space for the *Our Values* sticker. Read aloud the value (*We take care of our clothes*). Tell students that it is good to look after your clothes.
- Congratulate students for having worked well today learning about fabrics and award. Award them with the *Our Values* sticker to stick in the space on page 30.

Finisher

- Play *Four in a row*. See Ideas Bank (Teacher's Book page 141) for instructions. Use flashcards from Units 1–3.

Further practice
Workbook page 22

3 Review

1 Look and write. Draw the secret word.

boots   jacket   shorts   shoes   skirt

	s	h	o	r	t	s		
		s	h	o	e	s	s	
		j	a	c	k	e	t	
		s	k	i	r	t		
b	o	o	t	s				

Put on your s o c k s !

2 Make your flip book. Play and say. ✂ Page 115

Look, a hat, a sweater, shorts ...

31

3 Complete your picture dictionary. Page 83

Review page 31
Classroom Presentation Tool

Objectives
To review the linguistic content of the unit.

Language and structures
Active: *jacket, socks, hat, pants, boots, shoes, T-shirt, sweater, shorts, skirt, wool, cotton; Put on your (boots), Take off your (sweater).*
Passive: *secret word; Make your flip book.*

Materials
Unit 3 flashcards; Craft cut-out Unit 3 Review; scissors, colored pens

Warmer
- Play *Guess the flashcard*. See Ideas Bank (Teacher's Book page 140) for instructions.

1 Look and write. Draw the secret word.
- Point to the word box and ask the class to read the words aloud.
- Ask students to look at the clothes pictures on the left of the word puzzle. Tell them to write the words in the puzzle.
- When they have completed the horizontal clues, point to the highlighted vertical column and ask *What's the secret word? (Socks!)*
- Tell students to write the word in the space provided and to draw a picture of socks.

> **TEACHING TIP**
> With a less confident class, ask students to tell you the names of the clothes pictured before they write them.

2 Make your flip book. Play and say.
- Tell students they are going to make a flip book. Point to the pictures and ask

students what they need to make one (scissors, glue, colored pens).
- Tell students to turn to page 115 and cut the Craft cut-out from their Student Books. Model how to make a flip book by coloring it in, cutting out the pages, then gluing them together along the side.
- Make sure students have all the materials. Move around the class offering help if necessary. Ask students questions about their flip book, e.g. *What's he wearing? Is it a hat? Are they pants? What color is it / are they? Is it wool?*
- Ask the class to line up in a single line. Pair students up with the person next to them. Ask them to move to a space in the room and sit on the floor. Students play together with their flip books, selecting different combinations of clothes. They tell their partner *Look! A hat, a T-shirt, shorts, and shoes.*

> **Extension activity**
> Ask students to take turns using their clothes flip book to give their partner instructions, e.g. *Put on your (socks)*. They listen and follow, using the flip book.

3 Complete your picture dictionary.
- Tell students to turn to page 83 of their Student Books and look at the Picture Dictionary section for Unit 3.
- Point to each of the pictures and ask students to say the words.
- Students color the items in the Picture Dictionary. Move around the class as they work, asking questions, e.g. *What is it? Is it (a T-shirt)? What are they? Are they (shorts)?*

Finisher
- Play *Mime the word*. See Ideas Bank (Teacher's Book page 140) for instructions.

> **Culture note**
> One of the most famous fashion exports of the USA are blue jeans. They first became popular as work clothes in the 1850s and later became popular with American teenagers. They were introduced by Levi Strauss who was originally from Germany but emigrated to San Francisco. Now they are popular with people of all ages and all backgrounds around the world and are worn for both work and leisure!

| Further practice
| Unit 3 Test
| Workbook page 23

Unit 4 Home, Sweet Home
Lesson 1 pages 32—33
Classroom Presentation Tool

Objectives
To present and practice six new items of vocabulary.

To review vocabulary from a previous unit.

Language and structures
Active: *bedroom, bathroom, living room, dining room, kitchen, yard*; *boots*

Materials
Unit 1, 2, 3, and 4 flashcards; Class Audio CD 1; Megabyte puppet; stickers section

Warmer
- Play *Musical flashcards* with the Unit 1, 2, and 3 flashcards. See Ideas Bank (Teacher's Book page 141) for instructions.

1 Listen and point. Say. 💿 1·40
- Books closed. Introduce the new words using the Megabyte puppet and the flashcards. Draw a basic house outline on the board. Place the flashcards on the board inside the house. Use Megabyte to point to the flashcards and say the words for students to repeat.
- Books open. Play the recording for students to listen and point to the rooms in the picture. Play the recording again for students to listen, point, and repeat the words.

Extra activity
With a more confident class, ask students to take turns calling out home words for the rest of the students to point to and say slowly then quickly.

Transcript
bedroom, bathroom, living room, dining room, kitchen, yard

living room, bedroom, yard, kitchen, bathroom, dining room

4 Home, Sweet Home
Lesson 1

1 Listen and point. Say. 1.40

bedroom

living room

dining room

32 **Vocabulary** bedroom, bathroom, living room, dining room, kitchen, yard

2 Stick.
- Ask students to turn to the stickers section in the Student Book. Hold up your book and point to each of the home stickers in turn. Encourage students to say the words. Then say the words for students to point to the correct stickers.
- Students stick the stickers in the correct spaces on page 33. When they have finished, ask students to point to the stickers and say the words.

Fast finishers
Put students into pairs to take turns pointing to the stickers and telling their partner the words, e.g. *It's a (kitchen).*

3 Chant. 💿 1·41
- Play the chant once for students to listen and point to the flashcards on the board.
- Play the chant again and encourage students to point to the correct rooms in their Student Books.

- Place the flashcards on the walls around the room. Play the chant once more. When students hear the words, they walk to the correct flashcard.

Chant
kitchen, kitchen, kitchen
living room, living room, living room
dining room, dining room, dining room
yard, yard, yard
bedroom, bedroom, bedroom
bathroom, bathroom, bathroom

21ST CENTURY SKILLS:
Communication
Students reinforce their understanding of new vocabulary using a chant.

EXTRA VOCABULARY:

bathtub
bed
cabinet
doll
lion
rocket
sink
sofa
stove
superhero
swing

Further practice
**CD-ROM: Vocabulary and Grammar Worksheet
Unit 4 Lesson 1
Workbook page 24**

Notes

Find it!
- Point to Jack's drawing pad and ask students what they can see (boots). Ask students to find the boots in the main picture. (On the superhero in the kitchen on page 33.)
- Tell students to turn to the Picture Dictionary for Unit 4 (Student Book page 83) and find the boots. Ask students to color the boots in the Picture Dictionary the same colors as the main artwork on Student Book page 33.

Extension activity
Make a class miniature house over the course of Unit 4. Bring five shoeboxes or similar to class. Use sticky tape to attach them together, with three boxes along the bottom and two on top. Ask students to take turns throughout the unit to decorate the rooms, painting the walls and making furniture out of colored card. Glue the furniture in the rooms. Make sure each student has a turn at painting or making something. This could be used as a reward for good behavior in class and for fast finishers.

Finisher
- Play *Tic-Tac-Toe*. See Ideas Bank (Teacher's Book page 141) for instructions.

Lesson 2 pages 34–35

Classroom Presentation Tool

Objectives

To present a new grammar structure.

To practice the new grammar structure with the Lesson 1 vocabulary.

To sing a song using the Lesson 1 vocabulary and the new grammar.

To do a personalization activity that involves a simple craft activity.

To talk about a value.

Language and structures

Active: *Where's (Uncle Alex)? (He's in the (yard); bedroom, bathroom, living room, dining room, kitchen, yard*

Passive: *What is it? Put the people in the house. We clean up after craft.*

Materials

Unit 4 flashcards, Lucy and Jack flashcards; Class Audio CD 1; Craft Worksheet Unit 4 Lesson 2; scissors, glue, colored pens; Our Values sticker

Warmer

- Play the chant from Unit 4 Lesson 1 page 33 🔊 1.41 for students to listen and join in.
- Place the home flashcards around the room and ask students to point to the correct room as they say the chant.

1 Listen and read. Say. 🔊 1·42

- Point to the picture and ask students to say the names of the course characters they can see (Jack, Lucy, Uncle Alex, and Ellie).
- Play the recording for students to listen. Then play it again and encourage students to repeat the grammar structure.
- Place the home flashcards on the board. Point to a flashcard and ask *What is it? (The kitchen.)* Repeat with the other flashcards.
- Place the Lucy flashcard next to a room and ask the class *Where's Lucy?* Elicit *She's in the (bedroom).* Repeat with the other rooms. Play again with Jack. Ask *Where's Jack?* Elicit *He's in the (bathroom).* Remind students we use *He* for a boy and *She* for a girl.

Extension activity

Ask students to come to the front and place Lucy and Jack in a room and ask *Where's (Jack)?* etc. The rest of the class responds. With a more confident class, place Lucy and Jack in the same room and ask *Where are they? They're in the (bathroom)* to introduce this structure.

4 Lesson 2

1 Listen and read. Say. 1.42

Learn with **Lucy** and **Jack**

Where's Uncle Alex? — He's in the yard.

Where's Ellie? — She's in the kitchen.

2 Listen and circle. 1.43 Listen again and repeat.

34 Where's Uncle Alex? He's in the yard.

---

2 Listen and circle. 🔊 1·43 Listen again and repeat.

- Point to the rooms in the house and elicit the names of the rooms.
- Ask students to look at the picture and ask *Where's Megabyte?* Elicit *He's in the yard.* Explain that he's playing a game of Hide and Seek. The children are hiding from him. Ask *Where's Ellie?* Elicit *She's in the living room* and show students the circled example answer.
- Tell students to listen and circle the hiding places. Play the recording twice or pause after each item if necessary.
- Check answers by asking *Where's (Lucy)?* Encourage students to reply using the structure *She's in the (kitchen).*

Transcript

A: Where's Lucy?
Megabyte: She's in the kitchen.
A: Where's Jack?
Megabyte: He's in the bathroom.
A: Where's Ellie?
Megabyte: She's in the living room.
A: Where's Uncle Alex?
Megabyte: He's in the bedroom.

4 Put the people in the house. Play and say.

- Tell students that they are going to cut out and make a house.
- Make sure each student has scissors, glue, and colored pens.
- Students cut out their houses and the family members, and color them in.
- As they make their houses, move around the room asking questions, e.g. *Which room is it? What color is it?* etc.
- Ask students to tidy up their materials before putting them into pairs. They take turns hiding the family members and asking *Where's (Dad)? He's in the (bedroom).*

> **21ST CENTURY SKILLS:**
> **Collaboration**
> Students engage with each other in a speaking activity to practice the grammatical structures and vocabulary.

Our Values

- Show the class the space for the *Our Values* sticker. Read out the value (*We clean up after craft time*). Tell students that it is good to clean up after they do craft time.
- Tell students they have used lots of materials for craft time today, and it's important to put things away so the room is left clean. Congratulate students for cleaning up and award them with the *Our Values* sticker to stick in the space on page 35.

Finisher

- Play *Mime the word*. See Ideas Bank (Teacher's Book page 140) for instructions. Ask *Where's (Daniel)?* for each person who mimes and encourage the class to guess using *He's in the (bathroom).*

Further practice
Extra Practice Student Book page 92
Workbook page 25

3. Sing. 1·44

- Play the *My Computer House* song once for students to listen. See page 143 for the lyrics.
- Play the song again, modeling actions: use your finger to click and drag an imaginary mouse. Place the home flashcards on the board for students to point to as they sing.
- Play the song once more for students to join in, do the actions, and point to the flashcards.

My Computer House

Click and drag! Click and drag!
A computer house for our family!
Oh, where's Dad?
Click and drag!
Look in the kitchen! He's in the kitchen!
In my computer house, Dad's in the kitchen.
Oh, where's Mom?
Click and drag!
Look in the dining room! She's in the dining room!
In my computer house, Mom's in the

dining room.
Oh, where's Grandpa?
Click and drag!
Look in the bedroom. He's in the bedroom!
In my computer house, Grandpa's in the bedroom.
Oh, where's Grandma?
Click and drag!
Look in the living room! She's in the living room!
In my computer house, Grandma's in the living room.
Oh, where's Anna?
Click and drag!
Look in the bathroom. She's in the bathroom!
In my computer house, Anna's in the bathroom.
Oh, where's Mac?
Click and drag!
Look in the yard. He's in the yard!
In my computer house, Mac's in the yard.
Click and drag! Click and drag!
A computer house for our family!

Lesson 3 (pages 36–37)

Classroom Presentation Tool

Objectives

To present new vocabulary in the context of the story.

To practice the new vocabulary using the grammar from Lesson 2.

To practice a short Everyday English role play taken from the story.

Language and structures

Active: *bed, sofa, bathtub, table; I'm scared! Don't worry. It's my turn! Look! It's a … What's … ?*

Passive: *Here's a … Where's the … ?*

Materials

Unit 4 flashcards; Class Audio CD 1; Megabyte puppet

Warmer

• Play the *My Computer House* song from Unit 4 Lesson 2 page 35 🔊 1.44 for students to listen and join in if possible.

1 Watch or listen. 🔊 1·45 Act it out.

• Point to the first frame of the story and ask students who they can see in the picture (Jack, Lucy, Ellie, and Megabyte). Point to Frame 1 and ask *Where are the students? (Camping.)*

• Play the recording. Encourage students to point to the correct pictures as they listen.

• Play the recording again and ask students questions about each frame.

  Frame 1: *Are the children happy? (Yes.) Is Megabyte happy? (No.)*

  Frame 2: *Where are the children? (In the tent.) Is Megabyte happy? (No, he's thinking about the sofa at home.)*

  Frame 3: *What are the children doing? (Making shadow shapes with their hands.)*

  Frame 4: *What is Megabyte doing? (Making shadow shapes.)*

  Frame 5: *Is Ellie scared? (No.) What does she do? (She sprays water at Megabyte.)*

  Frame 6: *Where is Megabyte? (In the water.) What is he thinking about? (The bathtub at home.)*

• Divide the class into groups to act out the story. Allow students time to practice in their groups. Then invite groups to act out the story for the class.

2 Listen and point. Say. 🔊 1·46

• Introduce the new words with Megabyte using the flashcards. Slowly reveal the flashcards from behind a piece of paper and place them on the board. Point to the flashcards and say the words for students to repeat.

• Play the recording for students to listen and point to the correct items in their Student Books. Play the recording again for students to listen, point, and repeat the words.

• Ask students to point to the items in the story and say the words.

Transcript

bed, sofa, bathtub, table
table, bed, bathtub, sofa

2 Listen and point. Say. `1.46`

1. bed
2. sofa
3. bathtub
4. table

3 Listen and circle *A* or *B*. `1.47`

A | B

1 **A** B 2 A **B** 3 A **B** 4 A **B** 5 A **B** 6 A **B**

Everyday English!

4 Listen and repeat. `1.48`

5 Act it out.

I'm scared!

Don't worry.

Vocabulary bed, sofa, bathtub, table

Practice ▶ Page 93   37

Finisher

- Play *Bingo!* See Ideas Bank (Teacher's Book page 141) for instructions.

Further practice

Extra Practice Student Book page 93
CD-ROM: Vocabulary and Grammar Worksheet Unit 4 Lesson 3
Workbook pages 26–27

Notes

---

3 Listen and circle *A* or *B*. 🔊 1·47

- Divide the class into two teams. Ask each team to look at either picture A or picture B and take turns saying things they can see, e.g. *Look! It's a (bathtub)*.
- Point to the numbers 1–6 below the pictures. Tell students to listen and circle A or B depending on which picture is being described in the recording.
- Play the recording. Pause after the first item. Ask *Is it A or B? A!* Refer students to the example answer.
- Play the recording for students to listen and circle. Play the recording again for students to check or complete their answers.

Transcript

1 Where's the bed? It's in the bedroom.
2 Where's the sofa? It's in the kitchen!
3 Where's the table? It's in the dining room.
4 Where's the sofa? It's in the living room.
5 Where's the bed? It's in the yard!
6 Where's the bathtub? It's in the dining room!

4 Listen and repeat. 🔊 1·48

- Play the recording for students to listen. Then play it again. Pause after each line for students to repeat the phrases.

5 Act it out.

- Model the dialogue a few times with the Megabyte puppet, or with more confident students.
- Ask pairs of students to practice the exchange together. Encourage them to act out being scared. Move around the class making sure students are speaking and responding appropriately.
- Tell students they can use this exchange whenever they want to make someone feel better when they feel scared/sad/upset/worried.

> **21ST CENTURY SKILLS:**
>
> **Social and cross-cultural interaction**
> Students learn an everyday phrase in English to express fear and to comfort others.

Lesson 4 page 38

Classroom Presentation Tool

Objectives

To present a CLIL concept (History).

To practice the unit vocabulary and grammar through a CLIL concept.

Language and structures

Active: *old, new; It's in the old/new (kitchen).*

Passive: *This (living room)'s new/old; new things, old bedroom. Draw a new bedroom.*

Materials

Unit 4 flashcards; Class Audio CD 1; CLIL stickers; CLIL Worksheet Unit 4 Lesson 4; ball (optional); colored pens

Warmer

- Play *True or False*. See Ideas Bank (Teacher's Book page 141) for instructions. Use a balled up piece of paper if you don't have a ball.

1 Listen and point. 🔘 1·49 Stick.

- Point to the old house in the Student Book. Say *This house is old*. Write *old* on the board. Ask students to say *old*. Point to the new house and say *This house is new*. Write *new* on the board. Ask students to say *new*.

- Ask students to tell you what things they can see in the old house. Then ask what they can see in the new house.

- Play the recording. Pause after each item. Ask students to point to either the old house or the new house. Ask students to check with their partner.

- Ask students to turn to the stickers section in the Student Book. Hold up your book and point to each of the CLIL stickers in turn. Encourage students to name the items.

- Play the recording again for students to listen and stick the stickers in the correct spaces on page 38.

Transcript

This living room's old. This living room's new. This bathroom's new. This bathroom's old. This bedroom's old. This bedroom's new. This kitchen's new. This kitchen's old.

2 Listen and find. 🔘 1·50 Ask and answer.

- Tell students to look at the pictures again. Read the first line of the recording from the transcript. Students listen and point to the item. Check that they are pointing to the correct object.

- Play the recording. Pause after each question for them to listen, find, and point to the items in the pictures.

4 Lesson 4

History

1 Listen and point. ^{1.49} Stick.
2 Listen and find. ^{1.50} Ask and answer.

OLD NEW

3 Look and circle five new things. Listen and check. ^{1.51}

4 Look at the old bedroom. Draw a new bedroom.

38 **Vocabulary** old, new

- Put students into pairs. Ask them to take turns asking about different furniture for their partner to find and say, i.e. *Where's the (new table)? It's in the (new kitchen).*

Transcript

Where's the old sofa? / Where's the new bed? / Where's the old bathtub? / Where's the new table? / Where's the new sofa? / Where's the old bed? / Where's the new bathtub? / Where's the old table?

3 Look and circle five new things. Listen and check. 🔘 1·51

- Point to the picture. Ask the class *What things are old?* Listen to students' ideas. Ask *What things are new?* Listen again to students' ideas.

- Tell students to listen and circle the things that are new.

- Play the recording once. Ask students to check their answers in pairs. Play the recording again for students to complete or check their answers.

- Check answers by pointing to an item and eliciting, e.g. *It's a (new) (sofa).*

Transcript

This picture's new. / This T-shirt's new. / This toy helicopter's new. / This sofa's new. / This scooter's new.

4 Look at the old bedroom. Draw a new bedroom.

- Hand out CLIL worksheets. Look at the picture together. Students identify familiar vocabulary in the old room (*bed, chair, picture, candle, teddy, bike,* etc.)

- Tell students to draw and color a new bedroom in the empty frame.

- Ask individual students about their room, e.g. *Is there a (bed) in your bedroom? (Yes, there is.) Is it the same or different?*

Finisher

- Play *Change places*. See Ideas Bank (Teacher's Book page 141) for instructions.

Further practice
Workbook page 28

4 Review

1 Follow and write. Ask and answer.

living room   kitchen   yard

1 Tim
2 Lea
3

yard

kitchen

living room

2 Make your game board. Play and say. ✂ Page 113

Where's the sofa?

It's in C1.

3 Complete your picture dictionary. Page 83

39

Review page 39

Classroom Presentation Tool

Objectives
To review the linguistic content of the unit.

Language and structures
Active: *bedroom, bathroom, living room, dining room, kitchen, yard, bed, sofa, bathtub, table, old, new; Where's (the sofa)? (It)'s in the (yard).*

Passive: *follow*

Materials
Unit 4 flashcards; Craft cut-out Unit 4 Review; scissors, colored pens

Warmer
- Play *Kim's game*. See Ideas Bank (Teacher's Book page 140) for instructions.

1 Follow and write. Ask and answer.
- Point to the three characters on the left. Ask *What's his/her name?* (Tim, Lea, robot.)
- Ask the class to read the words in the word box. Ask students to use their fingers like feet to follow the path and walk to the correct place. They write the correct word on the line below the picture.
- Check answers by asking *Where's (Tim)? He's in the (living room)*. Ask students to repeat the questions and answers in pairs.

TEACHING TIP
With a more confident class, put students into pairs. Ask them to take turns asking and answering as they walk their fingers to the places in the pictures.

2 Make your game board. Play and say.
- Tell students they are going to make a game board. Point to the pictures and ask students what they need to make one (paper, scissors, colored pens).
- Tell students to turn to page 113 and cut the Craft cut-out from their Student Books. Model how to make a game board by cutting out the grid and the furniture, and coloring them in.
- Make sure students have all the materials. Move around the class offering help if necessary. Ask students questions about their game board, e.g. *What is it? Is it a (table)? What color is it? Is it (blue)?* etc.
- Ask pairs of students to place a book between them as in the photo. Ask one student to place their furniture in the spaces in the grid. The other student leaves their board game empty and asks questions to find out where each item is, e.g. *Where's the (sofa)? It's in (C1)*. They place their items in the same place in their grid.
- When they have finished, ask students to take down the book and see if they placed their furniture in the correct place. The next student takes their turn asking.

3 Complete your picture dictionary.
- Tell students to turn to page 83 of their Student Books and look at the Picture Dictionary section for Unit 4.
- Point to each of the pictures and ask students to say the words.
- Students color the items in the Picture Dictionary. Move around the class as they work, asking questions, e.g. *What is it? Is it a (bathroom)?*

21ST CENTURY SKILLS:
Productivity and accountability
Students reflect on the language they have learned in the unit.

Finisher
- Play *What number is it?* See Ideas Bank (Teacher's Book page 140) for instructions.

TEACHING TIP
Students can play the game in small groups using the cut-out home vocabulary cards from their board game in exercise 2.

Further practice
Unit 4 Test
Workbook pages 29–31

Culture 2
Vacation! pages 40–41
Classroom Presentation Tool

Objectives
To present and practice four new items of vocabulary.

To think about what we do on vacation.

To review the vocabulary from a previous unit.

Language and structures
Active: *hotel, boat, motor home, tent; clothes*

Passive: *Where do you go on vacation? How many hats? count; Draw your clothes and your vacation.*

Materials
Class Audio CD 1; colored pens; Unit 3 and 4 flashcards

Warmer
- Play *Sharkman* to elicit the word *vacation*. See Ideas Bank (Teacher's Book page 142) for instructions.
- Ask students *Where do you go on vacation?*

1 Listen and point. Say. 1·52
- Read the words aloud and point to each photo. Repeat the words and ask students to listen and point to the correct photo.
- Play the recording for students to listen and point to the photos. Play the recording again for students to listen, point, and repeat the words.
- Say the words again and ask students to point to the correct photo. Start slowly, then get faster and faster.

Extra activity
With a less confident class, put students into pairs. Ask them to take turns saying a word pictured on page 40 for their partner to listen, point to, and repeat.

Transcript
hotel, boat, motor home, tent
tent, boat, motor home, hotel

2 Listen and number. 1·53
- Ask students to look at the photos again. Ask them *What can you see?* Elicit *hotel, boat, motor home, tent*, and any other words students know.
- Tell students to listen and write the numbers 1, 2, 3, and 4 in the correct boxes next to the photos.
- Play the recording, pausing after each item to give students time to write the numbers. With a less confident class, play the recording twice.

Culture 2 **Vacation!**

1 Listen and point. Say. 1.52
2 Listen and number. 1.53
3 Find and count. Say.
4 Draw your clothes and your vacation.

hotel **4**

boat **1**

motor home **3**

2 tent

40 Vocabulary hotel, boat, motor home, tent

Extra activity
With a more confident class, ask students which vacation home they prefer and why.

Transcript
1 Look, this is the boat. It's really great.
2 I'm on vacation in a tent. I am in the bedroom.
3 This is my vacation, in a motor home. Look, I'm in the bedroom with my sister and my brother.
4 I'm on vacation in a hotel. Look, this is me in the pool with my mom.

3 Find and count. Say.
- Review clothing vocabulary with the class. Play *Little by little* and slowly reveal the Unit 3 flashcards. Place them on the board. See Ideas Bank (Teacher's Book page 140) for instructions.
- Point to the picture of the bedroom on page 41. Ask the class *What room is it?* Elicit *The bedroom*. Ask students what clothes they can see and elicit the

clothing vocabulary (*hat, T-shirt, socks, shoes, shorts, pants, jacket*).

- Point to the suitcase on the right. Point to the hats and ask, *How many hats? Count*. Count the hats in the bedroom as a class. 1, 2, 3, 4, 5, 6! Say *There are six hats*. The class repeats. Tell students to color in six of the hats in the suitcase.
- Tell students to count the T-shirts, socks, and shoes and color them in. They tell their partner how many of each clothing item there are using the correct structure *There are (5 socks)*. etc.

TEACHING TIP
With a less confident class, count each clothing item together as a class. With a more confident class, allow students to work independently. Then check their answers in pairs.

4 Draw your clothes and your vacation.

- Ask *Can you remember the vacation words?* Draw pictures on the board to help elicit the Culture 2 vocabulary. Write the words clearly on the board.

- Tell students to choose the vacation they like the most and draw a picture of themselves on vacation in the space on page 41.

- Place the Unit 3 clothing flashcards on the board and ask students to call out the vocabulary as you do so. Tell them to draw the clothes they will take on vacation in the suitcase on page 41.

- As they draw and color, move around the class asking questions, *What is it? What color is it? Is it a (blue) (hat)?* etc.

Fast finishers

Ask students to label their picture with the clothes vocabulary.

21ST CENTURY SKILLS:

Creativity and innovation
Students learn how to express ideas through art.

Finisher

- Play *Which one is missing?* with the Unit 3 and 4 flashcards. See Ideas Bank (Teacher's Book page 140) for instructions.

Unit 5 At the Beach
Lesson 1 pages 42–43
Classroom Presentation Tool

Objectives
To present and practice six new items of vocabulary.

To review vocabulary from a previous unit.

Language and structures
Active: *swim, dive, sing, climb, cook, run; sofa*

Passive: *beach*

Materials
Unit 3, 4, and 5 flashcards; Class Audio CD 1; Megabyte puppet; stickers section

Warmer
- Play *Fast flashcards* with the Unit 3 and 4 flashcards. See Ideas Bank (Teacher's Book page 140) for instructions.

1 Listen and point. Say. 🔊 1·54
- Books closed. Introduce the new words using the Megabyte puppet and the Unit 5 flashcards. Place the flashcards on the board. Use Megabyte to act out the actions after you place each flashcard on the board.
- Use Megabyte to point to the flashcards and say the words for students to repeat and act out the actions.
- Books open. Play the recording for students to listen and point to the actions in the picture. Play the recording again for students to listen, point, and repeat the words.

Transcript
swim, dive, sing, climb, cook, run
cook, swim, climb, sing, run, dive

2 Stick.
- Ask students to turn to the stickers section in the Student Book. Hold up your book and point to each of the action stickers in turn. Encourage students to say the words. Then say the words for students to point to the correct stickers.
- Students stick the stickers in the correct spaces on page 43. When they have finished, ask students to point to the stickers and say the words.

5 At the Beach

Lesson 1

1 Listen and point. Say. 1.54

swim

sing

climb

cook

42 **Vocabulary** swim, dive, sing, climb, cook, run

Fast finishers
Put students into pairs to take turns saying the actions for their partner to act out.

3 Chant. 🔊 1·55
- Play the chant once for students to listen.
- Play the chant again, pointing to the flashcards on the board.
- Play the chant once more. Encourage students to act out the correct actions.

Extra activity
Divide the class into two teams. Place the flashcards in a pile at the front of the class. Ask a student from one team to come to the front, pick up a card, and mime it. If their team guesses the action correctly, they win a point. The next team takes their turn.

Chant
swim, swim, swim
climb, climb, climb
dive, dive, dive
sing, sing, sing
cook, cook, cook
run, run, run

Find it!
- Point to Lucy's tablet and ask students what they can see *(a sofa)*. Ask students to find the sofa in the main picture. *(It's made of sand on page 42.)*
- Tell students to turn to the Picture Dictionary for Unit 5 (Student Book page 84) and find the sofa. Ask students to color the sofa in the Picture Dictionary the same color as the main artwork on Student Book page 42.

2 Stick.

3 Chant. 🎵 1.55

dive

run

Find it! 43

Notes

21ST CENTURY SKILLS:

Information literacy
Students work with their Picture Dictionary to review vocabulary from a previous unit.

Finisher
- Play *Pass the flashcards* with the Unit 3, 4, and 5 flashcards. See Ideas Bank (Teacher's Book page 140) for instructions.

TEACHING TIP
Bring a bell or a whistle to class. Tell students that in lessons throughout this unit, you will randomly ring your bell/blow your whistle and call out an action. When you do, they must stand and mime it.

EXTRA VOCABULARY:
barbecue
climbing wall
crab
fish
guitar
inner tube
lifeguard
shell
starfish
the ocean
whale

Further practice
CD-ROM: Vocabulary and Grammar Worksheet
Unit 5 Lesson 1
Workbook page 32

Lesson 2 pages 44–45
Classroom Presentation Tool

Objectives
To present a new grammar structure.

To practice the new grammar structure with the Lesson 1 vocabulary.

To sing a song using the Lesson 1 vocabulary and the new grammar.

To do a personalization activity that involves a simple craft activity.

Language and structures
Active: *I can (swim). I can't (cook)*; *swim, dive, sing, climb, cook, run*

Passive: *check*; *What about you? Draw the things you can do.*

Materials
Unit 5 flashcards, Lucy, Jack, and Ellie flashcards; Class Audio CD 1; Craft Worksheet Unit 5 Lesson 2; colored pens

Warmer
- Play the chant from Unit 5 Lesson 1 page 43 🔊 1.55 for students to listen and join in.
- Ask students to do the actions as they say the chant.

TEACHING TIP
Reward well-behaved students by allowing them to take turns using Megabyte to do the actions as they listen to the chant.

1 Listen and read. Say. 🔊 1·56
- Point to the picture and ask students to say the names of the course characters (Lucy, Jack, and Megabyte).
- Play the recording for students to listen. Then play it again and encourage students to repeat the grammar structure.
- Place the action flashcards on the board and elicit the vocabulary as you go. Point to each flashcard and act them out using either the affirmative structure, e.g. *I can (swim)* or the negative structure, e.g. *I can't (cook)*. Repeat with the other flashcards.

Extension activity
Ask students to pick flashcards. Elicit the action from the class. Invite a confident student to mime that action either badly or well. Encourage them to say *I can/can't (climb)*. etc.

2 Listen and make a ✓ or an ✗. 🔊 1·57 Complete for you. Say.
- Place the Lucy, Jack, and Ellie flashcards on the left of the board in a column.

Place the flashcards for *cook, sing, dive,* and *climb* across the top of the board.

- Point to Lucy and say *I can't cook.* Draw an ✗ next to Lucy and under *cook* on the board. Point to Jack and say *I can cook* and draw a check under *cook*.
- Point to the grid in the Student Book. Say *Listen. Check for I can.* ✗ *for I can't.* Play the recording twice or pause after each item if necessary.
- Ask students to check their answers in pairs before checking together as a class. Point to the grid on the board and encourage students to use the structure to answer *I can't sing.*
- Say *What about you?* Tell students to check or put an ✗ next to the things they can and can't do in the final row in the table.
- Put students into pairs to take turns telling their partner about their answers using the structure.

Extension activity
With a more confident class, ask students to give you the answers using the third person, e.g. *She can't cook. He can swim.* Remind the class we use *He* for a boy and *She* for a girl.

Transcript
Lucy: I can't cook and I can't sing. I can dive and I can climb!
Jack: I can cook. I can't sing. I can't dive, but I can climb!
Ellie: I can't cook, but I can sing. I can dive and I can climb!

21ST CENTURY SKILLS:
Communication
Students use visual and audio media to learn a new grammatical structure in English.

Song lyrics > Page 104   Practice > Page 94   45

3 Sing. 🎵 1·58

- Play the *I Can Try* song once for students to listen. See page 143 for lyrics.
- Play the song again, modeling actions: nod your head for *yes*; shake your head for *no*; two thumbs up for *try*; and hands together, then unfolded like a book to read.
- Divide the class into six groups. Give each group an action, i.e. *read, swim, dive, run, sing,* and *cook.* Play the song once more. Each group does the action for their verse.

I Can Try

I can read. Yes, yes, yes.
Yes, I can read. Read, read, read.
I can swim. Yes, yes, yes.
Yes, I can swim. Swim, swim, swim.
But I can't dive. No, no, no.
No, I can't dive. But I can try.
I can try. Try, try, try.
Yes, I can try. Try, try, try.
I can run. Yes, yes, yes.
Yes, I can run. Run, run, run.
I can sing. Yes, yes, yes.

Yes, I can sing. Sing, sing, sing.
But I can't cook. No, no, no.
No, I can't cook. But I can try.
I can try. Try, try, try.
Yes, I can try. Try, try, try.

4 Draw the things you can do. Say.

- Tell students that they are going to make a poster of the things they can do.
- Make sure each student has colored pens. Students draw and color pictures of the things they can do.
- As they make their posters, move around the class monitoring and asking questions, e.g. *What's this? I can (swim). That's great!*
- Ask students to clean up their materials before putting them into pairs. They take turns telling their partner the things they can do using the structure, e.g. *Look! I can swim.* Their partner responds saying, *That's great!*

Extension activity

Play some music and ask the class to stand and walk around the room with their posters. Pause the music. Students turn to the person closest to them and tell them one thing they can do, e.g. *Look! I can read!* Their partner responds *Good job!* and says one thing they can do. Repeat several times.

Finisher

- Play *What card is missing?* See Ideas Bank (Teacher's Book page 140) for instructions.

Further practice

Extra Practice Student Book page 94
Workbook page 33

Lesson 3 (pages 46–47)
Classroom Presentation Tool

Objectives
To present new vocabulary in the context of the story.

To practice the new vocabulary using the grammar from Lesson 2.

To practice a short Everyday English role play taken from the story.

Language and structures
Active: *dance, jump, fly, catch; Oh no! Quick!*

Passive: *Watch out! Catch Megabyte!*

Materials
Unit 5 flashcards; Class Audio CD 1; Megabyte puppet; colored pens

Warmer
- Play the *I Can Try* song from Unit 5, Lesson 2 page 45 🔊 1.58 for students to listen and join in if possible.
- Encourage students to use the actions from Lesson 2.

1 Watch or listen. 🔊 1·59 Act it out.
- Point to the first frame of the story and ask the class *Where are the students? (At the beach.)* Ask *What can Ellie do? (Dive.) What can Jack do? (Swim.)*
- Play the recording. Encourage students to point to the correct pictures as they listen.
- Play the recording again. Ask students questions about each frame.

  Frame 1: *How does Megabyte feel? (Sad.) Why? (He can't swim.)*

  Frame 2–4: *What can Megabyte do? (Dance, jump, and climb.) Is he happy? (Yes.)*

  Frame 5: *Why does Lucy say 'Watch out, Megabyte!'? (Megabyte can't climb down.)*

  Frame 6: *Can Megabyte jump? (Yes.) Can Megabyte fly? (No.) How do the students help him? (They catch him.)*
- Divide the class into groups to act out the story. Allow students time to practice in their groups. Then invite groups to act out the story for the class.

21ST CENTURY SKILLS:
Information literacy
Students listen to and read a story, develop their understanding of the story, and then act it out.

2 Listen and point. Say. 🔊 1·60
- Introduce the new words with Megabyte using the flashcards. Place them on the board and use Megabyte to act out the actions for students to repeat.
- Play the recording for students to listen and point to the correct items in their Student Books. Play the recording again for students to listen, point, and say the actions.
- Call out an action from the story, i.e. *dive, swim, dance, jump, climb, fly,* and *catch.* Ask the class to point to each of the actions in the story and say the words.

Transcript
dance, jump, fly, catch
catch, dance, jump, fly

3 Match.
- Point to pictures 1–4 and elicit the actions (*dance, catch, jump, fly*). With a less confident class, call out the actions

and ask students to point to the correct picture and repeat the words.
- Point to pictures A–D and elicit which picture is *dance*. Point to the example line matching picture 1 to picture B.
- Read the sentences on the right, or invite a confident student to read them. Say *Match the sentences to the pictures.* Point to the example matching line.
- Allow students time to check their answers in pairs before checking together as a class, e.g. *Picture 1 I can dance!*

TEACHING TIP

With a less confident class, work through each item together and ask students to match the picture first, then match the speech bubbles.

---

4 Listen and repeat. 🔊 1·61
- Play the recording for students to listen. Then play it again, pausing after each line for students to repeat the phrases.

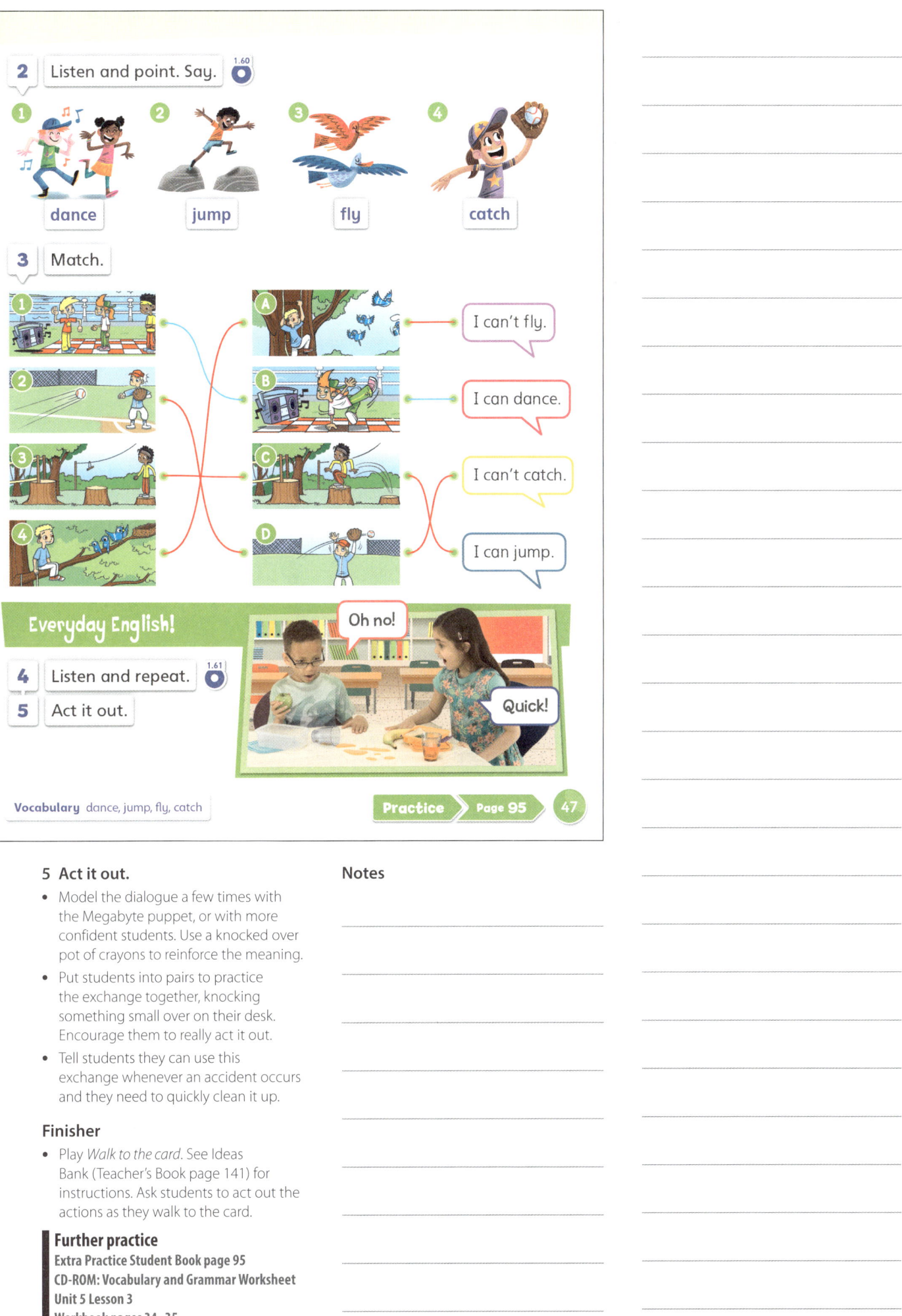

2 Listen and point. Say. 🔵 1.60

1 **dance** 2 **jump** 3 **fly** 4 **catch**

3 Match.

I can't fly.

I can dance.

I can't catch.

I can jump.

Everyday English!

4 Listen and repeat. 🔵 1.61

5 Act it out.

Oh no!

Quick!

Vocabulary dance, jump, fly, catch

Practice **Page 95** 47

5 Act it out.

- Model the dialogue a few times with the Megabyte puppet, or with more confident students. Use a knocked over pot of crayons to reinforce the meaning.

- Put students into pairs to practice the exchange together, knocking something small over on their desk. Encourage them to really act it out.

- Tell students they can use this exchange whenever an accident occurs and they need to quickly clean it up.

Finisher

- Play *Walk to the card*. See Ideas Bank (Teacher's Book page 141) for instructions. Ask students to act out the actions as they walk to the card.

Further practice
Extra Practice Student Book page 95
CD-ROM: Vocabulary and Grammar Worksheet
Unit 5 Lesson 3
Workbook pages 34–35

Notes

Lesson 4 (page 48)

Classroom Presentation Tool

Objectives

To present a CLIL concept (Social Studies).

To practice the unit vocabulary and grammar through a CLIL concept.

To talk about a value.

Language and structures

Active: *safe, dangerous, lifeguard, sign, flag; It's safe/dangerous. Swim. Don't swim.*

Passive: *We follow the rules.*

Materials

Unit 5 flashcards; Class Audio CD 1; ball (optional); CLIL stickers; CLIL Worksheet Unit 5 Lesson 4; colored pens, ball, scissors; Our Values sticker

Warmer

- Play *Hit the card!* See Ideas Bank (Teacher's Book page 140) for instructions. Use a balled up piece of paper if you don't have a ball.

1 Listen and point. 1·62 Stick.

- Write *dangerous* on the board and say the word. Pick up some scissors and point to the sharp sides, say *It's dangerous*. Ask students to give more examples of things that are dangerous. Write *safe* on the board and say the word. Point to the handles of the scissors and say *It's safe*. Ask students what *safe* is.

- Point to pictures 1 and 2. Ask students what they can see. Point to the *lifeguard, flag,* and *sign* in picture 1 and ask the class to repeat the words.

- Play the recording, pausing after each item for students to point to each picture.

- Put the flashcard for *swim* on the board. Draw a check next to it and say *I can swim*. Ask students *Is it safe or dangerous?* Replace the check with a ✗ and ask *Can you swim?* Elicit *No*. Say *Don't swim*.

- Ask students to look at each picture and ask *Is it safe or dangerous? Why?* Listen to students' ideas and praise them.

- Ask students to turn to the stickers section in the Student Book. Say *Point to the green flag*. Then say *Point to the red flag*. Say *Point to swim. Point to don't swim*.

- Play the recording again. Pause after each item to allow students to stick the stickers in the correct spaces.

Transcript

1 Look, can you see the lifeguard? And look at the sign. And there's a green flag, too. You can swim here. It's safe.

2 Look! There's a red flag at this beach. And look at the sign, it says 'don't swim'. Don't swim here. It's dangerous.

2 Point and say *safe* or *dangerous*.

- Point to each sticker in pictures 1 and 2. Ask *Is it safe or dangerous?* Encourage students to explain why.

3 Draw and color. Say *swim* or *don't swim*.

- Point to each picture in turn and ask *Swim or don't swim?* Ask *Is it safe or dangerous?*

- Point to the flag in the first picture and ask what color flag it needs (*red*). Point to the sign and ask which sign it needs (*don't swim*). Repeat with the second picture.

- Tell students to draw and color the flags and signs.

- Say *swim, don't swim, safe, dangerous* and encourage students to point to the correct pictures. Repeat several times.

Our Values

- Show the class the space for the *Our Values* sticker. Read out the value (*We follow the rules*). Tell students that rules keep us safe.

- Tell students they have learned about danger and safety today at the beach.

Congratulate students for listening to the rules in school. Award them with the *Our Values* sticker to stick in the space on page 48.

4 Make signs for your school.

- Hand out CLIL worksheets. Look at the signs and elicit what they mean.

- Look at the plan of the school. Point to each area (*corridor, classroom, gym, library, playground, soccerfield*). Ask students to choose an appropriate sign, e.g. *Don't run* (in the corridor). Encourage the class to say *Don't run*. Ask why.

- In pairs, students plan which signs they want to put and where. Give students time to draw them on the worksheet next to each area on the plan. Encourage them to talk about their signs: *Climb! It's safe!*

Finisher

- Play *Yes or No*. See Ideas Bank (Teacher's Book page 141) for instructions.

Further practice

Workbook page 36

5 Lesson 4 — Social Studies

1 Listen and point. 1.62 Stick.

2 Point and say *safe* or *dangerous*.

3 Draw and color. Say *swim* or *don't swim*.

don't swim

swim

Our Values — We follow the rules.

4 Make signs for your school.

48   Vocabulary   safe, dangerous, lifeguard, sign, flag

5 Review

1 Write and make a ✓ or an ✗ for you. Say.

swim run cook climb dance catch

run	dance	swim	catch	climb	cook

2 Make your dice. Play and say. ✂ Page 111

I can cook.

3 Complete your picture dictionary. Page 84

49

Review page 49
Classroom Presentation Tool

Objectives
To review the linguistic content of the unit.

Language and structures
Active: *swim, dive, sing, climb, cook, run, dance, jump, fly, catch; I can (cook). I can't (swim).*
Passive: *dice; Can you (dance)?*

Materials
Unit 5 flashcards; Craft cut-out Unit 5 Review; scissors, glue, colored pens

Warmer
- Play *Four in a row*. See Ideas Bank (Teacher's Book page 141) for instructions.

1 Write and make a ✓ or an ✗ for you. Say.
- Read the words in the word box aloud with the class. Ask students to look at the pictures and write the words on the lines below the correct picture.
- Allow students to check their answers in pairs before checking together as a class.
- Point to the spaces below the writing lines and tell students to draw a check or an ✗ for themselves if they can or can't do the action.
- When they are ready, put students into pairs. Ask them to tell their partner what they can or can't do using the correct structure, e.g. *I can (run). I can't (dance).*
- Ask confident students to tell the class about their partner.

TEACHING TIP
With a less confident class, place the action flashcards from exercise 1 on the board and elicit the vocabulary as you do so. Ask students to say the words again and write the correct word under each picture as it's elicited.

2 Make your dice. Play and say.
- Tell students they are going to make a dice. Point to the pictures and ask students what they need to make one (paper, scissors, glue, colored pens).
- Tell students to turn to page 111 and cut the Craft cut-out from their Student Books. Model how to make a dice by cutting it out, coloring it, and gluing it.
- Make sure students have all the materials. Move around the class offering help if necessary. Ask students questions, e.g. *What is it? Can you (dance)?*
- Put students into pairs to take turns rolling their dice and saying *I can* or *I can't* with the action the dice lands on.

Extension activity
Sit in a circle with students on the floor or on chairs. Throw a completed dice to a student. They catch it and say a sentence about themselves, holding up the picture on the dice, e.g *I can't cook.* They throw the dice to another student who makes another sentence using *can* or *can't*. Repeat until everyone in the class has had a turn.

21ST CENTURY SKILLS:
Communication
Students use a game to practice expressing what they *can* and *can't* do.

3 Complete your picture dictionary.
- Tell students to turn to page 84 of their Student Books and look at the Picture Dictionary section for Unit 5.
- Point to each of the pictures and ask students to say the words.
- Students color the items in the Picture Dictionary. Move around the class as they work, asking questions, e.g. *Can you (swim)?*

Finisher
- Play *Simon Says*. See Ideas Bank (Teacher's Book page 141) for instructions. If Simon says e.g. *I can (sing)*, students act out singing. If Simon says e.g. *I can't (run)*, students don't react.

Further practice
Unit 5 Test
Workbook page 37

Unit 6 Animal Fun!
Lesson 1 (pages 50–51)
Classroom Presentation Tool

Objectives
To present and practice six new items of vocabulary.

To review vocabulary from a previous unit.

Language and structures
Active: *horse, cow, goat, pig, chicken, duck; run*

Materials
Unit 5 and 6 flashcards; Class Audio CD 2; Megabyte puppet; stickers section

Warmer
- Play *Change places* using the Unit 5 flashcards. See Ideas Bank (Teacher's Book page 141) for instructions.

1 Listen and point. Say. 🔘 2·01
- Books closed. Introduce the new words using the Megabyte puppet and the flashcards. Place the flashcards on the board. Use Megabyte to point to the flashcards and say the words for students to repeat.
- Books open. Play the recording for students to listen and point to the animals in the picture. Play the recording again for students to listen, point, and repeat the words.

Transcript
horse, cow, goat, pig, chicken, duck
duck, cow, goat, chicken, pig, horse

Extra activity
Place the flashcards around the room. Play the recording again for students to act like the animal when they hear it, say the animal word and move to the correct flashcard. If you like, teach students the sounds the animals make in English: horse – neigh, cow – moo, goat – meh, pig – oink, chicken – cluck, duck – quack.

2 Stick.
- Ask students to turn to the stickers section in the Student Book. Hold up your book and point to each of the animal stickers in turn. Encourage students to say the words. Then say the words in a random order for students to point to the correct stickers.
- Students stick the stickers in the correct spaces on page 51. When they have finished, ask students to point to the stickers and say the words.

6 **Animal Fun!**

Lesson 1

1 Listen and point. Say. 2.01

horse

goat

chicken

pig

50 **Vocabulary** horse, cow, goat, pig, chicken, duck

Fast finishers
Put students into pairs to take turns saying the words for their partner to do the actions.

21ST CENTURY SKILLS:
Creativity and innovation
Students use different techniques, such as mime and sounds, in order to help memorize new vocabulary.

Finisher

- Play *Musical flashcards* using the Unit 5 and 6 flashcards. See Ideas Bank (Teacher's Book page 141) for instructions.

EXTRA VOCABULARY:
barn
birdhouse
bull
farm
feed (n.)
field
pigeon
pond
tractor

Further practice

CD-ROM: Vocabulary and Grammar Worksheet Unit 6 Lesson 1

Workbook page 38

Notes

---

3 Chant. 🔊 2·02

- Play the chant once for students to listen and point to the flashcards on the board.
- Play the chant again. Encourage students to act like the animals, e.g. pull up their noses for a pig, flap their wings for a duck, etc.
- Divide the class into six groups. Give each group one animal flashcard. Play the chant once more. When the group hears their animal in the chant they stand, say their word, and act like the animal.

Chant

cow, cow, cow
goat, goat, goat
horse, horse, horse
chicken, chicken, chicken
pig, pig, pig
duck, duck, duck

Find it!

- Point to Jack's drawing pad and ask students what they can see (*I can run*).

Ask students to find someone running in the main picture. (The boy on page 51 is running from the bull.)

- Tell students to turn to the Picture Dictionary for Unit 6 (Student Book page 84) and find the boy running. Ask students to color the boy in the Picture Dictionary the same colors as the main artwork on Student Book page 51.

Extension activity

Hold up the Unit 6 flashcards and say *A (chicken) can …* Elicit the actions it can do. Say *Yes, a (chicken) can (run/jump/fly)*. Hand out the flashcards to random students or pairs of students. Ask them to come to the front and place their animal next to an action that it *can* do. There may be more than one animal next to each action. Play again with what the animal *can't* do. Elicit sentences, e.g. *A horse can't fly.* etc.

Lesson 2 `pages 52–53`

Classroom Presentation Tool

Objectives

To present a new grammar structure.

To practice the new grammar with the Lesson 1 vocabulary.

To sing a song using the Lesson 1 vocabulary and the new grammar.

To do a personalization activity that involves a simple craft activity.

Language and structures

Active: *(A duck) can swim. Can (a cow) (swim)? Can it (fly)? Yes, it can. No, it can't*; *horse, cow, goat, pig, chicken, duck*

Passive: *fold, animal quiz machine*

Materials

Unit 5 and 6 flashcards, Lucy and Jack flashcards; Class Audio CD 2; Craft Worksheet Unit 6 Lesson 2; colored pens

Warmer

- Play the chant from Unit 6 Lesson 1 page 51 🔊 2•02 for students to listen and join in.
- Ask students to act like the animals as they say them in the chant.

> **TEACHING TIP**
> Reward well-behaved students by allowing them to take turns using Megabyte to hold up the animal flashcards as they listen to the chant.

1 Listen and read. Say. 🔊 2•03

- Point to the picture and ask students to say which animals they can see with Lucy and Jack.
- Play the recording for students to listen. Then play it again and encourage students to repeat the grammar structure.
- Place the *duck* flashcard next to the *swim* flashcard on the board. Ask *Can a duck swim?* Elicit *Yes, it can.* Draw a check. Place the *cow* flashcard on the board next to *swim* and ask the class *Can a cow swim?* Elicit *No, it can't.* Draw an ✗. Ask a second question *Can it run?* Elicit *Yes, it can.*
- Place a different animal flashcard on the board and invite students to choose the action flashcards. Ask the questions again. Elicit answers from the class. When students are confident with the answers, encourage the class to ask the questions.

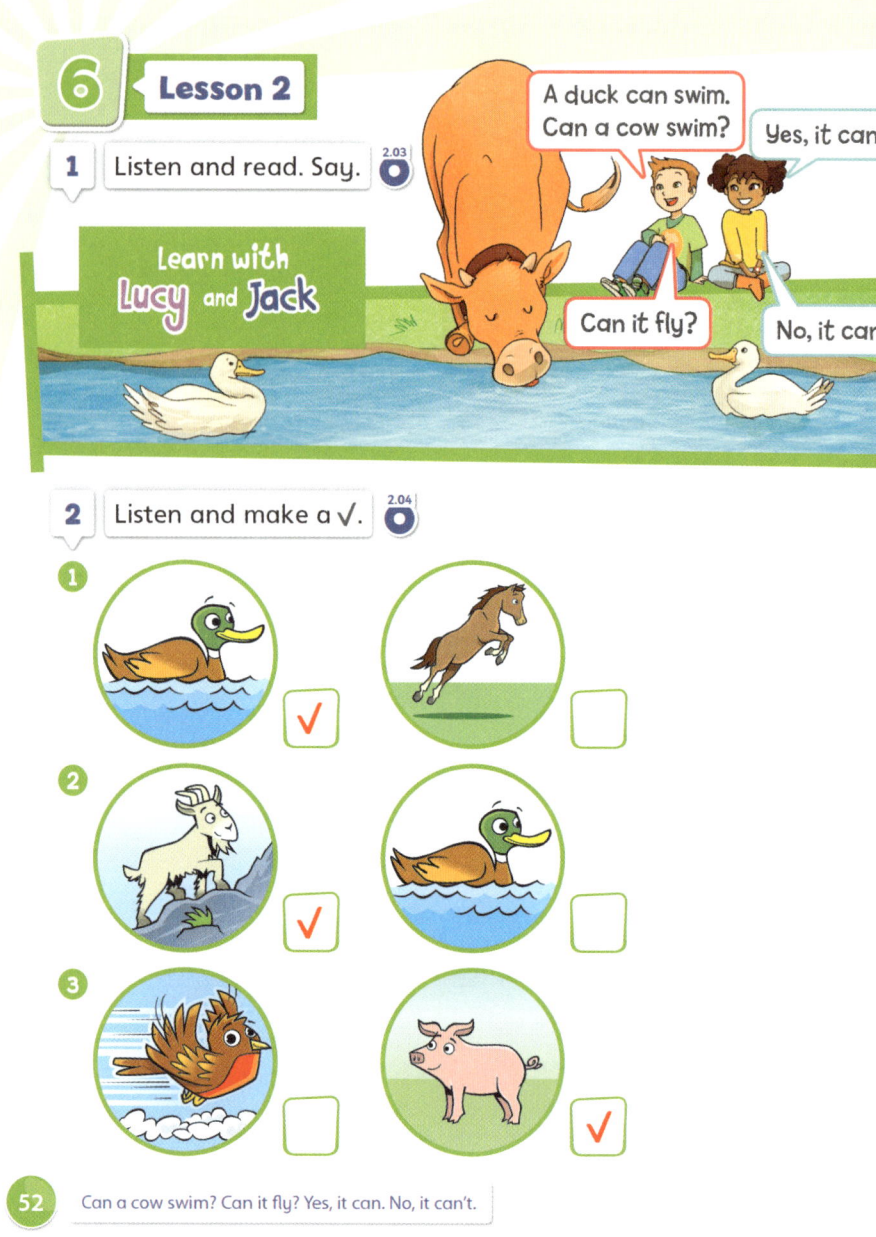

Extension activity

Divide the class into two teams. Place an animal flashcard and an action flashcard on the board. Write *Can it?* on the board for support. Ask one team to ask the question. The other team answers *Yes, it can* or *No, it can't.* Swap roles and repeat several times. If the teams ask and answer the questions correctly, they win a point.

2 Listen and make a ✓. 🔊 2•04

- Place the duck and horse flashcards on the board. Ask for each *What can it do?* Elicit the possible verbs, e.g. *run*, *swim*, *fly*, *jump*.
- Say *Listen.* Play the recording. Pause after the first item. Point to the two flashcards and ask *Which animal is it?* (*Duck!*)
- Point to the pairs of pictures on the page. Play the remainder of the recording. Ask students to listen and

check the correct animal. Pause after each item if necessary.

- Ask students to check their answers in pairs before checking together as a class.

Transcript

1 Can it jump? No, it can't. Can it fly? Yes, it can.

2 Can it fly? No, it can't. Can it climb? Yes, it can.

3 Can it fly? No, it can't. Can it run? Yes, it can.

3 Sing.  ▶ **Watch!**

Song!

4 Make your animal quiz machine! Play and say.

Can a pig dance?

No, it can't!

Song lyrics ➤ Page 104 | Practice ➤ Page 96 | 53

- Move around the class monitoring and checking students are speaking well.

Finisher
- Play *Simon Says*. See Ideas Bank (Teacher's Book page 141) for instructions.

Further practice
Extra Practice Student Book page 96
Workbook page 39

---

3 Sing. 2·05

- Play *The Cow Calypso* song once for students to listen to.
- Play the song again and encourage students to point to the animals in the picture in the Student Book.
- Play the song once more, modeling actions: shake your head and wiggle your finger for *No, it can't*; dance about and nod your head during the chorus.

The Cow Calypso
Can a pig cook? No, it can't.
Can a goat fly? No, it can't.
Can a duck climb? No, it can't.
Can a chicken catch? No, it can't.
Can a horse dive? No, it can't.
Can a cow sing? No, it can't.
But a cow can dance! Oh yes, it can.
A cow can dance a calypso!
Moooooooo! Moooooooo!
A cow can dance a calypso.
Moooooooo! Moooooooo!
And you can try it too!
Moooooooo! Moooooooo!
Moooooooove your body!

It's the cow calypso.
Moooooooo! Moooooooo!
Oh yes, a cow can dance.
Oh yes, a cow can dance.

4 Make your animal quiz machine! Play and say.

- Tell students that they are going to make an animal quiz machine.
- Make sure each child has scissors and colored pens. Students cut out the quiz machine and color the animal pictures. Model how to fold the quiz machine.
- Put students into pairs. One child chooses a number. The other child opens and closes their quiz machine, moving their fingers back and forth that number of times. The first child then chooses an animal. The other child lifts up the picture and asks a question using the verb given. Their partner answers accordingly, e.g. *Can a (pig) (dance)? No, it can't*. They play again with the other child's quiz machine.

Lesson 3 (pages 54–55)
Classroom Presentation Tool

Objectives

To present new vocabulary in the context of the story.

To practice the new vocabulary using the grammar from Lesson 2.

To practice a short Everyday English role play taken from the story.

Language and structures

Active: *bat, squirrel, frog, fox; What's your favorite animal? A (horse). Can (a frog) (swim)? Yes, it can. No, it can't. (A bat) can fly.*

Passive: *check, ask, answer; Look at me!*

Materials

Unit 6 flashcards; Class Audio CD 2; Megabyte puppet; colored pens

Warmer

- Play *The Cow Calypso* song from Unit 6 Lesson 2 page 53 🎵 2·05 for students to listen and join in if possible.

- Encourage students to use the actions from Lesson 2.

1 Watch or listen. 🎵 2·06 Act it out.

- Point to the first frame of the story and ask students who they can see in the picture (Jack, Lucy, Ellie, and Megabyte). Point to the clothes and ask *What clothes can you see? (Shorts, pants, T-shirt.)*

- Play the recording. Encourage students to point to the correct pictures as they listen.

- Play the recording again. Ask students questions about each frame.

  Frame 1: *What are the students looking at? (A squirrel.) Is Megabyte happy? (No.)*

  Frame 2: *What are Lucy and Jack looking at? (A book/A bat.) Does Megabyte like the squirrel?* (No.)

  Frame 3: *Can Megabyte fly? (No!) Why does Megabyte jump? (He wants to catch the squirrel.) Is Megabyte wet? (Yes.)*

  Frame 4: *What animal is in the book? (A frog.)*

  Frame 5: *Can a fox run? (Yes, it can.)*

  Frame 6: *Is it a fox? (No, it's Megabyte!) What's Lucy's favorite animal? (Megabyte!)*

- Divide the class into groups to act out the story. Allow students time to practice in their groups. Then invite groups to act out the story for the class.

2 Listen and point. Say. 🎵 2·07

- Introduce the new words with Megabyte using the flashcards. Place them on the board. Use Megabyte to point to the flashcards and say the words for students to repeat.

- Play the recording for students to listen and point to the correct animals in their Student Books. Play the recording again for students to listen, point, and repeat the words.

- Call out an animal from the story, e.g. frog, squirrel, bat, fox. Ask the class to point to each of the animals in the story and say the words.

Transcript
bat, squirrel, frog, fox
fox, frog, squirrel, bat

3 Match. Listen and check. 🎵 2·08 Ask and answer.

- Point to pictures 1–5 and elicit the names of the animals. With a less confident class, call out the animals

and ask students to point to them and repeat.

- Point to the frog and ask *Can it swim?* Elicit *Yes, it can*. Show students the example line from *Can it swim?* to *Yes, it can*. Tell students to match the questions to the correct answer. With a less confident class, allow students to work in pairs.

- Ask students to listen and draw a check next to the animal if they got it correct. Play the recording. Pause after each item for students to check their answers. Ask them to change their answer if it was incorrect.

- Invite confident pairs to read out the questions and the answers.

Transcript
1 Can it swim? Yes, it can.
2 Can it fly? No, it can't.
3 Can it run? No, it can't.
4 Can it jump? Yes, it can.
5 Can it swim? Yes, it can!

2 Listen and point. Say. [2.07]

1. bat
2. squirrel
3. frog
4. fox

3 Match. Listen and check. [2.08] Ask and answer.

1. Can it swim?
2. Can it fly?
3. Can it run?
4. Can it jump?
5. Can it swim?

Yes, it can.

No, it can't.

Everyday English!

4 Listen and repeat. [2.09]

5 Act it out.

What's your favorite animal?

A horse!

Vocabulary bat, squirrel, frog, fox

Practice ＞ Page 97   55

---

4 Listen and repeat. 2·09

- Play the recording for students to listen. Then play it again, pausing after each line for students to repeat the phrases.

5 Act it out.

- Model the dialogue a few times with the Megabyte puppet or with more confident students. Encourage students to give a personal answer.
- Ask students to stand. Play some music. Pause the music and ask students to turn to the child closest to them. They take turns asking and answering *What's your favorite animal?* Repeat several times.
- Tell students they can use this exchange whenever they want to ask about a person's favorite things.

> **21ST CENTURY SKILLS:**
>
> **Social and cross-cultural interaction**
> Students exchange information to learn more about each other's personal preferences.

Finisher

- Play *What number is it?* See Ideas Bank (Teacher's Book page 140) for instructions.

Further practice
Extra Practice Student Book page 97
CD-ROM: Vocabulary and Grammar Worksheet Unit 6 Lesson 3
Workbook pages 40–41

Lesson 4 page 56

Classroom Presentation Tool

Objectives

To present a CLIL concept (Science).

To practice the unit vocabulary and grammar through a CLIL concept.

Language and structures

Active: *night time, day time, awake, asleep; bat, squirrel, frog, fox*

Passive: *Choose an animal; animal viewer; It's (day time).*

Materials

Unit 6 flashcards; Class Audio CD 2; CLIL stickers; CLIL Worksheet Unit 6 Lesson 4; colored pens, scissors, glue; two boxes, a ball (optional)

Warmer

• Play *Guess the flashcard.* See Ideas Bank (Teacher's Book page 140) for instructions.

1 Listen and point. 🔊 2·10 Stick.

• Point to the pictures and ask students *What animals can you see?* Ask *What can a (squirrel) do?* Elicit *It can (run/climb).* Repeat for bat, frog, and fox.

• Ask students to listen and point to the pictures.

• Ask students to turn to the stickers section in the Student Book. Say, e.g. *Find the (fox).* Students find the stickers and stick them in the correct spaces on page 56.

Transcript

1 It's day time. Look at the squirrel. It's awake. A squirrel can climb in the day. Look at the frog and the fox. They're asleep. Look at the bat. It's asleep.

2 It's night time. Look at the squirrel. It's asleep. Look at the fox. It's awake. Look at the bat and the frog. They're awake. A fox can run, a bat can fly and a frog can jump at night time.

2 Point to the animals and say *awake* or *asleep.*

• Say *asleep* and act it out by closing your eyes and resting your head on your hands. Write *asleep* on the board. Ask students to say *asleep* and act asleep.

• Say *awake* and act it out by opening your eyes, stretching your arms up, and looking around. Write *awake* on the board. Ask students to say *awake* and act awake.

• Point to the squirrel in picture 1 and ask *Is it awake or asleep?* Elicit *awake.* Point to the other animals in pictures 1 and 2 and repeat.

• In pairs, ask students to take turns pointing to the animals in the pictures and saying *It's awake* or *It's asleep.*

3 Draw an animal in the night and the day. Write and circle.

• Draw some stars and the moon on the board and say *night time.* Write it on the board. Say *I am asleep at night time.* Draw the sun on the board and say *day time.* Write it on the board. Say *I am awake in the day time.*

• Point to the pictures in exercise 2 in turn. Ask *Is it day time or night time?*

• Put the animal flashcards on the board and elicit the words. Say *Choose an animal.* Point to the space in exercise 3 and tell students to write the name of their animal. Then draw a picture of the animal in the day time and the night time.

• Read the two sentences, or invite a confident child to read them. Students complete the sentences by circling the correct option.

4 Make the animal viewer. Play and say.

• Hand out CLIL worksheets. Look at the two pictures and ask students to find the animals. Elicit sentences, e.g. *It's a fox. It's asleep.* Elicit which picture shows day time and which shows night time.

• Tell students to color in the pictures and carefully cut out the slots in the center.

• They stick the two pictures together to make a cylinder with the pictures facing the inside. Students can look through the slots and look at either the day time scene or the night time scene.

• Put students into pairs. Ask them to take turns looking through their viewers and making sentences about what they can see, e.g. *I can see a (frog). It's (awake).*

Finisher

• Play *Hit the card!* See Ideas Bank (Teacher's Book page 140) for instructions.

Extra practice
Workbook page 42

---

6 Lesson 4   Science

1 Listen and point. 2.10 Stick.

2 Point to the animals and say *awake* or *asleep*.

3 Draw an animal in the night and the day. Write and circle.

A _____

It's day time. It's **awake / asleep**.

It's night time. It's **awake / asleep**.

4 Make the animal viewer. Play and say.

56   **Vocabulary** night time, day time, awake, asleep

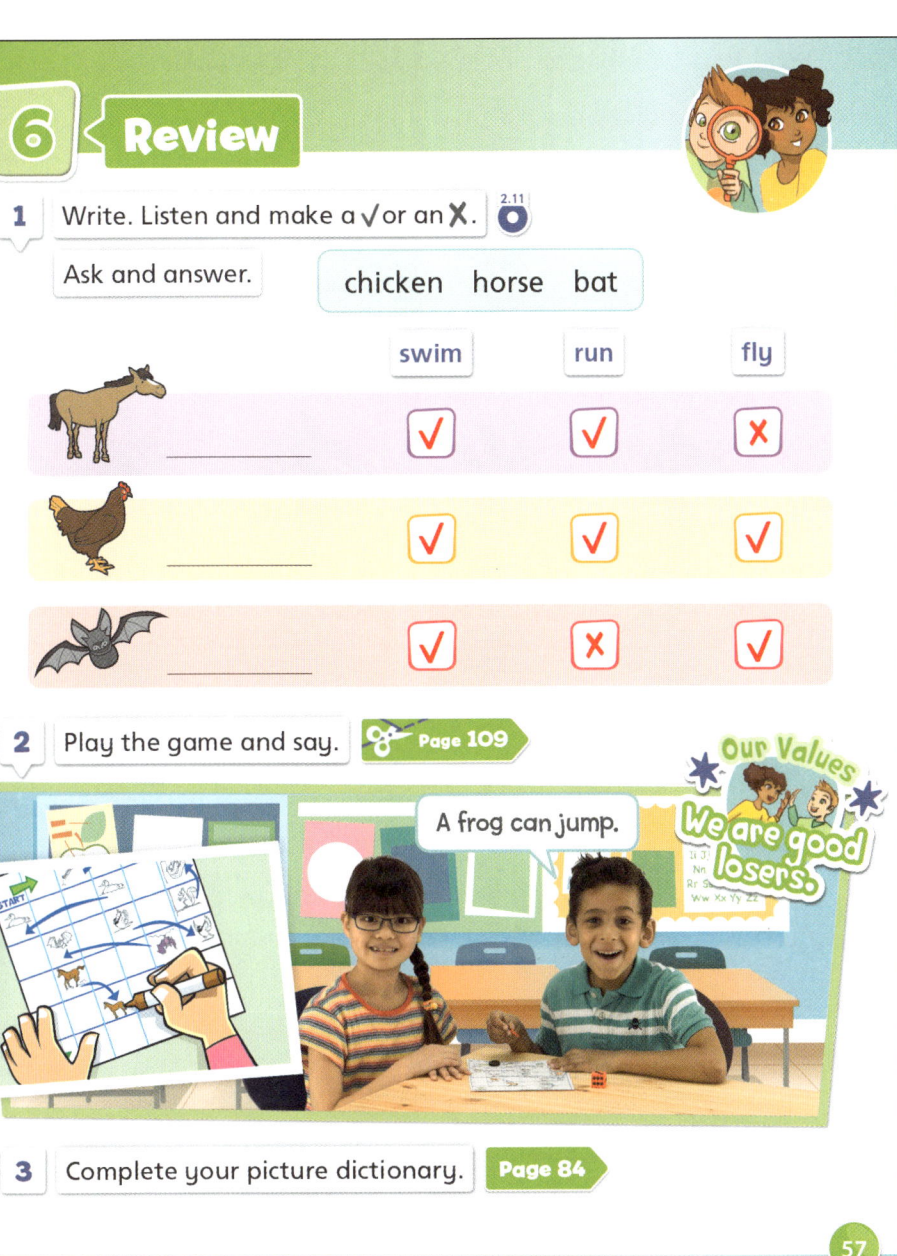

6 Review

1 Write. Listen and make a ✓ or an ✗. 2.11

Ask and answer.

chicken	horse	bat

	swim	run	fly
(horse) _____	✓	✓	✗
(chicken) _____	✓	✓	✓
(bat) _____	✓	✗	✓

2 Play the game and say. ✂ Page 109

A frog can jump.

Our Values
We are good losers!

3 Complete your picture dictionary. Page 84

57

Review (page 57)

Classroom Presentation Tool

Objectives

To review the linguistic content of the unit.

To talk about a value.

Language and structures

Active: *horse, cow, goat, pig, chicken, duck, bat, squirrel, frog, fox; Can a (cow) swim? Can it (fly)? Yes, it can. No, it can't; swim, dive, sing, climb, cook, run*

Passive: *We are good losers.*

Materials

Unit 5 and 6 flashcards; Class Audio CD 2; Craft cut-out Unit 6 Review; dice, counters, colored pens; Our Values sticker

Warmer

- Play *Odd one out* with the Unit 5 and 6 flashcards. See Ideas Bank (Teacher's Book page 140) for instructions.

1 Write. Listen and make a ✓ or an ✗. 2·11

- Ask the class to read aloud the words in the word box. Point to the picture of a horse and elicit the word. Tell students to write it on the line. Tell them to write the names of the other two animals.

- Say *Listen and make a check or an ✗*. Play the recording. Pause after the first item. Ask questions *Can a horse swim/run/fly?* and elicit the answers.

- Play the remainder of the recording. Play it twice or pause after each item. Check the answers as a class.

Transcript

1 **A:** What's your favorite animal?
B: A horse!
A: Great! Can a horse swim?
B: Yes, it can.
A: Can it run?
B: Yes, it can.
A: And can it fly?
B: No, it can't.
2 **A:** What's your favorite animal?
B: A chicken!

A: A chicken! Can a chicken swim?
B: Yes, it can.
A: Can it fly?
B: Yes, it can.
A: And can it run?
B: Yes, it can.
3 **A:** What's your favorite animal?
B: A bat!
A: Can a bat run?
B: No. A bat can't run.
A: Can it fly?
B: Yes, it can.
A: And can it swim?
B: Yes, it can!

2 Play the game and say.

- Tell students to turn to page 109 and cut the Craft cut-out from their Student Books. Ask them to color in the board.

- Put students into groups of four and give each group a dice and counters.

- Tell students to use one board. They take turns throwing the dice and moving their counters the correct number of spaces. When they land on an animal they name it, e.g. *It's a (frog)*. They can move forward following the arrows if they also correctly say an action, e.g. *A (frog) can (jump)*. If they land on a empty space, they don't need to say anything.

- Tell students to play fair. If they win, that's great. If they don't win, they have had fun playing the game. Move around the class offering help.

Our Values

- Show the class the space for the *Our Values* sticker. Read out the value (*We are good losers*). Tell students that it is important to enjoy a game no matter if you win or lose. It's also good to congratulate the winner.

- Tell students they have played well today. Congratulate students for being good losers and good winners. Award them with the *Our Values* sticker to stick in the space on page 57.

3 Complete your picture dictionary.

- Tell students to turn to page 84 of their Student Books and look at the Picture Dictionary section for Unit 6.

- Point to each of the pictures and ask students to say the words.

- Students color the items. Ask students questions, e.g. *What is it? What color is it? Is it a (cow)? Can it (fly)?* etc.

Finisher

- Play *What card is it?* See Ideas Bank (Teacher's Book page 140) for instructions. Give clues about the animal flashcard you are holding by saying what it can and can't do.

Further practice

Unit 6 Test
Workbook pages 43–45

Culture 3 Visitors In My Yard pages 58–59
Classroom Presentation Tool

Objectives

To present and practice four new items of vocabulary.

To think about animals we see in our yards.

To review the vocabulary from a previous unit.

Language and structures

Active: *snail, rabbit, chipmunk, butterfly; animals; swim, dive, climb, run, jump, fly, catch*

Passive: *What can a (rabbit) do? What's your favorite animal? How many (frogs)?*

Materials

Unit 6 flashcards, Unit 4 *yard* flashcard; Class Audio CD 2; colored pens; Culture 3 words (*snail, rabbit, chipmunk, butterfly*) written on word cards

Warmer

- Play *Mystery flashcard* with the Unit 4 flashcard *yard*. See Ideas Bank (Teacher's Book page 140) for instructions.
- Ask the class *Do you have a yard? What animals can you see in your yard?* Listen to students' ideas and praise them.

1 Listen and point. Say. 🔘 2•12

- Read the words aloud and point to each photo. Repeat the words and ask students to listen and point to the correct photo.
- Play the recording for students to listen and point to the photos. Play the recording again for students to listen, point, and repeat the words.
- Say the words again and ask students to point to the correct photo. Start slowly, then get faster and faster.

Transcript

snail, rabbit, chipmunk, butterfly
chipmunk, rabbit, butterfly, snail

2 Listen and number. 🔘 2•13

- Ask students to look at the photos again. Ask them *What can a (rabbit) do?* Elicit ideas from the class, e.g. *It can jump.*
- Tell students to listen and write the numbers 1, 2, 3, and 4 in the correct boxes next to the photos.
- Play the recording. Pause after each item to give students time to write the numbers. With a less confident class, play the recording twice.

Culture 3

Visitors In My Yard

1 Listen and point. Say. 🔘 2.12
2 Listen and number. 🔘 2.13
3 Circle seven words and match. Count and say.
4 Draw your favorite animal.

snail 3
rabbit 2
chipmunk 4
butterfly 1

58   **Vocabulary** snail, rabbit, chipmunk, butterfly

Transcript

1 Here's a butterfly.
2 In my yard I can see a rabbit. It can run – fast!
3 Look! Here's a snail in my yard.
4 In my yard I can see a chipmunk. It's hungry.

3 Circle seven words and match. Count and say.

- Point to the picture on page 59. Ask the class *What animals can you see? (Chipmunk, snail, butterfly, squirrel, frog, snake, rabbit.)*
- Point to the letters above and below the picture and tell students to find and circle six more animal words.
- Elicit the answers from the class and write the animals on the board.
- Point to the word *frog* and ask *How many frogs?* Count them with the students, i.e. *1, 2, 3, 4!* Say *There are 4 frogs.*

- Ask students to count the rest of the animals and check the number with their partner.
- Check answers by asking confident students to say, e.g. *There are (2) (rabbits).* etc.

gjgfrogjgfjfjsquirrelggjjalwchipmunkk

ajsnailkjlbutterflyjlairabbitghghsnake

My favorite animal!

59

TEACHING TIP

With a less confident class, play *Yes or No* to review the animals from Unit 6. Write the words on the board to help with spelling. See Ideas Bank (Teacher's Book page 141) for instructions.

21ST CENTURY SKILLS:

Learning to learn

Children use the word search and pictures to reinforce spelling and consolidate their understanding of the vocabulary.

4 Draw your favorite animal.

- Ask the class *What's your favorite animal?* Encourage students around the class to tell you.
- Tell students to draw a picture in the space on page 59 of their favorite yard animal.
- Have a show-and-tell session. Ask students to sit in a circle with their

pictures. Ask the child to your left *What's your favorite animal?* Elicit *My favorite animal is a (snail).* Say *That's great!* Then students ask the child to their left *What's your favorite animal?* Continue around the circle.

Extension activity

After the show-and-tell session ask *How many snails are there?* Count the snails that students have drawn and say together *There are (6) (snails).* Repeat with rabbits, butterflies, and chipmunks.

Finisher

Play *Mime the word* with the Unit 6 and Culture 3 words. See Ideas Bank (Teacher's Book page 140) for instructions.

Unit 7 Picnic Time!
Lesson 1 pages 60–61
Classroom Presentation Tool

Objectives
To present and practice six new items of vocabulary.

To review vocabulary from a previous unit.

Language and structures
Active: *chicken, rice, pasta, milk, salad, cheese; duck*

Passive: *picnic*

Materials
Unit 7 flashcards, Level 1 Unit 8 flashcards; Class Audio CD 2; Megabyte puppet; stickers section; food, basket and small blanket (optional)

Warmer
• Play *Pass the flashcards* using the Level 1 Unit 8 feelings flashcards. See Ideas Bank (Teacher's Book page 140) for instructions. Ask the class to mime the feelings.

1 Listen and point. Say. 2•14
• Books closed. Introduce the new words using the Megabyte puppet and the Unit 7 flashcards or real food. Place the flashcards, or food, in a basket and under a small blanket to help describe *picnic*. Say *It's picnic time! I'm hungry! What can we eat?*

• Use Megabyte to reveal the flashcards and place them on the board, or food on a table. Say the words for students to repeat.

• Books open. Play the recording for students to listen and point to the food in the picture. Play the recording again for students to listen, point, and repeat the words.

Transcript
chicken, rice, pasta, milk, salad, cheese
milk, chicken, rice, pasta, salad, cheese

Extra activity
Place the food flashcards on the board. Put students into pairs and ask them to choose three foods to take on a picnic and draw them. Ask confident students to tell you what food they want to take. With a more confident class, ask students to write the words next to each picture.

2 Stick.
• Ask students to turn to the stickers section in the Student Book. Hold up your book and point to each of the food stickers in turn. Encourage students to say the words. Then say the words in a random order for students to point to the correct stickers.

• Students stick the stickers in the correct spaces on page 61. When they have finished, ask students to point to the stickers and say the words.

21ST CENTURY SKILLS:
Initiative and self-direction
Students consolidate their understanding of new vocabulary (written and oral forms) using stickers.

3 Chant. 2•15
• Play the chant once for students to listen and point to the flashcards or food on the table.

• Play the chant again. Encourage students to mime eating/drinking each item.

• Divide the class into six groups. Give each group a flashcard. Play the chant once more. When the group hears their food in the chant they stand, say the word, and mime eating/drinking that food.

Transcript
chicken, chicken, chicken
salad, salad, salad
rice, rice, rice
cheese, cheese, cheese
milk, milk, milk
pasta, pasta, pasta

Find it!
• Point to Lucy's tablet and ask students what they can see. (*A duck.*) Ask students to find a duck in the main picture. (It's hiding in the reeds on the pond on page 60.)

• Tell students to turn to the Picture Dictionary for Unit 7 (Student Book

2 Stick.

3 Chant. 🎵 2.15

milk

cheese

Find it! 61

page 85) and find the duck. Ask students to color in the duck in the Picture Dictionary the same color as the main artwork on Student Book page 60.

Extra activity

Ask students to look at the picture of the picnic and write a list of the clothes they can see. With a less confident class, allow students to work in pairs or call out clothes words for students to listen and point to. Elicit what color the clothes are.

Finisher

• Play *Bingo!* or *Picture Bingo!* See Ideas Bank (Teacher's Book page 141) for instructions.

EXTRA VOCABULARY:

apple
banana
bowl
butterfly
forest
hill
kite
knives, forks, spoons
lake
pear
picnic blanket
plates
swing-ball

Further practice
CD-ROM: Vocabulary and Grammar
Worksheet Unit 7 Lesson 1
Workbook page 46

Notes

Lesson 2 pages 62–63

Classroom Presentation Tool

Objectives

To present a new grammar structure.

To practice the new grammar with the Lesson 1 vocabulary.

To sing a song using the Lesson 1 vocabulary and the new grammar.

To do a personalization activity that involves a simple craft activity.

Language and structures

Active: *I like (salad). I don't like (cheese);* *chicken, rice, pasta, milk, salad, cheese*

Passive: *plate*

Materials

Unit 7 flashcards, Lucy and Jack flashcards; Class Audio CD 2; Craft Worksheet Unit 7 Lesson 2; scissors, glue, colored pens; Megabyte puppet; paper plates (for exercise 4)

Warmer

- Play the chant from Unit 7 Lesson 1 page 61 🎵 2.15 for students to listen and join in.
- Place the Unit 7 flashcards on the walls around the room. Ask students to point to the correct food, or walk to the flashcard, when they hear it mentioned.

1 Listen and read. Say. 🎵 2·16

- Point to the picture and ask *Is Jack happy? (No.)* Ask *Is Lucy happy? (Yes. She's smiling.)*
- Play the recording for students to listen. Then play it again and encourage students to repeat the grammar structure. Encourage students to shake their head when they say *don't like* and nod their head when they say *like*.
- Place the food flashcards on the board and elicit the vocabulary as you go. Point to a food and ask *Do you like (milk)?* Elicit a student's answer using the correct structure, e.g. *I (don't) like (milk).* Praise the student and repeat with another student.

2 Listen and draw ☺ or ☹. 🎵 2·17 Complete for you. Say.

- Use Megabyte to place the food flashcards on the board from left to right in the order they are in exercise 2. Elicit the words as you go.
- Point to the pasta, and use Megabyte to say *I like pasta.* Draw a smiley face. Repeat with the cheese flashcard and say *I don't like cheese.* Draw a frowny face.
- Point to the picture of Ellie. Ask *What does Ellie say?* Elicit *I like pasta.*

- Say *Listen to Ellie and draw.* Play the recording. Pause after the second item. Point to the chicken and elicit Ellie's answer *I don't like chicken.* Check that students draw a frowny face. Check the remaining answers by pointing to each food flashcard on the board and saying *Ellie says …* Elicit, *I like/don't like …* Draw, or invite a confident child to draw, the answers on the board.
- Play the remainder of the recording and check answers for Uncle Alex.
- Tell students to draw the answers for themselves if they like or don't like the food.
- When they are ready, put students into pairs. Ask them to tell their partner what they like or don't like.
- Ask confident students to tell the class about their partner.

Transcript

Ellie: I like pasta. I don't like chicken. I like cheese. I don't like milk. I like rice. And, I like salad, yum!

Uncle Alex: Hmm … Yes. I like pasta, too. I like chicken. I like cheese. Ooh no. I don't like milk. I like rice. But I don't like salad.

3 Sing. [2.18] ▶ Watch!

Song!

they like and don't like and stick it under the correct headings on the plate.
- Put students into pairs. Ask them to talk about their plate, e.g. *I like cheese (and) I like pasta. I don't like milk (and) I don't like salad.* etc.

Finisher
- Play *Draw and guess.* See Ideas Bank (Teacher's Book page 141) for instructions. Use smiley/frowny faces to indicate like or don't like.

Further practice
Extra Practice Student Book page 98
Workbook page 47

4 Make your plate. Say. 🖥️

I like pasta!

Song lyrics ⟩ Page 104   Practice ⟩ Page 98   63

3 Sing. 2·18
- Play the *Pasta For The Picnic* song once through for students to listen. See page 143 for the lyrics.
- Play the song again, modeling actions: smiling faces, thumbs up and nodding for *I like* …; frowning, shaking head with thumbs down for *I don't like* …
- Play the song again for students to join in and do the actions.

Pasta For The Picnic
I like pasta.
Oh, I like pasta.
Pasta for the picnic, yeah, yeah.
Pasta for the picnic, please.
I don't like pasta.
But I like chicken.
Chicken for the picnic, yeah, yeah.
Chicken for the picnic, please.
I don't like chicken.
But I like cheese.
Cheese for the picnic, yeah, yeah.
Cheese for the picnic, please.
I don't like cheese.
But I like salad.

Salad for the picnic, yeah, yeah.
Salad for the picnic, please.
I don't like salad.
Oh, I like rice.
Rice for the picnic, yeah, yeah.
Rice for the picnic, please.
I like milk.
And I like milk.
Milk for the picnic, yeah, yeah.
Milk for the picnic, please.

21ST CENTURY SKILLS:

Communication
Students use music to learn a grammar structure and reinforce their understanding of target vocabulary.

---

4 Make your plate. Say.
- Tell students that they are going to make a plate of food.
- Make sure each child has a paper plate, colored pens, scissors, and glue.
- Students color the food pictures and cut them out. They choose which food

Lesson 3 pages 64–65
Classroom Presentation Tool

Objectives
To present new vocabulary in the context of the story.

To practice the new vocabulary using the grammar from Lesson 2.

To practice a short Everyday English role play taken from the story.

Language and structures

Active: *ice cream, fries, water, candy; What's wrong? I feel sick! I like (water). I don't like (candy).*

Passive: *fair, Are you hungry? I'm hungry.*

Materials
Unit 7 flashcards; Class Audio CD 2; Megabyte puppet; colored pens

Warmer
- Play the *Pasta For The Picnic* song from Unit 7 Lesson 2 page 63 🔊 2•18 for students to listen and join in if possible.
- Encourage students to do the actions from Lesson 2.

1 Watch or listen. 🔊 2•19 Act it out.
- Point to the first frame of the story and ask students who they can see in the picture (Jack, Lucy, Ellie, and Megabyte). Ask *Where are they? (At the fair.)*
- Point to Megabyte and say *I'm hungry!* Rub your tummy. Ask the class what food they think the children and Megabyte can eat at the fair. Listen to their ideas and praise them. Don't confirm any answers yet.
- Play the recording. Encourage students to point to the correct pictures as they listen.
- Play the recording again and ask students questions about the story.

  Frame 1: *Are the children hungry? (Yes.)*

  Frame 2: *What does Jack have? (Chicken.) Does Megabyte like chicken? (No!) What does he like? (Fries.)*

  Frame 3: *What food do the children have? (Pasta, ice cream, salad.)*

  Frame 4: *What can Megabyte see? (Candy.)*

  Frame 5: *Is Megabyte happy? (No.) Why? (He ate too much candy, ice cream and fries!)*

  Frame 6: *What does Megabyte like now? (He likes water.)*

- Divide the class into groups to act out the story. Allow students time to practice in their groups. Then invite groups to act out the story for the class.

21ST CENTURY SKILLS:
Critical thinking
Students use pictures to predict what happens in a story.

2 Listen and point. Say. 🔊 2•20
- Introduce the new words with Megabyte using the flashcards. Place them on the board. Use Megabyte to point to the flashcards and say the words for students to repeat.
- Play the recording for students to listen and point to the correct food/drink in their Student Books. Play the recording again for students to listen, point, and repeat the words.
- Ask students *Who likes (fries)?* and encourage them to find the food items and the correct frame in the story.

Transcript
ice cream, fries, water, candy
fries, ice cream, candy, water

3 Follow and write.
- Point to pictures 1–4 and elicit the food/drink, or call out each item and ask students to point to them and repeat.
- Look at the first photo of the girl. Use your finger to follow the line from her speech bubble to the food. Ask *What is it? Ice cream.* Point to the example answer and read the sentence aloud.
- Say *Follow and write.* With a less confident class, allow students to work in pairs.

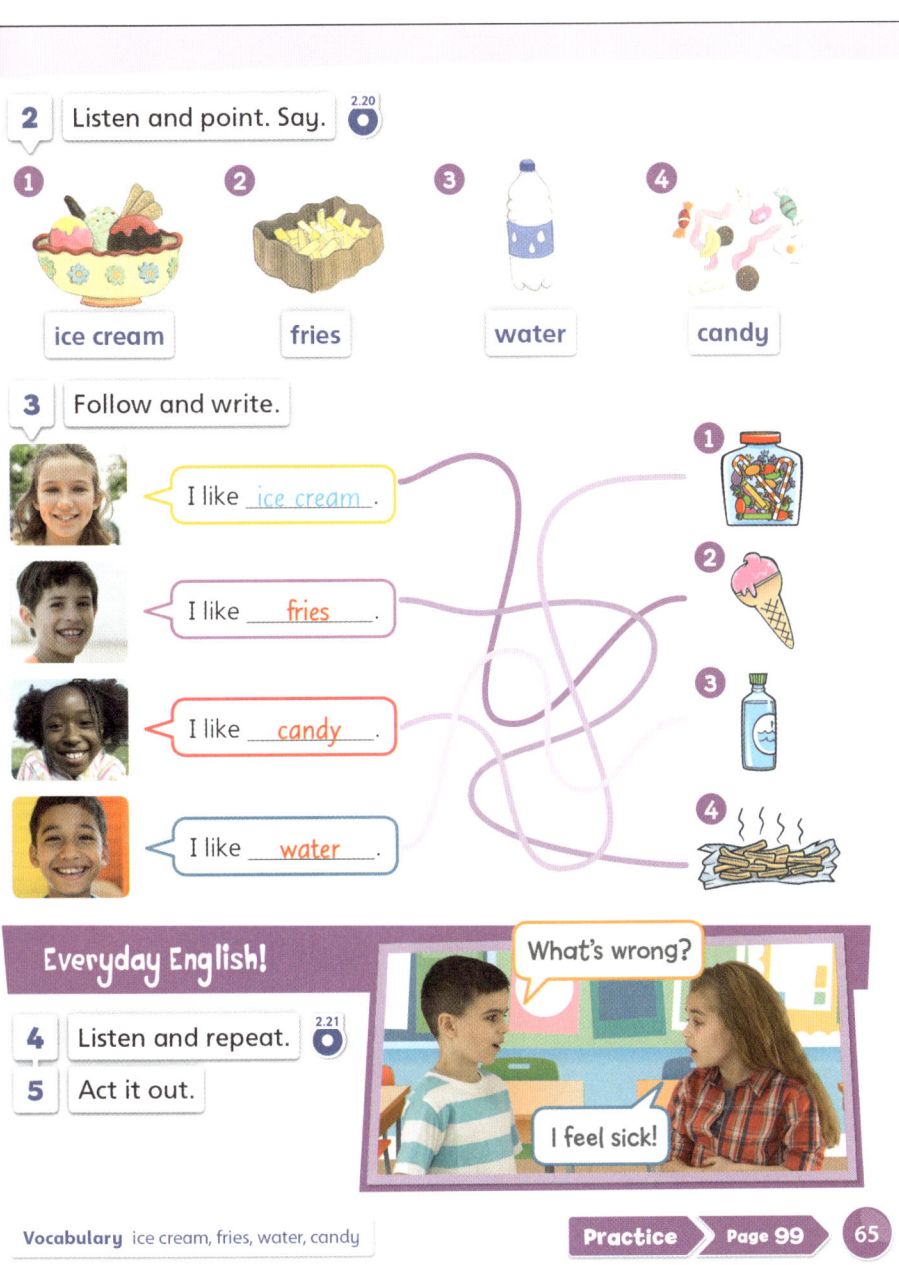

2 Listen and point. Say. 2.20

1. ice cream
2. fries
3. water
4. candy

3 Follow and write.

I like _ice cream_.

I like _fries_.

I like _candy_.

I like _water_.

Everyday English!

What's wrong?

I feel sick!

4 Listen and repeat. 2.21

5 Act it out.

Vocabulary ice cream, fries, water, candy

Practice ▷ Page 99 65

---

4 Listen and repeat. 🔊 2•21

• Play the recording for students to listen. Then play it again, pausing after each line for students to repeat the phrases.

5 Act it out.

• Model the dialogue a few times with the Megabyte puppet or with more confident students. When Megabyte says *I feel sick!* make him hold his tummy and act unwell.

• Ask students to stand. Divide the class into two teams: A and B. Team A put their hands palms up in a questioning pose. Team B hold their tummies. Say *Team B, find an A!* They race to find an opposing team member and ask and answer, e.g. *What's wrong? I feel sick!* Repeat several times. Then swap roles.

• Tell students they can use this exchange whenever they want to ask what's wrong with someone and when they want to say they feel unwell.

Finisher

• Play *Watch my lips.* See Ideas Bank (Teacher's Book page 140) for instructions.

Further practice
Extra Practice Student Book page 99
CD-ROM: Vocabulary and Grammar
Worksheet Unit 7 Lesson 3
Workbook pages 48–49

Lesson 4 page 66
Classroom Presentation Tool

Objectives
To present a CLIL concept (Science).
To practice the unit vocabulary and grammar through a CLIL concept.

Language and structures
Active: *grass, store; cow, milk, cheese*
Passive: *cream, sugar, flow chart; What can you see? Where does cheese come from? Cheese comes from milk.*

Materials
Unit 7 flashcards; Class Audio CD 2; CLIL stickers; CLIL Worksheet Unit 7 Lesson 4; colored pens, scissors, glue

Warmer
• Play *Kim's game*. See Ideas Bank (Teacher's Book page 140) for instructions.

1 Listen and point. 2·22
• Point to the photos. Ask students *What can you see?* Listen to students' ideas and praise them.
• Ask students to listen and point to the photos. Play the recording. Pause after each description for students to point to the correct photos.
• Say *cow* and ask the class to point to the cow in the photos. Repeat with the words *grass, milk, hot, cheese,* and *store.* Write the words on the board.
• Play the recording again. Encourage students to raise their hands when they hear the words on the board.
• Explain that these pictures show the process of making cheese.

Transcript
1 This is a cow. It likes grass.
2 This is milk. Milk comes from cows.
3 This is milk, too. Now it's very hot.
4 This is cheese. Look! It's white. Cheese comes from milk.
5 This is a cheese store. I like cheese!

2 Draw and stick.
• Ask students to look at the pictures showing how we make cheese. Go through each picture and talk about what they can see.
• Ask students to turn to the stickers section in the Student Book. Hold up your book and point to each of the CLIL stickers in turn. Encourage students to say what it shows, e.g. *milk, hot milk, milk changes to white cheese.* They stick the stickers in the correct spaces on page 66.
• Ask the class what is missing from the process and point to the blank spaces in the flow chart. Look back at

exercise 1 for help. (*The cow eats grass. This is a cheese store.*) Ask students to draw these two pictures.

3 Make a flow chart about ice cream. Point and say.
• Hand out CLIL worksheets. Say *I like ice cream!* Go round the class and elicit who likes ice cream.
• Say *Ice cream comes from milk.* Point to the pictures on the worksheet and explain that they show how we make ice cream.
• Go through each picture and make sure students understand what happens at each stage. (*Cows like grass; Milk comes from cows; This is milk, cream and sugar; Now they're hot; This is ice cream. Look! It's cold; This is an ice cream store.*) Point to the flow chart and show students the direction of the steps.
• In pairs or small groups, students cut out the pictures and place them onto the flow chart in the order they think is correct. Tell students not to glue them yet.

• Move around offering help and check that students have the items in the correct order. Tell them to glue each step onto the flow chart and color them in.
• Ask a few confident groups to present to the class by pointing to each picture and telling the class what it shows.

Extension activity
Act out how we make cheese and ice cream. Ask the class to stand. Say *This is how we make (cheese)!* Say the stages of the process and ask the class to act them out, e.g. *The cow eats grass* (students act like cows eating grass).

Finisher
• Play *Musical flashcards*. See Ideas Bank (Teacher's Book page 141) for instructions.

Further practice
Workbook page 50

---

7 **Lesson 4**   **Science**

1 Listen and point. 2.22

2 Draw and stick.   *Where does cheese come from?*

3 Make a flow chart about ice cream. Point and say.

66   Vocabulary grass, store

7 Review

1 Look and write. Find Jack's favorite food.

cheese   fries   milk
chicken   candy   rice
salad   water

1 c h i c k e n
2 c h e e s e
3 f r i e s
4 c a n d y
5 r i c e
6 w a t e r
7 s a l a d
8 m i l k

I like _ice cream_.

2 Make your food book. Play and say. ✂ Page 107

I like salad.

Our Values
We choose healthy food.

3 Complete your picture dictionary. Page 85

67

Review (page 67)

Classroom Presentation Tool

Objectives
To review the linguistic content of the unit.

To talk about a value.

Language and structures
Active: *chicken, rice, pasta, milk, salad, cheese; ice cream, fries, water, candy; I like (salad). I don't like (cheese).*

Passive: *We choose healthy food. What's number 1?*

Materials
Unit 7 flashcards; Craft cut-out Unit 7 Review; scissors, colored pens; Our Values sticker; a large piece of card/paper (optional)

Warmer
- Play *What card is missing?* See Ideas Bank (Teacher's Book page 140) for instructions.

1 Look and write. Find Jack's favorite food.
- Point to pictures 1–8. Ask *What's number 1? Chicken!* Point to the grid and tell students to write *chicken* next to number 1. Refer students to the words in the word box.
- Ask students to complete the crossword. With a less confident class, allow students to work in pairs.
- Ask students to check their answers in pairs before checking together as a class.
- Point to the secret word in blue and ask *What's Jack's favorite food? (Ice cream.)* Tell students to write it in the space.

2 Make your food book. Play and say.
- Tell students they are going to make a food book. Point to the pictures and ask students what they need to make one.
- Tell students to turn to page 107 and cut the Craft cut-out from their Student Books. Model how to fold the book. Students can decorate the cover with a picture and write their name. They draw foods they like and don't like, and one healthy food.
- Move around the class offering help if necessary. Ask students questions about their food book, e.g. *What is it? Do you like (ice cream)? What is your favorite food/drink? Is it healthy?* etc.
- Put students into pairs. Ask them to show their books to their partner and talk about the pictures, e.g. *This is my food book. I like (rice). I don't like (candy). My healthy food is (salad).* Check students are using the correct structures and pronunciation.
- Pair up students with a new partner and repeat.

Extra activity
Draw a large mouth on a piece of card or on the board. Ask students to place the flashcards showing healthy foods on the mouth or the board, e.g. *rice, salad, pasta, milk, water,* and *chicken.* Ask students to add to this by drawing additional foods/drinks that are healthy.

Our Values
- Show the class the space for the *Our Values* sticker. Read out the value (*We choose healthy food*). Tell students it is important to eat healthy food to take care of themselves.
- Tell students they have all chosen a healthy food in their book today. Congratulate students for doing so. Award them with the *Our Values* sticker to stick in the space on page 67.

3 Complete your picture dictionary.
- Tell students to turn to page 85 of their Student Books and look at the Picture Dictionary section for Unit 7.
- Point to each of the pictures and ask students to say the words.
- Students color the items in the Picture Dictionary. Move around the class asking questions, e.g. *What is it? Is it healthy?*

Finisher
- Play *Tic-Tac-Toe.* See Ideas Bank (Teacher's Book page 141) for instructions.

Further practice
Unit 7 Test
Workbook page 51

Unit 8 Numbers Everywhere!

Lesson 1 pages 68–69

Classroom Presentation Tool

Objectives

To present and practice the numbers 11–20.

To review vocabulary from a previous unit.

Language and structures

Active: *eleven, twelve, thirteen, fourteen, fifteen, sixteen, seventeen, eighteen, nineteen, twenty; ice cream*

Materials

Unit 8 flashcards, Starter Unit flashcards; Class Audio CD 2; Megabyte puppet; stickers section; a ball (optional)

Warmer

- Play *Hit the card* with the Starter Unit flashcards to review the numbers 1–10. See Ideas Bank (Teacher's Book page 140) for instructions. Use a balled up piece of paper if you don't have a ball.

1 Listen and point. Say. 2•23

- Books closed. Use Megabyte to place the Starter Unit flashcards on the board and ask students to count from 1–10.
- Introduce the new numbers with the Unit 8 flashcards and encourage the class to continue counting.
- Use Megabyte to point to the numbers in a random order and say the words for students to repeat.
- Books open. Play the recording for students to listen and point to the numbers in the picture. Play the recording again for students to listen, point, and repeat the numbers.

TEACHING TIP

With a less confident class, use Megabyte to point to the numbers in order several times, before you point to them in a random order.

Transcript

eleven, twelve, thirteen, fourteen, fifteen, sixteen, seventeen, eighteen, nineteen, twenty
nineteen, thirteen, sixteen, eleven, eighteen, fourteen, twenty, fifteen, twelve, seventeen

Extension activity

Discuss the picture on pages 68–69. Ask the class to shout out things they can see in English, e.g. *toys, clothes, playground, trees, flowers, children, kite, balloon,* etc. Ask *Do you like skateboarding?* etc. With a less confident class, call out items from the picture for students to point to and repeat, e.g. tree, flowers, rope ladder, etc.

2 Stick.

- Ask students to turn to the stickers section in the Student Book. Hold up your book and point to each of the number stickers in turn. Encourage students to say the numbers. Then say the numbers in a random order for students to point to the correct stickers.
- Students stick the stickers in the correct spaces on page 69. When they have finished, ask students to point to the stickers and say the words.

Fast finishers

Put students into pairs to take turns saying a number for their partner to point to.

21ST CENTURY SKILLS:

Communication

Students extend their knowledge of counting in English.

EXTRA VOCABULARY:

cart
helmet
hot air balloon
rope ladder
skateboard
skateboard ramp
swing
tower
zip line

Further practice

CD-ROM: Vocabulary and Grammar
Worksheet Unit 8 Lesson 1
Workbook page 52

Notes

_____

_____

_____

_____

_____

_____

_____

_____

_____

_____

_____

_____

_____

_____

_____

_____

_____

_____

3 Chant. 2·24

- Play the chant once for students to listen and point to the number flashcards on the board.
- Hand out the Unit 8 flashcards to pairs of students. Play the chant again and ask students to stand with their flashcard when they hear their number.
- Play the chant once more and ask students to write the numeral in the air as they say the word.

Transcript

eleven, eleven, eleven
twelve, twelve, twelve
thirteen, thirteen, thirteen
fourteen, fourteen, fourteen
fifteen, fifteen, fifteen
sixteen, sixteen, sixteen
seventeen, seventeen, seventeen
eighteen, eighteen, eighteen
nineteen, nineteen, nineteen
twenty, twenty, twenty

Find it!

- Point to Jack's drawing pad and ask students what they can see (ice cream). Ask students to find the ice cream in the main picture. (The girl behind the swing on page 68 is eating one.)
- Tell students to turn to the Picture Dictionary for Unit 8 (Student Book page 85) and find the ice cream. Ask students to color the ice cream in the Picture Dictionary the same colors as the main artwork on Student Book page 68.

Finisher

- Play *Musical flashcards* with the Starter Unit and Unit 8 flashcards. See Ideas Bank (Teacher's Book page 141) for instructions.

Lesson 2 (pages 70–71)
Classroom Presentation Tool

Objectives
To present a new grammar structure.

To practice the new grammar with the Lesson 1 vocabulary.

To sing a song using the Lesson 1 vocabulary and the new grammar.

To do a personalization activity that involves a simple craft activity.

Language and structures
Active: *Look! I have (eleven) (shoes). I don't have (eleven) (shoes). How many … ? Numbers 11–20; colors; shoes, socks, hat, robot, car, picture*

Materials
Unit 8 flashcards; Class Audio CD 2; Craft Worksheet Unit 8 Lesson 2; colored pens, scissors

Warmer
- Play the chant from Unit 8 Lesson 1 page 69 2•24 for students to listen and join in.
- Place the Unit 8 flashcards on students' desks around the room. Ask students to hold up the correct number flashcard when they hear the word. Play the chant again.

1 Count. Listen and read. Say. 2•25
- Point to the picture and ask students to tell you what clothes items they can see. Ask *How many shoes does Lucy have?* Ask students to count as a class (*1, 2, 3 …11!*)
- Play the recording for students to listen to. Then play it again and encourage students to repeat the grammar structure. Divide the class into two to repeat either Jack or Lucy's lines.
- Hold up 12 pencils and ask *How many pencils do I have?* Count them as a class and elicit *You have twelve pencils.*
- Give a confident child three pencils and ask them to hold them up. Hold up your 12 pencils again. Say *Look! I have twelve pencils!* Elicit *How many?* from the class. Then encourage the child holding the three pencils to say *I don't have twelve pencils. I have three pencils!*
- Repeat with three or four more sets of objects.

2 Count and circle. Listen, check, and repeat. 2•26
- Ask students to look at the picture and tell you what they can see (*bedroom, cars, robots, pictures, balloons, hats,* etc.)
- Ask students to count the pictures on the bedroom wall in pairs or count

them as a class. Elicit the structure *I have fourteen pictures.* Point to the first sentence below the picture and show students the example answer.
- Ask the class to read the second sentence. Students count the hats and circle the correct number in the sentence below.
- Then the class completes the remaining items. With a less confident class, count each object together.
- Allow students to check their answers in pairs. Encourage them to use the structure, e.g. *I have eleven (hats).*
- Say *Listen and check your answers.* Play the recording. Pause after each item and ask the class to repeat the sentences.

Transcript
1 I don't have fifteen pictures. I have fourteen pictures.
2 I don't have thirteen hats. I have eleven hats.
3 I don't have twenty balloons. I have twelve balloons.
4 I don't have nineteen cars. I have seventeen cars.
5 I don't have eighteen robots. I have sixteen robots.

2 Count and circle. Listen, check, and repeat. 2.26

1 (fourteen pictures) / fifteen pictures
2 thirteen hats / (eleven hats)
3 twenty balloons / (twelve balloons)
4 (seventeen cars) / nineteen cars
5 (sixteen robots) / eighteen robots

70 I have eleven shoes. I don't have eleven shoes.

3 Sing. 2.27 Watch! *Song!*

4 Make your bingo card. Play and say.

Bingo! I have thirteen, fourteen, seventeen ...

BINGO!

Song lyrics ▸ Page 104   Practice ▸ Page 100   71

---

3. Sing. 🔊 2·27
- Play the *Twenty Socks!* song once through for students to listen to.
- Play the song again. Ask students to hold up their fingers and count the numbers as they sing. They can flash their ten fingers twice for the number 20.

Twenty Socks!
Twenty socks! Twenty socks! I have twenty socks.
One, two, three, four, five, six, seven, eight, nine, ten – eleven, twelve, thirteen, fourteen, fifteen, sixteen, seventeen, eighteen, nineteen, twenty.
Twenty socks! Twenty socks! I have twenty socks.
I have red socks: 1, 2, 3, 4.
I have blue socks: 1, 2, 3, 4.
I have black socks: 1, 2, 3, 4.
I have white socks: 1, 2, 3, 4.
How many pink socks?
1, 2, 3 …1, 2, 3 pink socks.
Oh no! How many green socks? 1!
Oh no!

3 pink socks and 1 green sock!
Oh no!
Twenty socks! Twenty socks! I have twenty socks.
One, two, three, four, five, six, seven, eight, nine, ten, eleven, twelve, thirteen, fourteen, fifteen, sixteen, seventeen, eighteen, nineteen, twenty.
Twenty socks! Twenty socks! I have twenty socks.

4 Make your bingo card. Play and say.
- Tell students that they are going to play *Bingo!*
- Make sure each child has colored pens and scissors. They color and cut out the numbers and the bingo card.
- Students place six numbers from 11–20 on their card. Call out random numbers. When students hear their number they can turn it face down. When they have all six numbers face down on their card, they shout *Bingo!* Then students say the numbers they have, e.g. *I have twelve, eighteen …*

- With a more confident class, invite students to call out the numbers.

21ST CENTURY SKILLS:
Collaboration
Students learn to play a game in a group, remembering to play fair and the value of being a good loser.

Finisher
- Play *Which one is missing?* See Ideas Bank (Teacher's Book page 140) for instructions.

Further practice
Extra Practice Student Book page 100
Workbook page 53

Notes

_____

_____

_____

_____

_____

_____

_____

_____

_____

_____

_____

_____

_____

_____

_____

Lesson 3 (pages 72–73)
Classroom Presentation Tool

Objectives
To present new vocabulary in the context of the story.

To practice the new vocabulary using the grammar from Lesson 2.

To practice a short Everyday English role play taken from the story.

Language and structures
Active: *trampoline, hula hoop, jump rope, skateboard; I have a (skateboard). I don't have a (hula hoop). You can do it!*

Passive: *Sports day; Look! It's Sports Day! Don't worry! Go Lucy! Jump on! Come on!*

Materials
Unit 1 and 8 flashcards; Class Audio CD 2; Megabyte puppet; a hula hoop and/or jump rope (optional)

Warmer
- Play the *Twenty Socks!* song from Unit 8 Lesson 2 page 71 🔊 2•27 for students to listen and join in if possible. Encourage students to do the actions.

1 Watch or listen. 🔊 2•28 Act it out.
- Point to the first frame of the story and ask *Where are the children today? (At school.)*
- Play the recording. Encourage students to point to the correct pictures as they listen.
- Play the recording again and ask students questions about the story.

  Frame 1: *What is happening today at school? (It's Sports Day.)*

  Frame 2: *What does Lucy have? (A hula hoop and a jump rope.) Why is she sad? (She doesn't have a trampoline.)*

  Frame 3: *What sport is it? (Hula hoop.) Can Lucy do it? (Yes.)*

  Frame 4: *What sport is it? (Jump rope.) How many jumps can Ellie do? (Eleven.)*

  Frame 5: *What doesn't Jack have? (A skateboard.)*

  Frame 6: *How does Megabyte help him? (He is a skateboard!)*

- Divide the class into groups to act out the story. Allow students time to practice in their groups. Then invite groups to act out the story for the class.

2 Listen and point. Say. 🔊 2•29
- Introduce the new words with Megabyte using the flashcards. Place them on the board. Use Megabyte to point to the flashcards and say the words for students to repeat.
- Play the recording for students to listen and point to the correct items in their Student Books. Play the recording again for students to listen, point, and repeat the words.
- Ask pairs of students what they have or don't have at home, e.g. *I have a trampoline. I don't have a hula hoop.*

Transcript
trampoline, hula hoop, jump rope, skateboard
jump rope, trampoline, skateboard, hula hoop

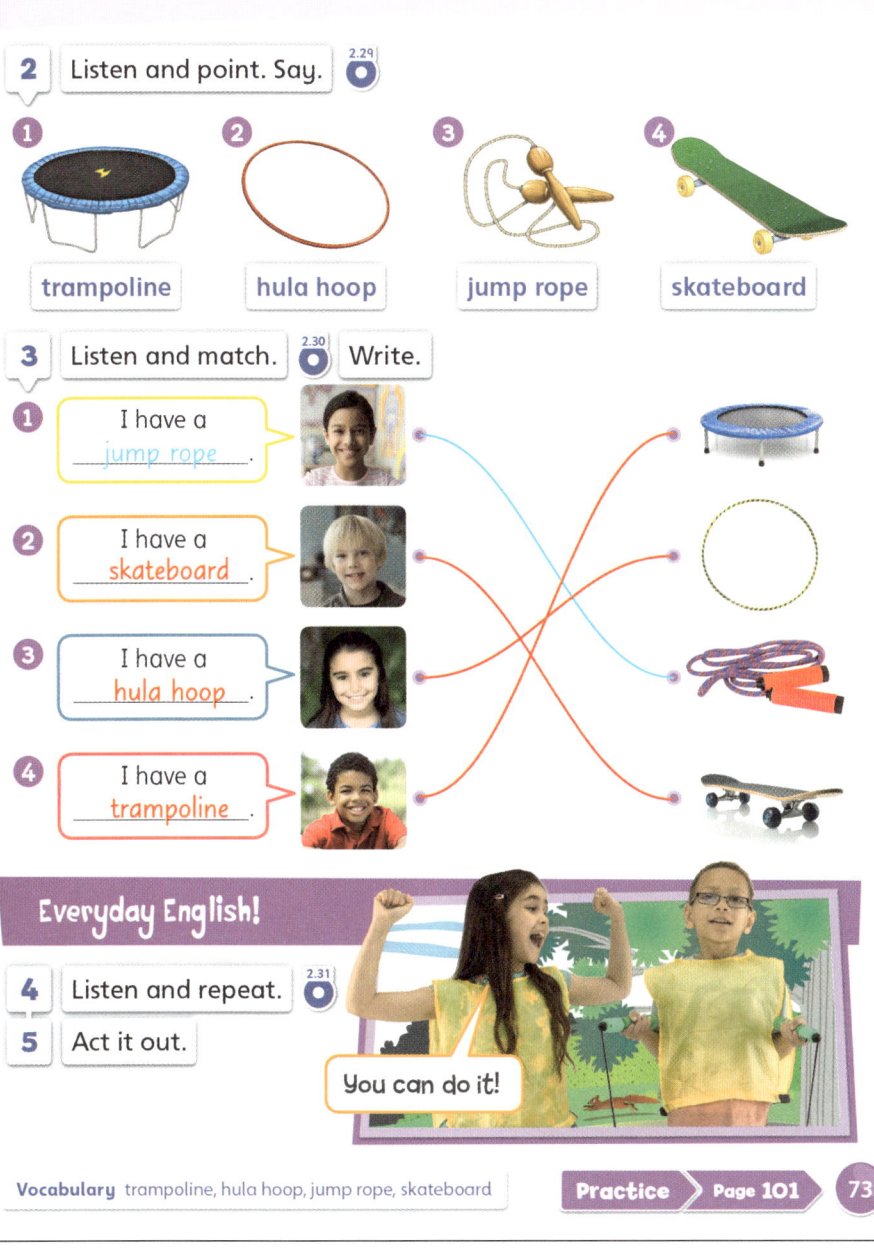

2 Listen and point. Say. 2.29

1 trampoline
2 hula hoop
3 jump rope
4 skateboard

3 Listen and match. 2.30 Write.

1 I have a ___jump rope___.
2 I have a ___skateboard___.
3 I have a ___hula hoop___.
4 I have a ___trampoline___.

Everyday English!

4 Listen and repeat. 2.31
5 Act it out.

You can do it!

Vocabulary trampoline, hula hoop, jump rope, skateboard

Practice ▷ Page 101 73

- Divide the class into two groups: competitors and spectators. If you have a jump rope or hula hoop, give it to the competitors' group. If not, encourage the group to pretend to do a sport. The competitors mime the sport while the spectators enthusiastically jump, cheer, and say *You can do it!* Swap roles.
- Tell students they can use this exchange whenever they want to encourage someone.

> **21ST CENTURY SKILLS:**
> **Social and cross-cultural interaction**
> Students learn an everyday phrase to help motivate others.

Finisher
- Play *What number is it?* See Ideas Bank (Teacher's Book page 140) for instructions.

> **Further practice**
> **Extra Practice Student Book page 101**
> **CD-ROM: Vocabulary and Grammar**
> **Worksheet Unit 8 Lesson 3**
> **Workbook pages 54–55**

Notes

---

3 Listen and match. 2·30 **Write.**
- Point to the photos and ask the class to name the toys. With a less confident class, call out the toys and ask students to point to them and repeat the words.
- Look at the first photo and invite a confident child to read the sentence aloud. Use your finger to follow the line to the jump rope. Say *I don't have a hula hoop. I have a jump rope.*
- Say *Listen and match.* Play the recording. Pause after each item or play the recording twice if necessary. Check that students are drawing matching lines and not writing yet.
- Tell students to write the words. Refer them to the spelling of the words in exercise 2.
- Allow students to check answers in pairs before checking together as a class. With a more confident class, encourage students to also say what the students don't have.

Transcript
1 I don't have a hula hoop. I have a jump rope.
2 I don't have a trampoline. I have a skateboard.
3 I don't have a skateboard. I have a hula hoop.
4 I don't have a jump rope. I have a trampoline.

4 Listen and repeat. 2·31
- Play the recording for students to listen to. Then play it again, pausing after each line for students to repeat the phrase.

5 Act it out.
- Model the dialogue with the Megabyte puppet, or with more confident students. Mime starting a race (in a crouched position on the starting blocks). Encourage the class to shout *You can do it!*

Lesson 4 (page 74)

Classroom Presentation Tool

Objectives
To present a CLIL concept (Math).

To practice the unit vocabulary and grammar through a CLIL concept.

Language and structures
Active: *block, graph, students; colors; I have a (hula hoop). I don't have a (trampoline).*

Passive: *How many (toys)? Talk to ten friends.*

Materials
Unit 6, 7, and 8 flashcards; Class Audio CD 2; CLIL stickers; CLIL Worksheet Unit 8 Lesson 4; a pen or pencil, colored pens; Megabyte puppet

Warmer
- Play *Odd one out* with the Unit 6, 7, and 8 flashcards. See Ideas Bank (Teacher's Book page 140) for instructions.

1 Listen, point, and answer. 2·32 Stick.
- Point to the block graph and read the title. Ask students *What toys can you see? (Trampoline, hula hoop, skateboard, jump rope)*. Elicit the colors of the blocks.
- Play the recording for students to listen and point to the toys in the graph as they hear them.
- Play the recording again, pausing after each sentence. Ask the class *What is it? (A block graph.)* Say *Point to the blocks*. Ask *How many students have a (trampoline/hula hoop/skateboard)?* Elicit *(Five) students have a (trampoline)*. Finally repeat the question from the recording *What do nine students have? (A jump rope!)*
- Ask students to turn to the stickers section in their Student Books. They stick the stickers in the correct spaces on page 74.

Transcript
This is a graph. It's a block graph.
A block is a colored square.
There are five red blocks. Five students have a trampoline.
There are seven green blocks. Seven students have a hula hoop.
There are three purple blocks. Three students have a skateboard.
There are nine blue blocks. What do nine students have?

2 How many toys? Talk to ten friends and write.
- Point to the photo and ask the class what the two students are doing (*asking each other about toys*).

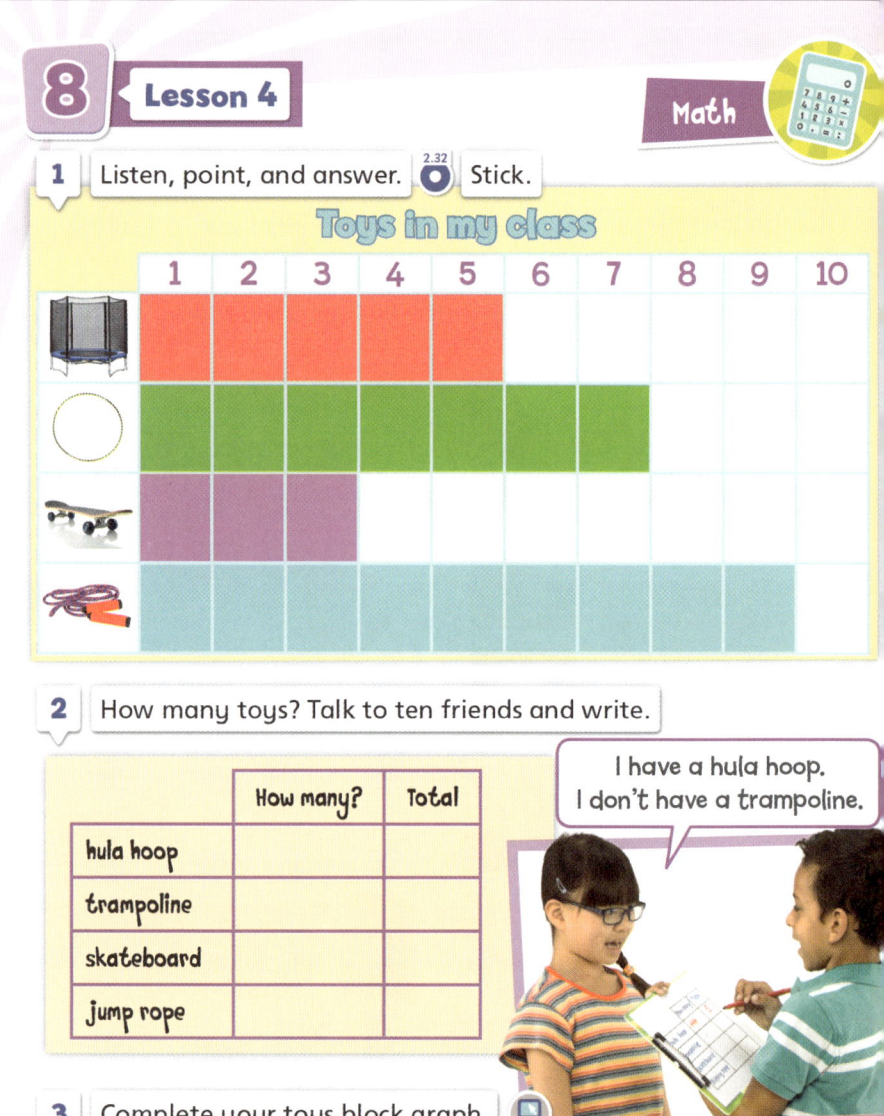

8 ◀ **Lesson 4**   **Math**

1 Listen, point, and answer. 2.32 Stick.

Toys in my class

	1	2	3	4	5	6	7	8	9	10
trampoline	■	■	■	■	■					
hula hoop	■	■	■	■	■	■	■			
skateboard	■	■	■							
jump rope	■	■	■	■	■	■	■	■	■	

2 How many toys? Talk to ten friends and write.

	How many?	Total
hula hoop		
trampoline		
skateboard		
jump rope		

I have a hula hoop. I don't have a trampoline.

3 Complete your toys block graph.

74   **Vocabulary** block, graph, students

- Write the question *What do you have?* on the board. Put the flashcards of a *hula hoop, trampoline, skateboard,* and *jump rope* on the board. Use Megabyte or a confident child to demonstrate asking and answering questions.
- Say e.g. *Hello David/Megabyte. What do you have?* Megabyte/the child replies, e.g. *I have a (hula hoop). I don't have a (trampoline)*. Draw a check on the board next to each item they have.
- Point to the table in exercise 2. Tell students to move around the class and talk to ten students. They put a check under *How many?* if the child they speak to has that item.
- When the class is ready and seated again, ask *How many students have hula hoops?* Students count the number of checks they have in their table and say the number. Answers will differ. They write their number in the space in the table. Repeat with the remaining toys.

3 Complete your toys block graph.
- Hand out CLIL worksheets. Point to the toys, the numbers down the left-hand side, and the words in the word box.
- Tell students they are going to create a block graph to show the results of their class survey about toys. They look at the table in exercise 2 on page 74 of the Student Book and find the *Total* number of students they have recorded for each toy. They mark that number of blocks in their graph and color them in. Tell students to choose a different color for each toy.
- Put students into pairs to talk about their results, e.g. *There are (five) (pink) blocks. (Five) students have a (jump rope)*.

Finisher
- Play *Four in a row* with the Unit 6, 7, and 8 flashcards. See Ideas Bank (Teacher's Book page 141) for instructions.

Further practice
Workbook page 56

8 Review

1 Look and color. Count and write.

jump ropes [green] →   skateboards [yellow] →
hula hoops [purple] →   balls [red] →

1 I have ___11 jump ropes___ .   3 I have ___13 skateboards___ .

2 I have ___14 hula hoops___ .   4 I have ___15 balls___ .

2 Spot the difference. Count and write. Say.   ✂ Page 105

I have sixteen hula hoops.

I have eighteen hula hoops!

Our Values
We work together!

3 Complete your picture dictionary.   Page 85

75

Review (page 75)

Classroom Presentation Tool

Objectives
To review the linguistic content of the unit.
To talk about a value.

Language and structures
Active: numbers 11–20; trampoline, hula hoop, jump rope, skateboard; I have (sixteen) (hula hoops). I don't have a (trampoline).

Passive: We work together. How many (jump ropes)? Spot the difference.

Materials
Unit 8 flashcards; Craft cut-out Unit 8 Review; scissors, glue, colored pens; two shoe boxes; Our Values sticker

Warmer
• Play *Change places*. See Ideas Bank (Teacher's Book page 141) for instructions. Use flashcards from any units you wish to review language from this level.

1 Look and color. Count and write.
• Point to the picture. Ask *What toys can you see?* Elicit the names of the toys.
• Point to the words in the word box and ask students to tell you which color is paired with each toy. Say *Color the jump ropes green. Color the skateboards yellow.* etc.
• When the class is ready, ask *How many (jump ropes)?* Elicit answers with, e.g. *I have (eleven) jump ropes.* Point to the numbered sentences below and tell students to count and write the items.
• Check answers by asking *How many (skateboards)?* and elicit *I have (thirteen) (skateboards).*

2 Spot the difference. Count and write. Say.
• Tell students they are going to play a game called *Spot the difference.*

• Tell students to turn to page 105 and cut the Craft cut-out from their Student Books. Point to the pictures and ask students what they can see (*a school gym*). Elicit as much vocabulary from the class as possible.
• Put students into pairs and tell them to cut picture A from picture B. One student takes picture A and the other student takes picture B. Tell students to sit back-to-back as in the photo on page 75, or with a book between them.
• They tell each other what they have in their picture in order to spot the differences, e.g. A: *I have sixteen hula hoops.* B: *I don't have sixteen hula hoops. I have eighteen hula hoops!* They write the number in the box next to each toy.
• Move around the class monitoring and praising students' speaking.

Fast finishers
Ask fast finishers to color their pictures and write complete sentences about what they have in each picture, e.g. *I have sixteen hula hoops.*

Our Values
• Show the class the space for the *Our Values* sticker. Read out the value (*We work together*). Tell students that it is important to work well with others.
• Tell students they have all worked well together today and throughout the course. Congratulate students for doing so. Award them with the *Our Values* sticker to stick in the space on page 75.

3 Complete your picture dictionary.
• Tell students to turn to page 85 of their Student Books and look at the Picture Dictionary section for Unit 8.
• Point to each of the pictures and ask students to say the words.
• Students color the items in the Picture Dictionary. Move around the class as they work, asking questions, e.g. *What is it? Do you have a (trampoline)?* etc.

Finisher
• Play *True or False*. See Ideas Bank (Teacher's Book page 141) for instructions. Use flashcards from any units that you wish to review language from. If you don't have shoe boxes, draw a check and an ✗ on a table.

Further practice
Unit 8 Test
Workbook pages 57–59

Culture 4
Lunch at School pages 76–77
Classroom Presentation Tool

Objectives
To present and practice four new items of vocabulary.

To think about what we eat at school.

To review the vocabulary from a previous unit.

Language and structures
Active: *school lunch, banana, sandwich, packed lunch; chicken, rice, pasta, milk, salad, cheese, ice cream, fries, water, candy*

Passive: *lunch; What's your favorite food for lunch? What do you have? I have/don't have a (school lunch).*

Materials
Unit 7 flashcards (food); Class Audio CD 2; colored pens; a lunchbox (optional)

Warmer
- If you have a lunchbox, place it open on your desk. If not, draw a large box on the board with the word *Lunch* on the side.
- Put the Unit 7 flashcards in the lunchbox or place them face down in the box on the board. Take a flashcard and mime eating or drinking the item. Ask the class to guess the food word. When they guess it correctly, stick it face up on the board.
- Ask the class if they eat lunch at school or if they bring their lunch from home. Listen to their responses and ask *What's your favorite food for lunch?*

1 Listen and point. Say. 2·33
- Read the words aloud and point to each photo. Repeat the words and ask students to listen and point to the correct photo.
- Play the recording for students to listen and point to the photos. Play the recording again for students to listen, point, and repeat the words.
- Say the words again and ask students to point to the correct photo. Start slowly, then get faster and faster.

Transcript
school lunch, banana, sandwich, packed lunch

packed lunch, school lunch, sandwich, banana

Culture 4 **Lunch at School**

1 Listen and point. Say. 2.33
2 Listen and number. 2.34
3 Listen and make a ✓. 2.35
4 Draw your lunch. Say.

A school lunch 2

B banana 3

C sandwich 1

D packed lunch 4

76 **Vocabulary** school lunch, banana, sandwich, packed lunch

Extra activity
If your school has both lunch options (packed lunch and school lunch), do a quick survey around the class. Ask students to put their hands up if they have a school lunch. Then ask those who have a packed lunch to raise their hands. Ask students what is different about school lunches and packed lunches. Consider discussing the choice of foods, what is hot or cold, the taste, etc.

2 Listen and number. 2·34
- Ask students to look at the photos again. Ask them *What can you see?* Elicit the Unit 7 and Culture 4 vocabulary.
- Tell students to listen and write the numbers 1, 2, 3, and 4 in the correct boxes next to the photos.
- Play the recording. Pause after each item to give students time to write the numbers. With a less confident class, play the recording twice.

Transcript
1 I've got a sandwich for lunch today.
2 Today, I've got a school lunch. I've got chicken, rice, and salad.
3 I've got a banana in my lunch today.
4 Today, I've got a packed lunch.

3 Listen and make a ✓. 2·35
- Point to the pictures of the food and drink on page 77 and elicit the food items (*school lunch, chicken and rice, milk, water, packed lunch, pasta, banana*).
- Point to the two students on the left. Say *This is Lisa, and this is Khaled.* Explain to the class that they are going to hear what Lisa and Khaled have for lunch.
- Play the recording, pausing after the second sentence. Repeat the sentence, *I have a school lunch. I have chicken and rice.* Point to the example check next to Lisa.
- Play the remainder of the recording about Lisa for students to listen and check. Allow students to check their answers in pairs.

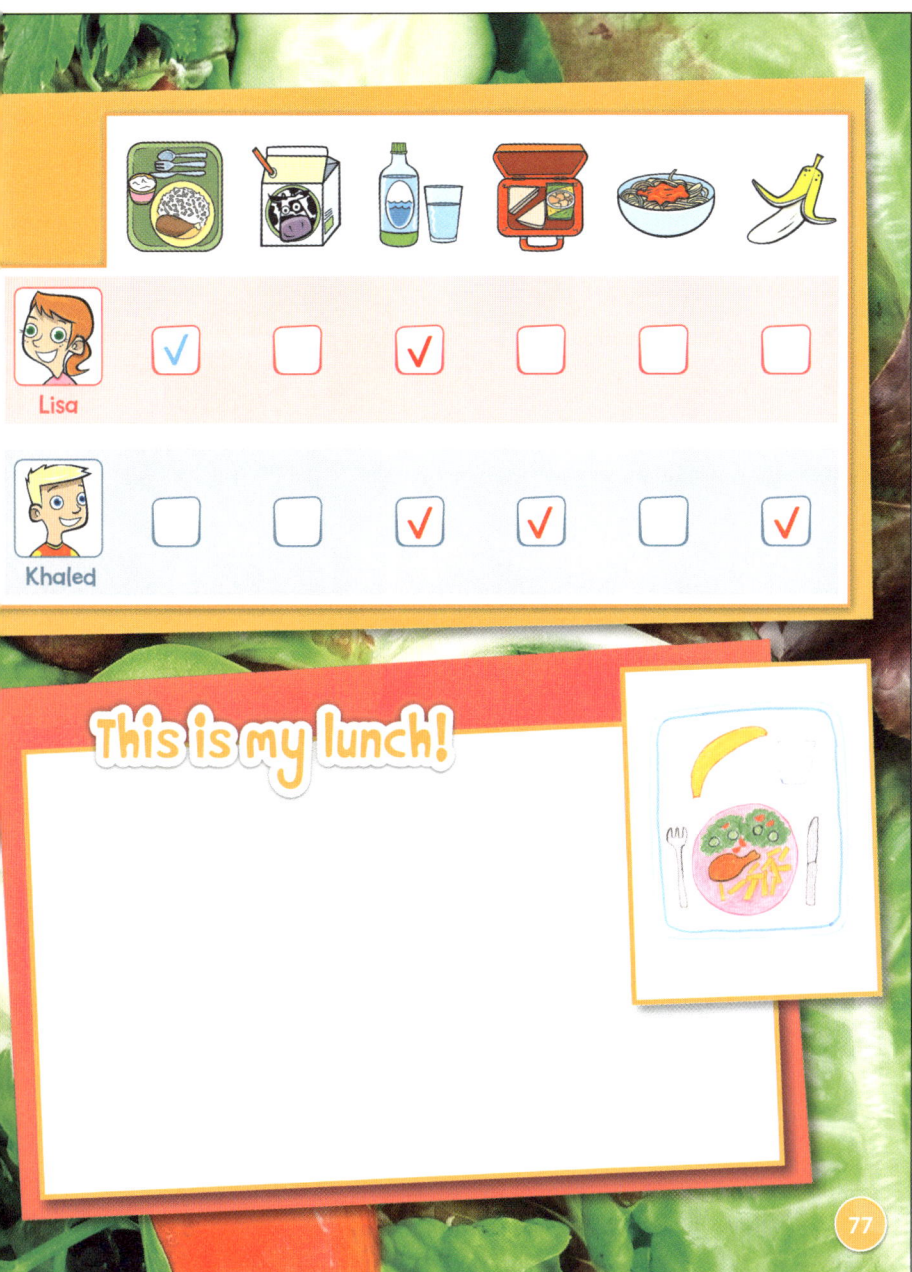

This is my lunch!

- Play the recording for Khaled. Ask students to check their answers in pairs before checking together as a class. Elicit sentences, e.g. *I have a school lunch*.

Transcript

Lisa: I have a school lunch. I have chicken and rice. I don't have any fruit today, but I have water.

Khaled: I don't have a school lunch today. I have a packed lunch. I have a cheese sandwich. I have fruit – look, a banana! I have water, too!

4 Draw your lunch. Say.

- Ask students to draw a picture of their favorite lunch. It can be the lunch they have today, or the lunch they had yesterday. Then students draw their favorite lunch in the space on page 77.
- Have a show-and-tell session. Ask students to sit in a circle with their pictures. Ask the student to your left *What do you have for lunch?* Elicit *I have a (sandwich, a banana, and water).*

They ask the student to their left *What do you have?* Continue around the circle, praising students for their use of language.

Extension activity

Use the students' pictures to practice numbers. Ask *How many apples do we have?* Count the apples in the students' pictures as a class and say together *We have five apples.* Repeat with other food and drink items.

21ST CENTURY SKILLS:

Communication

Students express ideas through the medium of art.

Finisher

- Play *Draw and guess* with the Unit 7 and Culture 4 words. See Ideas Bank (Teacher's Book page 141) for instructions.

Holidays
Mother's Day pages 78–79
Classroom Presentation Tool

Objectives
To present and practice four new items of vocabulary.

To review vocabulary from previous units.

To do a personalization activity that involves a simple craft activity.

Language and structures
Active: *hug, cookies, flowers, breakfast; present, card*

Passive: *Holidays, Mother's Day; Here are (some cookies) for you! Here's a (hug) for you!*

Materials
Unit 1–4 flashcards; Class Audio CD 2; Mother's Day Holidays Worksheets; colored pens, scissors, Mother's Day card in an envelope (optional)

Warmer
• Bring a Mother's Day card in an envelope to class or draw a card on the board. Ask *What is it?* Elicit ideas. Tell the class *It's a Mother's Day card.* Write *Mother's Day* on the board. Ask questions about Mother's Day in your country, e.g. *When is it? What do you do?*

1 Listen and point. Say. 🔘 2.36
• Read the words aloud and point to each photo. Repeat the words and ask students to listen and point to the correct photo.

• Play the recording for students to listen and point to the photos. Play the recording again for students to listen, point, and repeat the words.

• Say the words again and ask students to point to the correct photos. Start slowly, then get faster and faster.

Transcript
hug, cookies, breakfast, flowers cookies, flowers, hug, breakfast.

2 Listen and number. 🔘 2.37
• Ask students to look at the photos again. Tell them these are different ways children in the USA celebrate Mother's Day. Ask them *What can you see?* Elicit the vocabulary, i.e. *flowers, breakfast, cookies, hug,* and any other words they may know, e.g. *T-shirt, bedroom, kitchen, happy,* etc.

• Tell students to listen and write the numbers 1, 2, 3, and 4 in the correct boxes next to the photos.

• Play the recording. With a less confident class, pause after each item or play the recording twice.

• Ask students to check their answers in pairs, before checking together as a class, e.g. *What's number (1)? cookies!*

Transcript
1 Here are some cookies for my mom on Mother's Day!
2 **Girl:** Happy Mother's Day, Mom! Here are some flowers for you.
   Mom: Beautiful! Oh thank you so much!
3 I have breakfast for my mom. Look!
4 Happy Mother's Day, Mom. Here's a big hug for you!

3 Follow and number.
• Call out the Mother's Day words. Ask students to point to the items in the maze on page 79. Then invite confident students to read the words on the right.

• Show students the start of the maze and explain that they need to follow the maze and find the Mother's Day items. Ask students to follow the maze

with their finger. Ask *What's number 1? (Flowers.)* Point to the example answer in the box.

• Ask students to continue to follow the maze and write the correct numbers in the boxes. With a less confident class, allow students to work in pairs.

2 card

4 cookies

1 flowers

6 hug

3 present

5 breakfast

79

4 Chant. ⊚ 2.38

- Play the chant once for students to listen.
- Play the chant again and encourage the class to make up actions, e.g. draw a heart in the air for *I love you, Mom,* hug yourself for *hug,* mime offering a bunch of flowers, etc.

Chant

I love you Mom, I want to say:
Happy Mother's Day!
Flowers and hugs are on the way,
Happy Mother's Day!
I love you Mom, I want to say:
Happy Mother's Day!
Flowers and hugs are on the way,
Happy Mother's Day!

5 Make a Mother's Day card.

- Tell students that they are going to make a Mother's Day card.
- Hand out worksheets and make sure students have colored pens.

- Students cut out the hands, decorate them, and write a message.
- Move around the class offering help and asking questions: *What is it? Do you like hugs?*

> **TEACHING TIP**
>
> Elicit a message to write in the Mother's Day cards as a class, e.g. *Happy Mother's Day, Mom! I love you! From (Sara).*

> **21ST CENTURY SKILLS:**
>
> **Cultural awareness and expression**
> Students learn how to express ideas through art.

Finisher

- Play *Pass the flashcards.* See Ideas Bank (Teacher's Book page 140) for instructions.

Further practice
Workbook page 60

Holidays
Halloween pages 80–81

Classroom Presentation Tool

Objectives

To present and practice four new items of vocabulary.
To review vocabulary from the course.
To do a personalization activity that involves a simple craft activity.

Language and structures

Active: *skeleton, ghost, mask, pumpkin; cat, candles, balloons, cake, candy*
Passive: *Halloween mask, trick-or-treating*

Materials

Class Audio CD 2; *colored pens, scissors, string, tape*

Warmer

- Draw a pumpkin (or Jack-o-lantern) on the board. Ask the class *What holiday is it?*
- Write *Halloween* on the board. Say the word and ask students to repeat. Ask the class *What is Halloween? When is Halloween?* Ask the class if they celebrate around this time and what they do.

1 Listen and point. Say. 🔘 2·39

- Read the words aloud and point to each photo. Repeat the words and ask students to listen and point to the correct photo.
- Play the recording for students to listen and point to the photos. Play the recording again for students to listen, point, and repeat the words.
- Say the words again and ask students to point to the correct photos. Start slowly, then get faster and faster.

Transcript

skeleton, ghost, mask, pumpkin
ghost, skeleton, pumpkin, mask

2 Listen and number. 🔘 2·40

- Ask students to look at the photos again. Tell them that these are ways children in the USA celebrate Halloween. Children go trick-or-treating. Ask *What can you see?* Elicit the vocabulary and any other words they may know, e.g. candy, donut, orange, pumpkin, face: eyes, mouth, nose.
- Tell students to listen and write the numbers 1, 2, 3, and 4 in the correct boxes next to the photos.
- Play the recording. Pause after each item to give students time to write the numbers. With a less confident class, play the recording twice.

- Check answers by asking, e.g. *What's number (1)? Pumpkin!* etc.

Transcript

1 Look at my orange pumpkin with big eyes!
2 I'm a skeleton!
3 I have a mask. Look!
4 Look, I'm a ghost. (Ha ha ha!)

Culture note

It is very common for children and their parents to go trick-or-treating on Halloween night. Groups walk from house to house in their neighborhood, dressed in Halloween costumes. People give them candy and treats. In the past, if children didn't get a treat, they would play a trick on the person.

3 Number the pictures. Circle the words.

- Point to the pictures next to the puzzle on page 81. Elicit the words (*candle, ghost, skeleton, pumpkin, balloons, cake, mask, cat*).
- Point to the words in the word box. Say *Write the numbers next to the picture.* Point to the word *cat* and ask *Where is the cat?* Students point to the picture of the cat. Show them the example number 1 in the box.
- Point to the puzzle and the circled word cat. Say *Circle the words.*
- Move around the class as students complete the activity, offering help if necessary.

TEACHING TIP

Ask fast finishers to write the words of the objects under the pictures around the puzzle.

1 cat   2 candle   3 balloons   4 pumpkin
5 skeleton   6 ghost   7 mask   8 cake

p	u	m	p	k	i	n	c	k	l
d	g	a	h	j	k	l	a	c	b
x	c	s	k	e	l	e	t	o	n
v	b	k	n	m	p	o	i	u	g
c	y	t	r	e	w	q	a	s	h
a	b	a	l	l	o	o	n	s	o
k	d	f	g	h	j	k	l	z	s
e	x	c	c	a	n	d	l	e	t

2   6   5   1   7   4   3   8

81

Extension activity

Sing the *Rat-a-Tat-Tat* song again with the students wearing their masks.

Finisher

- Play *Draw in the air*. See Ideas Bank (Teacher's Book page 141) for instructions. Use Halloween words.

Extension activity

To review language from the course: Divide the class into groups of four to six students. Give each group a set of flashcards from any previous unit. Ask them to play a flashcard game with their set, e.g. *Little by little, Mime the word*, or *Watch my lips*. Within each group they take turns to be the teacher. Play for two minutes. Ask students to stand and walk to the next set of flashcards. They play another game with this new set of flashcards.

Further practice
Workbook page 62

4 Sing. 🎵 2•41

- Play the *Rat-a-Tat-Tat* song once for students to listen.
- Play the song again, modeling actions: flap your arms like a bat; wiggle your fingers for a spider; mime putting on a mask, etc.
- Divide the class into six groups. Give each group the name of one of the Halloween words. Play the song once more. When the group hears their word, they stand, say the line and do the action.

Rat-a-Tat-Tat
It's Halloween!
Rat-a-tat-tat!
What's this?
It's a cat!
A bat, a spider,
A pumpkin, too.
A witch and a ghost.
Woo! Woo! Woo!
It's Halloween!
Rat-a-tat-tat!
What's this?

It's a cat!
A bat, a spider,
A pumpkin, too.
A witch and a ghost.
Woo! Woo! Woo!

> **21ST CENTURY SKILLS:**
> **Cultural awareness and expression**
> Students learn how to express ideas through music and by miming actions.

5 Make a Halloween mask.

- Tell students that they are going to make a Halloween mask.
- Hand out worksheets and make sure students have colored pens, scissors, string, and tape. Students can make both masks or just one. They color their masks and cut them out.
- Move around the class offering help if necessary. Ask questions: *What is it? What color is it? Are you a (pumpkin)?* etc.

Unit 1 Happy Birthday!
Lesson 2 page 86

1 Circle the odd one out.

- Books closed. Draw a balloon on the board (a circle with a string attached to it). Ask *What is it? A balloon!*
- Draw three more balloons in a line next to the first. Make sure one balloon doesn't have a string. Ask *How many balloons? Four.* Ask *Which one is different? Why? (It has no string.)* Circle this balloon.
- Books open. Point to the completed example in number 1. Point to the other items on the page and elicit the words (*cake, present, card, candle, clown*).
- Point to the cakes in number 2 and say *Circle the odd one out.* Give students time to look and decide. Then students check with a partner. Elicit the answer (*cake 2*) and ask *Why? (It has three layers, the others have four.)*
- Students complete the remaining items. With a more confident class, allow students to work independently. Then check their answers in pairs. With a less confident class, allow students to work in pairs. Ask them to think about *why* they are different.
- Move around the class offering help if necessary.

Fast finishers

Ask fast finishers to color in the pictures. They choose one color for the items that are the same, e.g. blue balloons, and use a different color for the odd one out, e.g. a red balloon.

Extra activity

Hand out the Unit 1 flashcards to groups of students. Ask them to draw their own odd one out activity on a piece of paper. Allow them to be creative and decide what feature is different, e.g. They receive the clown flashcard: they could draw three clowns with a red nose and one clown with a blue nose, or three clowns with hair, one clown without. The groups then swap pictures with another group and find the odd one out.

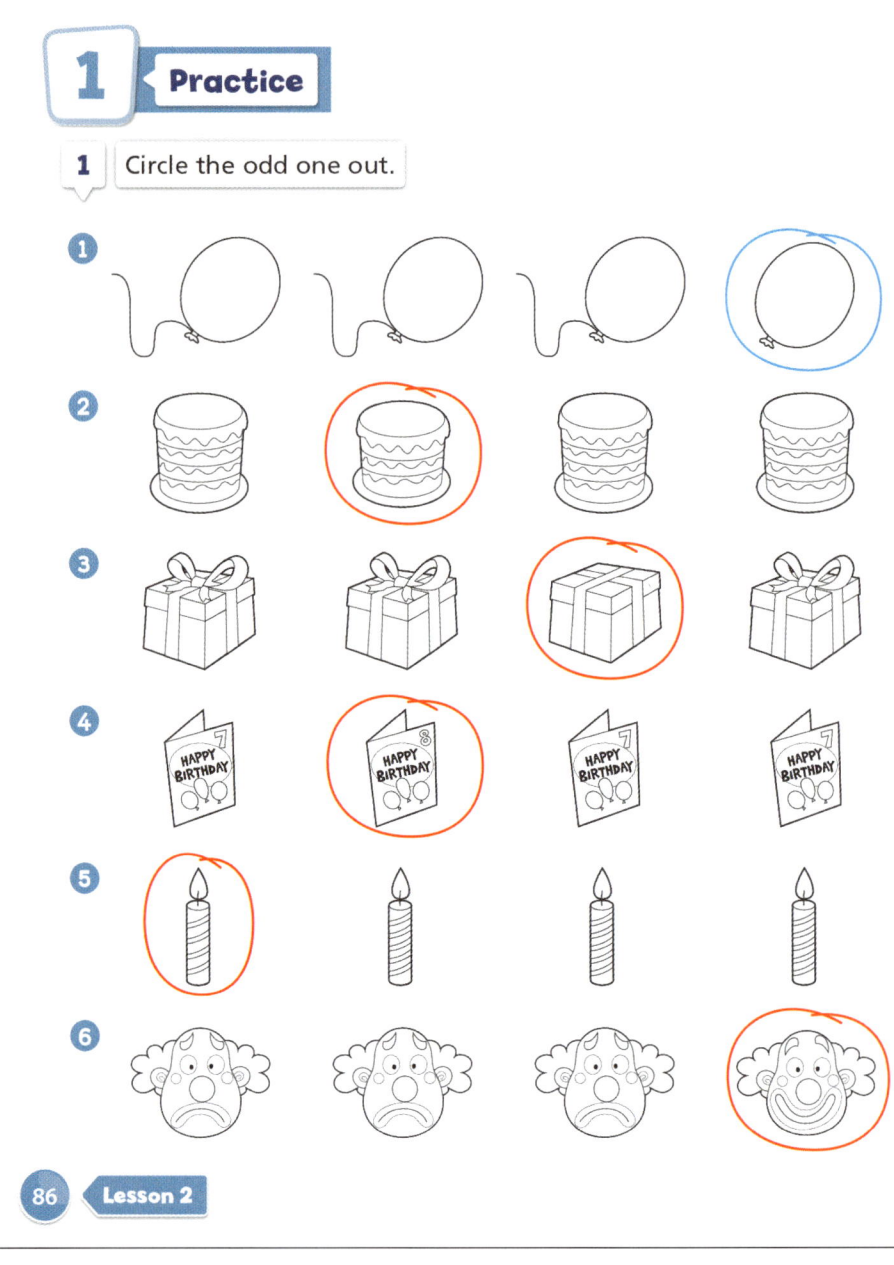

Notes

1 Draw. Count and circle.

1 3 cars / (2 cars)

2 (1 cake) / 2 cakes

3 (4 basketballs) / 3 basketballs

4 (2 robots) / 1 robot

5 6 puzzles / (3 puzzles)

6 7 candles / (5 candles)

Lesson 3 **87**

Notes

_____   _____

_____   _____

_____   _____

_____   _____

_____   _____

_____   _____

_____   _____

_____   _____

Lesson 3 page 87

1 Draw. Count and circle.

- Books closed. Slowly draw a basketball on the board line by line. After each line ask *What is it?* Take ideas from students. When they guess correctly, say *Yes! It's a basketball.* Complete the drawing.
- Draw two more basketballs and ask *How many basketballs?* Count them as a class, e.g. 1, 2, 3. Say *Well done!* Write *3 basketballs* below the picture.
- Books open. Point to the pictures and ask students what they can see. Refer them to the words below if they do not recognize the picture (*car, cake, basketball, robot, puzzle, candle*).

TEACHING TIP

Accept answers without the plural 's'. You might like to go through and elicit the plural forms of the words with students and practice the pronunciation, e.g. *puzzles*.

- Point to the cars in number 1 and say *Draw.* Tell students to start at number 1 and draw following the numbers in the correct order. When students are ready, say *Count the cars.* Elicit *There are 2 cars* and point to the circled example answer below the picture.
- Students complete the remaining items. Move around the class monitoring and offering help if necessary.
- Allow students to check answers in pairs before checking together as a class.
- To review numbers 1 through to 10, play *Lets count!* with students. See Ideas Bank (Teacher's Book page 141) for instructions.

Fast finishers

Ask fast finishers to color in the pictures. Ask them *What color is it?* as they color.

Extra activity

Put students into pairs. Ask them to take turns holding up a number of objects, or simply fingers, for their partner to count. They may use pens, pencils, books, etc. They ask their partner *How many?* Their partner answers using the plural 's' when necessary, e.g. *Five fingers*.

Unit 2 What Weather!
Lesson 2 page 88

1 What's the weather like? Read and draw.

- Books closed. Ask a pair of more confident students to come to the front of the class. Say *Draw it's sunny*. The two students each draw a sun picture on the board.

- Point to picture number 1 and ask students *What's the weather like?* Elicit *It's sunny*. Repeat a few times, inviting different pairs of students to draw rainy, stormy, and snowy.

TEACHING TIP

Being chosen to come up and draw is a nice reward for students who have worked well during the lesson.

- Books open. Point to the sentence below the first picture and say *Read*. Students read aloud the sentence *It's sunny*. Ask *What's the weather like?* Students repeat *It's sunny!* Say *Yes! Draw sunny*. Move around the class monitoring.

- When students are ready, ask them to read the remaining sentences and draw the correct weather in the pictures.

- Move around the class, offering help if necessary and giving praise.

- Check answers by asking students to exchange their books with a partner. Allow students time to look at what their partner has drawn. Encourage students to praise each other.

- Once students have finished, ask them to color their pictures in.

Extra activity

Give students a piece of paper. At the top ask them to write *What's the weather like?* Write the question on the board for students to copy. Ask students to choose their favorite type of weather and draw a picture of themselves (or with their friends and family), the weather and what they like to do when the weather is like that. They can choose the scene: they might be indoors, outdoors, at home, at school, in the park, etc. Have a show-and-tell session. Students ask *What's the weather like?* The child showing their picture answers and talks more about their picture.

2 **Practice**

1 What's the weather like? Read and draw.

It's sunny.

It's rainy.

It's snowy.

It's stormy.

88 Lesson 2

Notes

_____   _____

_____   _____

_____   _____

_____   _____

_____   _____

_____   _____

_____   _____

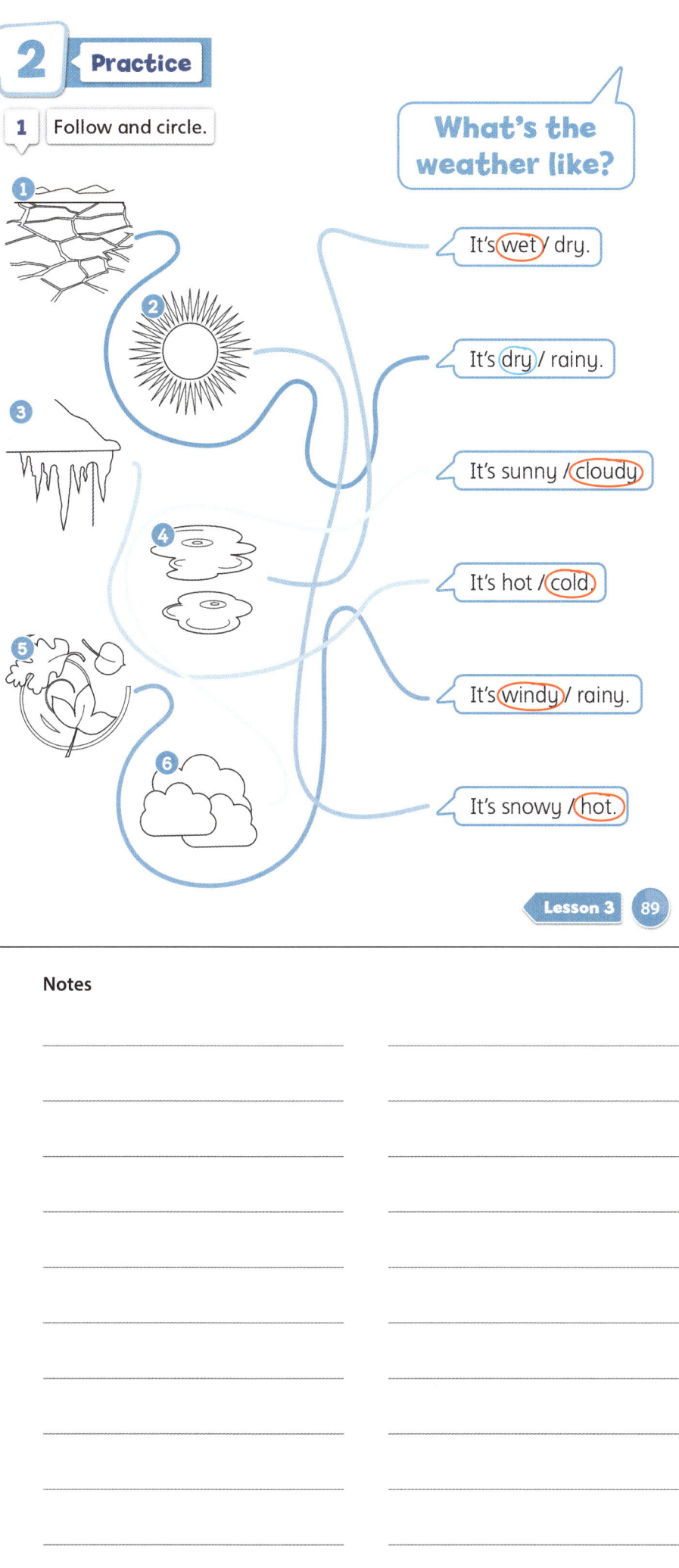

2 Practice

1 Follow and circle.

What's the weather like?

It's (wet) / dry.

It's (dry) / rainy.

It's sunny / (cloudy).

It's hot / (cold).

It's (windy) / rainy.

It's snowy / (hot).

Lesson 3 89

Notes

_____   _____

_____   _____

_____   _____

_____   _____

_____   _____

_____   _____

_____   _____

_____   _____

Lesson 3 page 89

1 Follow and circle.

- Books closed. Place the Unit 2 flashcards in a random order on the left of the board. On the right of the board write *It's wet/dry*. Draw a line connecting the flashcard *wet* to the sentence. Ask students to read aloud the sentence you've written.

- Point to the flashcard *wet* and ask students *What's the weather like? Is it wet* or *Is it dry?* Elicit *It's wet*. Say *Yes!* Draw a circle around *It's wet*.

- Books open. Point to the speech bubbles on the right and invite confident students to read each sentence aloud. Read both sentences, e.g. *It's wet. It's dry.*

- Point to picture number 1. Say *Follow and circle*. Students follow the line with a finger. Point to the circled example answer *It's dry*.

- Ask students to complete the remaining items. With a more confident class, allow students to work independently. Then students check their answers in pairs. With a less confident class, allow students to work in pairs.

- Move around the class monitoring and offering help if necessary.

- Check answers by asking *What's number (2)? It's hot.*

- Once students have finished, ask them to color their pictures in.

Extra activity

Put students into pairs. Ask one child to choose a weather condition they can see on page 89, but to keep it secret from their partner. They ask their partner *What's the weather like?* Their partner tries to guess which weather condition they have chosen by making guesses, e.g. *It's rainy*. If they guess correctly, it's their turn to choose the weather. If they guess incorrectly, they guess again.

Unit 3 My Clothes!
Lesson 2 page 90

1 Circle six words.

- Point to the letters and ask students to find and circle six clothes words.
- Point to the example circled answer *boots*.
- Ask students for the answers and write them on the board.

2 Read and write.

- Books closed. Review the clothes vocabulary.
- Books open. Point to the word *hat* in sentence 4 and then ask students to look at sentence 4 and read the word *hat*.
- Say *Read the sentence and finish the word*. Look at the first sentence and read as a class, i.e. *Put on your …* Elicit *shoes*. Point to the shoes and say *Finish the word*. Ask *Which number is it?* Elicit *1*. Repeat with the second sentence, i.e. *Put on your … boots!*
- Monitor the activity and check that students are doing it correctly. If necessary, write the word on the board to help with spelling.
- Ask students to work independently and to give answers in pairs. Elicit the answers from the pairs. At the end of the activity, students can color the pictures.

Extra activity

For fast finishers, put students into pairs. Ask them to take turns giving each other instructions to mime, e.g. *Put on your hat! Take off your shoes! Take off your jacket!* etc. If time, play as a class for two to three minutes.

1 Circle six words.

dwboots̲zaphat̲jgsjacket̲lsnshoesakesocksqot̲pants̲sn

2 Read and write.

1 Put on your s̲ h̲ oe s̲ !

2 Put on your b o̲ o t s̲ !

3 Put on your j̲ ack e̲ t̲ !

4 Take off your h̲ at!

5 Put on your p̲ a̲ n̲ t̲ s!

6 Take off your s̲ o c̲ k̲ s!

90 **Lesson 2**

Notes

3 Practice

1 Read and circle. Draw.

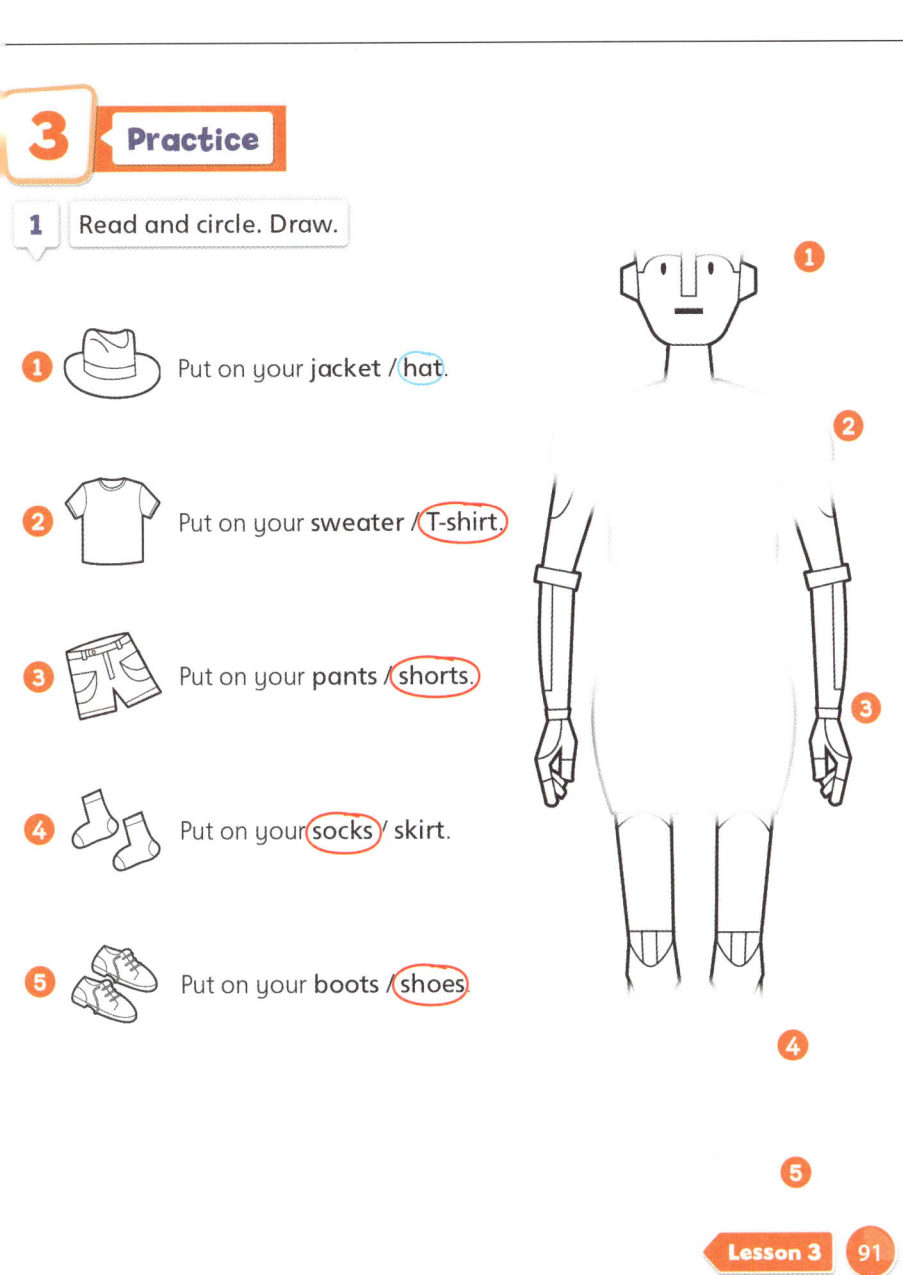

1 Put on your **jacket** / (**hat**).

2 Put on your **sweater** / (**T-shirt**).

3 Put on your **pants** / (**shorts**).

4 Put on your (**socks**) / **skirt**.

5 Put on your **boots** / (**shoes**).

Lesson 3 91

Lesson 3 page 91

1 Read and circle. Draw.

- Books closed. Draw a hat on the board. Write *Put on your jacket/hat* next to it. Point to the hat and ask *What is it? Hat!* Point to the sentence. Elicit the correct sentence *Yes! Put on your hat. Circle hat!* Circle the word hat on the board.

- Books open. Point to the clothes on the left-hand side of the page and elicit the words (*hat, T-shirt, shorts, socks, shoes*). Say *Read and circle.* Say *Do not draw yet.*

- Ask students to complete the remaining sentences. With a more confident class, allow students to work independently. Then students check their answers in pairs. With a less confident class, allow students to work in pairs.

- Move around the class checking that students are working correctly and are not drawing.

- Check answers by asking *What's number (2)? Put on your T-shirt.*

- Point to the robot on the right-hand side of the page and tell students to draw a picture of each item of clothing next to the correct number.

- If you have time, allow students to color in the clothes.

Extra activity
Do a guided coloring exercise. Say *Color the hat yellow. Color the T-shirt green.* etc. With a more confident class, put students into pairs to guide one another when they color. They take turns telling their partner what color each clothing item should be.

Notes

_____   _____

_____   _____

_____   _____

_____   _____

_____   _____

_____   _____

_____   _____

Unit 4 Home, Sweet Home
Lesson 2 page 92

1 Look and circle. Match.

- Books closed. Write *he* and *she* on the board. Say *She!* Ask the girls to stand up. Say *He!* Ask the boys to stand up. Repeat randomly for the girls and boys to stand up accordingly.

- Books open. Point to the first picture of the woman. Ask *He or she?* Elicit *She.* Read the first sentence and elicit which is the correct option. *She's in the kitchen. Yes!* Point to the circled example answer.

- Students complete the remaining sentences. Say *Do not match yet.*

- Move around the class checking that students are working correctly and are not matching the rooms.

- Allow students to check answers in pairs before checking together as a class.

- Point to picture number 1 and say *She's in the kitchen. Where's the kitchen?* Follow the example line to picture C. Ask students to match the remaining pictures. With a less confident class, work through each answer together.

- If you have time, allow students to color in the pictures.

Extra activity

Put students into pairs. Ask them to take turns calling out a room or person for their partner to point to, e.g. *Kitchen!* They point to the picture of the kitchen, or *She's in the dining room.* They point to the girl eating spaghetti, etc.

Notes

4 Practice

1 Draw. Read and write.

bed sofa bathtub table

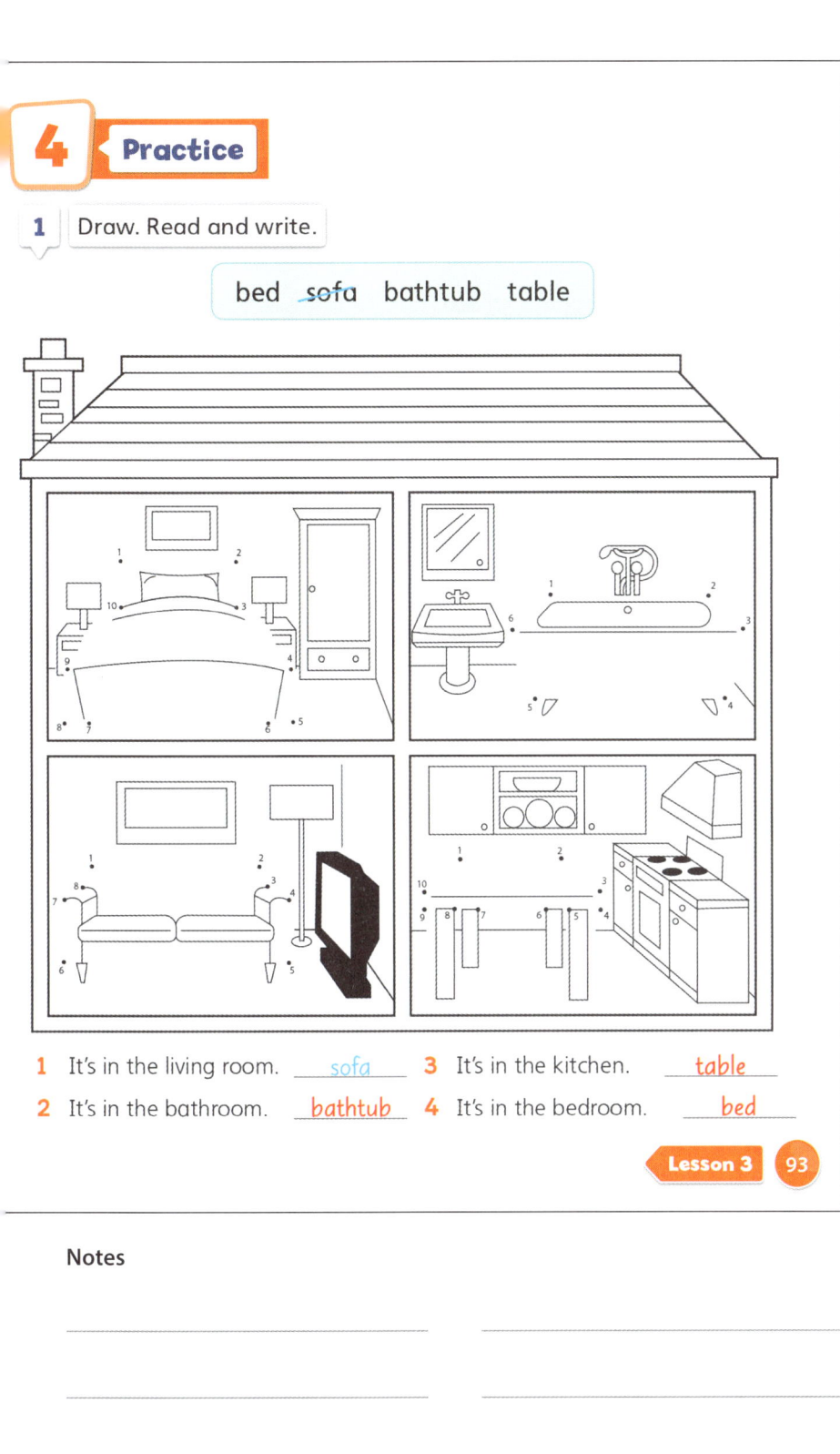

1 It's in the living room. _____sofa_____

2 It's in the bathroom. _____bathtub_____

3 It's in the kitchen. _____table_____

4 It's in the bedroom. _____bed_____

Lesson 3 93

Lesson 3 (page 93)

1 Draw. Read and write.

• Books closed. Write the numbers 1–10 in a circle on the board. Ask a confident child to come to the front of the class. Say *Follow the numbers and draw*. Ask students to count along with the child as s/he draws. Praise the child. Ask students *What is it? It's a ball!*

• Books open. Point to the house and say *Point to the bedroom*. Repeat with the other rooms. Then say *Follow the numbers and draw*.

• Move around the room checking that students are working correctly.

• Point to the bed and ask *What is it?* Elicit *Bed!* Then point to the bathtub, sofa, and table.

• Point to the first sentence below the picture and invite a confident child to read it aloud. Ask *What's in the living room?* Elicit *Sofa*. Say *Yes, here's a sofa*. Refer students to the words in the word box.

• Ask students to read the remaining sentences and write the correct words next to them. With a more confident class, allow students to work independently. Then check their answers in pairs. With a less confident class, allow students to work in pairs.

• If you have time, allow students to color in the pictures.

• If you like, play *Draw and roll* with students. See Ideas Bank (Teacher's Book page 142) for instructions.

Extra activity

Bring in some home magazines to class. Ask students to cut out pictures of sofas, bathtubs, tables, etc. and stick them on a piece of paper to create their own house collage. With a more confident class, ask students to label the furniture that they stick on.

Notes

_____

_____

_____

_____

_____

_____

_____

Unit 5 At the Beach
Lesson 2 page 94

1 Read and write. Find and circle.

- Books closed. Place the Lesson 1 action verb flashcards on the board. Elicit the words as you do so. Mime doing an action well, e.g. swim. Elicit *I can swim* from students. Repeat with another action. Then mime two actions badly to elicit *can't*, e.g. *I can't climb*.
- Books open. Point to the picture and ask students what they can see. Elicit as many actions as possible.
- Point to the two people diving off the platform in the water. Ask students if the two can dive. Elicit the sentences *I can dive* for one and *I can't dive* for the other.
- Point to the first sentence below the picture and invite a confident child to read it aloud. Ask *How do you spell dive?* Elicit *d-i-v-e*. Say *Yes!*
- Point to the two small pictures next to the sentence and ask students to find the two men again in the main picture. Say *I can't dive* and point to the circled example answer.
- Work through another example together. Point to the two dogs in number 2 and ask *Where are the dogs?* Students look in the main picture and find them. Read the sentence and elicit the action (run). Say *Write the letter r*. Say *I can run* and ask students which dog can run. They circle the correct picture.
- Move around the class monitoring and checking answers.

Extra activity

Play the miming game as in the beginning of the exercise. Divide students into two teams. Ask a child from the first team to act out a verb badly/well. Their team must answer using the correct structure and verb, e.g. the child acts swimming badly – their team shouts *I can't swim!* They win a point. A child from the next team takes their turn.

1 Read and write. Find and circle.

94 Lesson 2

1 I can't _d_ ive.

2 I can _r_ un.

3 I can't _c_ ook.

4 I can _s_ wim.

5 I can't _s_ ing.

6 I can _c_ limb.

Notes

_____ _____

_____ _____

_____ _____

_____ _____

_____ _____

_____ _____

_____ _____

5 Practice

1 Read and circle.

1 I **can** / **can't** swim.

2 I **can** / can't run.

3 I **can** / can't jump.

4 I can / **can't** fly.

5 I can / **can't** catch.

6 I **can** / can't dance.

Lesson 3 95

Lesson 3 page 95

1 Read and circle.

- Books closed. Hold up the Lesson 1 and 3 action verb flashcards one at a time and elicit the words. Start slowly, then get faster and faster.
- Divide students into two teams. Show one team one of the flashcards and tell them to all mime the action. The other team watches and shouts out the action, e.g. *dance*. If they are correct, they take a turn. Repeat a few times.
- Continue playing the game. This time draw a check and an ✗ on two separate pieces of paper. Show each team a flashcard and either the check or the ✗. They mime doing the action badly or well. The other team must elicit the correct action using the correct structure, e.g. *I can/can't jump!*
- Books open. Point to the first picture. Ask *Can he swim?* Elicit *No!* Say *Read the sentence.* Elicit *I can't swim.*
- Students complete the remaining sentences.
- Allow students to check their answers in pairs before checking together as a class.
- Allow students time to color in the pictures.

Fast finishers
Ask students to draw their own pictures to illustrate the opposite sentences, e.g. Number 1– *I can swim.* Students draw a person swimming really well.

Notes

Unit 6 Animal Fun!
Lesson 2 page 96

1 Look and write.

- Books closed. Act out each of the farm animals from Unit 6, Lesson 2 to elicit the animal words. As students guess, write the words on the board.
- Books open. Point to the picture and say *Look at all the animals!* Point to the word box and ask students to read the words aloud.
- Point to picture number 1 and elicit the animal *chicken*. Point to the example answer and the word crossed through in the word box. Say *Write the words.*
- Students complete the remaining items. With a more confident class, allow students to work independently. Then students check their answers in pairs. With a less confident class, allow students to work in pairs.
- Check answers by asking *What's number (2)? A cow!*

2 Read and write.

- Books closed. Place the chicken flashcard on the board. Ask *Can it fly?* Write *Yes* and *No* on the board. Elicit the correct answer using the structure *Yes, it can.*
- Books open. Read the first sentence or invite a confident child to read it aloud. Point to the example answer. Say *Read and write.*
- Students complete the remaining sentences. With a more confident class, tell students to write the answers with the full structure *Yes, it can / No, it can't.* With a less confident class, allow students to write *Yes* or *No.*
- Monitor and check that students are working correctly.
- Ask students who worked independently to check their answers in pairs. Elicit answers from pairs of students who have answered correctly.

Fast finishers
Ask fast finishers to color in the animals. If students finish quickly, do a guided coloring exercise. Say *Color the horse brown.* Say *Color the chicken red and yellow.*

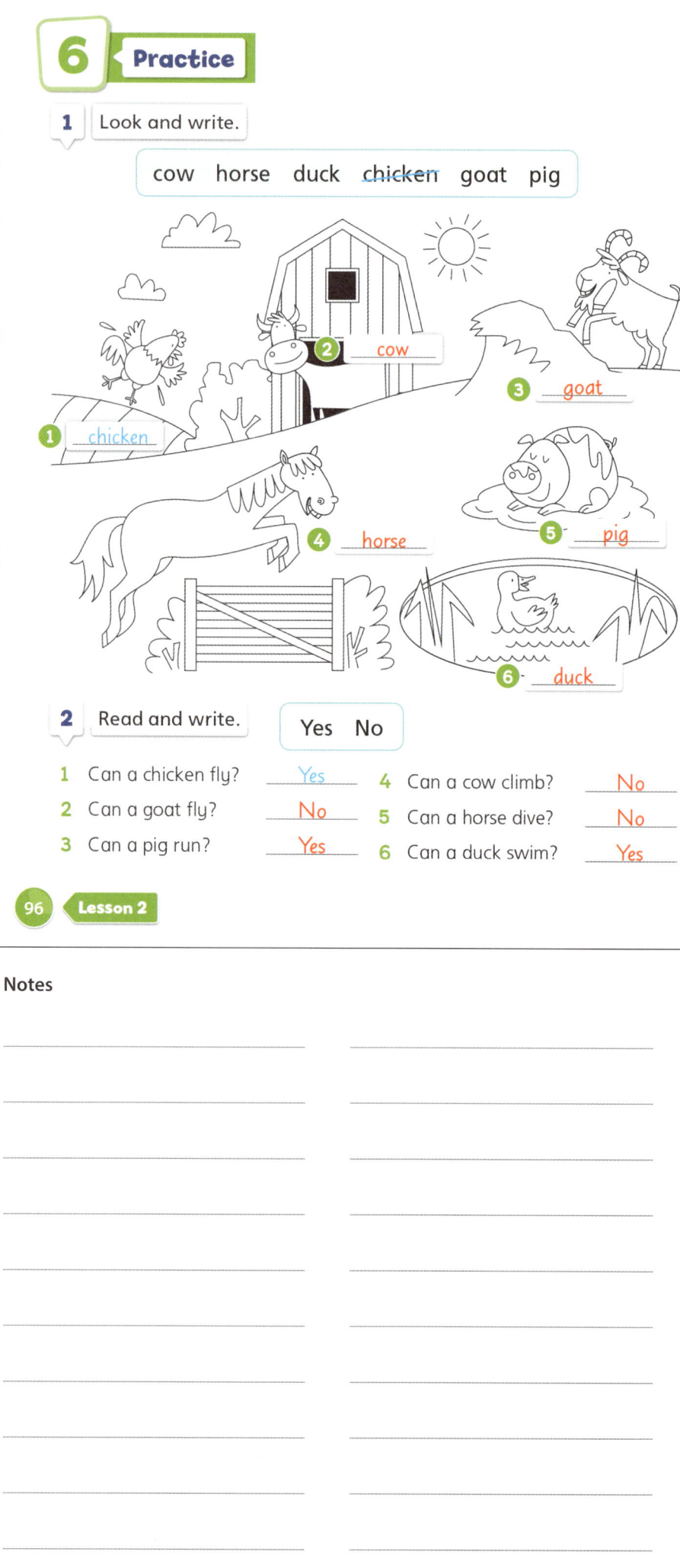

Notes

6 Practice

1 Read, make a ✓, and write.

bat fox frog squirrel

1 Can it fly? Yes, it can.

✓ bat ☐ _____

2 Can it climb? Yes, it can.

✓ squirrel ☐ _____

3 Can it fly? No, it can't.

☐ _____ ✓ frog

4 Can it jump? Yes, it can.

✓ fox ☐ _____

Lesson 3 97

Lesson 3 page 97

1 Read, make a ✓, and write.

- Books closed. Draw four circles on the board and write *fly, jump, swim,* and *run* in each circle. Hold up the fox flashcard. Ask *Can it run?* Elicit the answer *Yes, it can.* Hold up the frog flashcard and ask *Can it run?* Elicit *No, it can't.* Repeat with the bat and squirrel. Ask again using the other verbs: *fly, jump,* and *swim.*

- Books open. Invite a confident child to read the first question and answer. Hold up the bat and fox flashcards and elicit which animal can fly (bat). Point to the example answer and the ✓ next to the picture of the bat.

- Say *Read the question and answer. Make a check.* Refer students to the words in the word box. Say *Write the words.*

- Allow students to work independently. Then students check their answers in pairs.

- Move around the class offering help if necessary.

- Allow students to color in the pictures.

Fast finishers

With a more confident class, ask students to write the questions and answers about the other animal in the pair, e.g. Number 1 Fox – *Can it fly? No, it can't.*

Extension activity

Ask students to draw an animal poster. Ask them to draw one animal from Unit 6. Ask them to label it with the actions that it can and can't do, e.g. Fox – *It can run. It can jump. It can't fly. It can swim.* etc.

Notes

_____ _____

_____ _____

_____ _____

_____ _____

_____ _____

_____ _____

_____ _____

Unit 7 Picnic Time!
Lesson 2 page 98

1 Read and draw. Look and write the names.

- Books closed. Place the food flashcards from Lesson 1 on the board. Elicit the words as you do so. Draw a large plate/circle on the board.

- Ask two confident students to come to the front of the class. Tell them to listen and put two flashcards on the plate. Tell them only to put the food you like on the plate. Say, e.g. *I like pasta. I don't like rice. I like chicken*. Students place the pasta and chicken flashcards on the board. Repeat with different pairs of students.

- Books open. Point to Jo and invite a confident child to read the speech bubble. Ask *What does Jo like?* and elicit *cheese* and *salad*. Repeat with Anna and Tim.

- Say *Read and draw the food the children like*. Check that students understand to only draw the food the children like.

- Allow students to complete the pictures. Move around the class checking answers and giving praise. Say, e.g. *Yes! Jo is happy. I like cheese and I like salad*.

- Point to the table below the three children. Elicit the food items along the top (*pasta, chicken, cheese, milk, rice, salad*).

- Work through the first row in the table. Point to each food item and invite a student to look and see if there is a smiley face or a frowny face. They say e.g. *I like pasta. I like chicken. I don't like cheese*. Go through all the food items. Then ask *Who is it?* Give students time to work in pairs and read Jo, Anna, and Tim's speech bubbles again and decide which person it is (Anna). Tell students to write Anna's name in the table.

- Students work in pairs to complete the other two names. Move around the class offering help if necessary.

- Check answers by inviting students to go through each food item and make a sentence, e.g. *I like (pasta)*. etc. Finally ask students *Who is it?*

Extra activity

Put students into pairs. Ask them to go through the food items in the table and tell their partner what they like and don't like, e.g. *I like pasta. I don't like chicken*. etc. Their partner listens and draws the appropriate face below each food item. Ask students to repeat with a new partner if you have time.

Notes

_____   _____

_____   _____

_____   _____

_____   _____

_____   _____

_____   _____

_____   _____

7 **Practice**

1 What do you like? Draw ☺ or ☹ and write.

| like   don't like |

1 I _____ ice cream.

2 I _____ candy.

3 I _____ water.

4 I _____ fries.

5 I _____ milk.

6 I _____ cake.

2 What's your favorite food? Draw.

Lesson 3 99

Lesson 3 (page 99)

1 What do you like? Draw ☺ or ☹ and write.

- Books closed. Place all the food flashcards from Unit 7 on the board. Elicit the words as you do so. Write *I like* on the left-hand side of the board and *I don't like* on the right-hand side of the board. Draw a smiley face under *I like* and a frowny face under *I don't like*.
- Hold up each flashcard and place it in one of the columns, e.g. *I like rice* (place the rice flashcard in the *like* column). *I don't like chips* (place the chips flashcard in the *don't like* column).
- Ask five or six confident students to stand and say a sentence for themselves. Listen and place the flashcards in the correct column for them.
- Books open. Point to the food in the table and elicit the food words. Ask *Do you like (ice cream)?* Tell students to draw a happy face for *like* and a frowny face for *don't like*.
- Move around the room giving help if necessary and asking *Do you like (candy)?*
- When students are ready, point to the sentences below. Say *Write like or don't like.* Refer students to the words in the word box.

2 What's your favorite food? Draw.

- Tell students to look at the food and drink items they have said they like in exercise 1. Ask *What's your favorite food?* Encourage students to choose one of the items in exercise 1 or any other food.
- Point to the space on the right-hand side of the page and say *Draw your favorite food*.
- Give students time to draw and color in their picture. Then put them into pairs to tell their partner what their favorite food is.

- Go around the class and ask students *What's your favorite food?* and see if the class has similar or different tastes.

Unit 8 Numbers Everywhere!
Lesson 2 page 100

1 Count. Read and circle.

- Books closed. Ask students to count from 1 to 20 as a class. Play *Missing numbers*. See Ideas Bank (Teacher's Book page 141) for instructions. Encourage students to say the numbers in the sequence as you play.

- Hold up three pencils and count them, i.e. *1, 2, 3*. Say *I have three pencils*. Hold up five books and count them as a class, e.g. *1, 2, 3, 4, 5*. Elicit *I don't have three books*.

- Books open. Point to the first picture and say *Count the pencils*. Count the pencils together as a class. Elicit *twenty*. Say *I have twenty pencils*. Point to the circled example answer.

- Students count the remaining items and circle the correct answers. Move around the class checking answers and offering help if necessary.

- Allow students to check their answers in pairs before checking together as a class. Check answers by counting the items in each picture together as a class.

- Allow students to color in the objects.

Extra activity

Write the following items on the board: *bags, balls, dolls, sisters, brothers, dogs, cats, cars, shoes, sweaters*. Put students into pairs. Ask them to tell their partner what they have and don't have and how many, e.g. *I have seven bags. I don't have two brothers. I have eleven sweaters.* etc. Go around the class and find out who has the most of each item. Ask a student to tell you how many sisters they have. Elicit their answer, e.g *I have two sisters*. Ask another student. If their answer is different, elicit *I don't have two sisters. I have one sister*. Continue around the class until you find out who has the most sisters, etc.

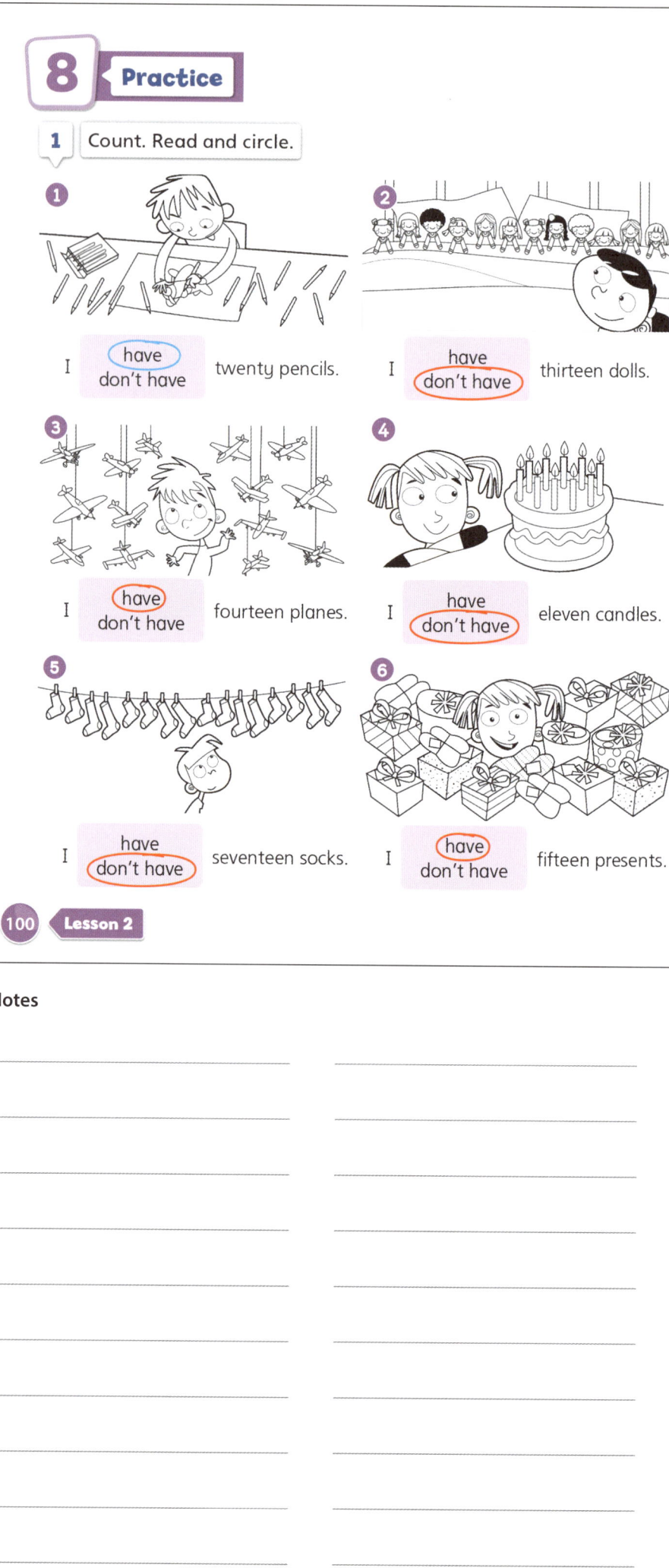

8 Practice

1 Complete the sentences. Draw.

> I have   I don't have

1 ✗ I don't have a trampoline.

   ✓ ___I have___ a skateboard.

2 ✗ ___I don't have___ a hula hoop.

   ✓ ___I have___ a jump rope.

3 ✗ ___I don't have___ a jump rope.

   ✓ ___I have___ a trampoline.

4 ✗ ___I don't have___ a skateboard.

   ✓ ___I have___ a hula hoop.

Lesson 3 **101**

Lesson 3 page 101

1 Complete the sentences. Draw.

- Books closed. Place the toys flashcards from Lesson 3 on the board. Elicit the words as you do so. Hold up a flashcard, e.g. skateboard, and say *I have a skateboard*. Place it on the board and draw a ✓ below it. Pick up the hula hoop flashcard and say *I don't have a hula hoop*. Place it on the board and draw an ✗ below it. Repeat with another pair of flashcards.

- Books open. Point to the first two sentences and say *Complete the sentence*. Say *An ✗ is for …* Elicit *I don't have*. Say *A ✓ is for …* Elicit *I have*. Refer students to the words in the word box for support.

- Move around the class monitoring and checking students are completing the exercise by referring to the ✓ or ✗ next to each sentence.

- Allow students to check their answers in pairs before checking together as a class.

- Say *Draw the toys*. Give students time to draw the items each child has in each picture. Move around the class praising students.

- Allow students time to color in the students and their toys.

> **Extra activity**
>
> Ask students to draw a picture of their favorite toy from home. Help them to write a sentence under it if it's a toy they don't know the name of, e.g. *I have a computer game. I have a scooter.* etc. Ask them to show their pictures to the class and talk about them. For example, *I have a scooter. It's red. I like my scooter.* etc.

Notes

Ideas Bank

Vocabulary games

All of the following games are excellent ways of reinforcing vocabulary in a stimulating way. Furthermore, all of them are ideal ways to start a lesson to revise lexical sets which you have already presented. Any one of them would make a useful warmer or finisher routine for your class. Consider this section as a bank of flexible Warmer and Finisher resources.

Flashcard games

Little by little

Cover a flashcard with a sheet of paper and hold it up in front of the class. Start to move the paper very slowly to reveal the card and ask students: *What is it?* Carry on revealing the flashcard, pausing to ask students *What is it?* and to allow the class to offer their ideas. Repeat with another flashcard when a student guesses correctly.

Mystery flashcard

Put a flashcard inside a large envelope and show the class the envelope. Ask students to draw what they think is inside the envelope. When everyone has finished, ask students to say what they have drawn. Then open the envelope and reveal the mystery flashcard.

Fast flashcards

Show a set of flashcards, one after the other, fairly fast. As you run through each flashcard say the word for one of the flashcards. Students call "stop" when the word and the picture match.

Find the flashcards

Ask five students to leave the classroom. Then ask the class to help you hide five flashcards somewhere in the classroom. Bring the five students back into the room and ask them to find the missing flashcards and say what they are.

Pass the flashcards

Arrange students in a circle and hand out the flashcards to different students. Play a song from the Class Audio CD while students pass the flashcards around the circle. Stop the music at random points. Each student with a flashcard holds it up and says the correct word. Alternatively, when you stop the music, you can call out a word, and the student with that flashcard must hold it up.

Kim's game

Put up a set of flashcards on the board. Point to each flashcard and ask the class: *What is it?* Repeat the correct word for each flashcard with students. Then turn each flashcard over. When the flashcards are all face down, ask again and see how many students can remember which flashcard is which.

What number is it?

Put up a set of flashcards of words you want to review with students. Below each one put a number flashcard. Say the name of a toy and ask: *What number is it?* Alternatively, say the number and ask: *What is it?*

Mime the word

Divide the class into two teams. Tell one team to choose a flashcard/word from the new vocabulary set and mime the word for the opposite team. If the opposite team guesses the word correctly and pronounces the word correctly, they score a point, otherwise the point goes to the team performing the mime.

Which one is missing?

Tell students to stand in a circle. Put a number of flashcards face up on the floor in the middle of the circle. Give students a couple of minutes to memorize them. Then tell them to turn their backs while you remove one of the flashcards. Tell students to turn back and ask them which flashcard is missing. The student who guesses first has a turn to remove one of the flashcards. Repeat several times.

Odd one out

Choose three flashcards from one lexical set (e.g. toys) and one card from a different category (e.g. classroom objects). Students have to say which flashcard does not belong with the others in the group.

Watch my lips

This activity helps students to concentrate on the mouth movements necessary to pronounce certain words. Put five flashcards up around the classroom. Explain to students that you are going to mouth a word silently and that they have to point to the right flashcard. Say the word silently, exaggerating your mouth movements. The student who points to the correct flashcard can try saying a word silently for the rest of the class to guess.

Hit the card!

Put up three or more flashcards on the board. Then invite three students to the front of the class and stand them in a line facing the board (don't position them too close). Give each of the students a small sponge ball and explain that the game is a bit like hitting the target. (Instead of sponge balls, you could use any small soft object, or make paper balls.) Say the word for one of the flashcards on the board. The players have to throw their ball at the right card and try to hit it.

What card is it?

Hide a flashcard behind your back and ask the class: *What card is it?* Listen to their answers and then show the flashcard.

What card is missing?

Show a set of flashcards one after the other. Then take one out and show the set again. Students have to identify the one that is missing.

Guess the flashcard

Put up the flashcards on the board face down, and write a number next to each one. Ask the class: *What's number (one)?* Invite a student to the front of the class and ask him/her to try and guess. After hearing the answer, lift up a corner of the flashcard and say *No* if it is wrong and *Yes* if the student guessed right. If the student guesses correctly, turn the card face up. If the student does not guess the flashcard, leave it where it is and invite another student to guess. Continue the game until all the flashcards have been guessed and are face up.

Walk to the card

Put up a few flashcards around the classroom. Explain that you are going to name the flashcards one after the other. Choose two or three students to walk as quickly as they can to the flashcard you name and stand next to it. The first person to the card is the winner.

Change places

Put up some flashcards around the classroom. Divide the class into as many groups as there are flashcards. Position the groups near their flashcard. Name two flashcards. Students in those two groups have to move and change places.

Musical flashcards

Put up some flashcards around the classroom and play some music. Students wander freely around until you stop the music and name a flashcard. They then have to go to the flashcard you named.

True or False

Bring in two shoe boxes. Label one box with a big check and the other box with a big X. Invite two students to the front of the class. Position them at some distance from the boxes and give each of them a sponge or paper ball. Show a flashcard and say a word. If the word and the flashcard match, students have to throw their ball into the box with the check on the side. If not, they throw it into the box with the X on the side. This can also be played as a team game with one team member playing against a student from the other team. The player who throws the ball into the correct box wins a point for the team.

Tic-Tac-Toe

Divide the class into two teams. Draw a 3x3 grid on the board and stick a flashcard in each cell. Each team takes a turn saying a word for one of the flashcards. If they are correct, they draw an X or an O in the cell. The first team to get three in a row wins.

Yes or No

Hold up flashcards from previous lessons and say a word (sometimes the correct word, and sometimes the wrong word). Students say whether or not the word matches the flashcard (Yes or No). Invite students to hold up flashcards and say correct or incorrect words for the rest of the class.

Four in a row

Invite a student (or a pair of students) to the front of the class. Hand the student (or students) four flashcards from previous lessons. Call out the words for the flashcards. The student (or students) stick(s) the cards on the board in the correct order. Repeat with other students and other flashcards.

Other word games

Draw and guess

Divide the class into two teams. Start drawing a known item on the board. Students from each team call out and guess what the item is. The student who guesses correctly wins a point for their team and takes a turn to draw an item on the board. If you have different colored pens, use them and ask students to name the colors too.

Memory game

Place various classroom objects of different colors on your desk. Invite students to look at the items for one minute and try to remember all the objects and what color they are. Cover or remove the items on your desk. Invite students to name as many objects (with their colors) as they can remember.

Let's count!

Ask a student to choose a number from one to ten. The student next to him/her counts up from one to that number. If this student counts correctly, they stay in the game. If a student says the wrong number or can't remember the next number, he or she is out of the game. The last student left in the game is the winner.

How many?

Draw a number (1–10) of simple objects (balls, flowers, apples, etc.) on the board. Ask students around the class to count the objects and say the correct number. This can also be played as a team game.

Draw in the air

"Draw" an object in the air with your finger. The first student to guess the object takes a turn to "draw" something else.

Bingo!

Ask students to draw a 3 x 3 grid. Ask students to write a number or word in each space from a vocabulary set. Call out the numbers or words in a random order. When a student hears their word or number they cross it out. When all of their words or numbers have been crossed out, they shout Bingo!

Picture Bingo!

Ask students to draw four vocabulary items from the unit. Call out words from that unit in random order. If a student has the matching picture, they can cross out that picture. The first student to cross out all of their pictures wins the game.

Missing numbers

Write a sequence of four numbers on the board, with one number missing (draw a line for this number to go on). Invite students to come to the board and write the missing number, or to call out the missing number for you to write. If you like, you can use flashcards and ask students to stick the correct flashcard on the board to complete the sequence.

Simon Says

Tell students that if you say 'Simon says' they should follow the instruction you give. If you do not say 'Simon says' they should remain still. Begin by saying, e.g. Simon says, touch your nose and check to see if everybody is following the instruction. Give another command. This time without Simon says. Check again. Keep giving the class instructions with or without Simon says. If students follow an instruction that doesn't start with 'Simon says' or if they fail to do what Simon says, they are out of the game. Play until one student is left.

Picture it!

Describe an animal / a monster / a person / an object to the class and tell them to draw what you are describing. See how accurately the students draw what you are describing. With a more confident class, you can invite a student to describe something to the class.

Draw and roll

Divide the class into two teams. Invite a student from one team to come to the front of the class and draw an item on the board. The students in the other team try to guess the word. If they guess correctly, they can roll a dice. The number on the dice is the number of points they score for their team.

Card games

Minute race!

Seat the students in a circle. Set a timer for one minute using iTools on the board, or your phone, or simply use a sand timer. Call out a vocabulary set, e.g. clothes. The students take turns calling out an item of clothing around the circle. They have to try and get around the circle before the minute is up. Alternatively, in a large class, they have to say as many words as they can in one minute. Play the game again. See if they can beat their record with the same vocabulary or you could change to a different set of words.

Sharkman

Draw a set of six steps leading into the sea with a stick man at the top of the steps. Draw a shark's fin poking out of the sea. Think of a word to elicit. Write lines for each of the letters in the word. Ask the students to call out letters they think are in the word, e.g. *E!* If there is an 'e', write it in the correct place in the word. If they don't get it correct, move the stick man down a step toward the sea. The students must try to finish the word before they reach the sea and the shark.

Lyrics and actions for the *Shine On!* song

Starter Unit: Hello!

Hello! Hello!
It's English time!
Hello! Hello! It's time to shine!
Let's be friendly and wave hello!
We can shine, shine on!

Hello! Hello! It's English time!

Students raise their hand and wave in time with the music.

Let's be friendly and wave hello!

Students turn to each other and wave. They can wave in pairs or groups, as long as they are looking at each other and waving

Come on, everyone!
Let's sing our song.
Shine on! Shine on!
It's time to shine!
It's time to shine!
Shine, shine on!

Come on, everyone!

Students raise their arm and move their hand as if beckoning someone towards them.

Shine, shine on!

Students raise their arms above their heads as if they are drawing a big sun around themselves.

Hello! Hello!
It's English time!
Hello! Hello!
It's time to shine!
Let's work together, you and me.
We can shine, shine on!

Let's work together, you and me.

First, students extend their hand towards another student and then bring it in and touch their chest.

Come on, everyone! Let's sing our song.
Shine on! Shine on!
It's time to shine! It's time to shine!
Shine, shine on!
(Repeat)

Wordlist

Starter Unit
eight
five
four
I'm (sad/happy).
Is it D?
Look! New neighbors.
Nice to meet you!
nine
one
seven
six
ten
three
two
Welcome!
Who's that?

Unit 1
balloon
basketball
cake
candle
car
card
clown
How old are you?
I'm eight.
Look!
Me, too!
present
puzzle
robot
There are (five) cards.
There's a (present)!

Unit 2
cloudy
cold
dry
hot
I don't understand!
It's (rainy).
Let's check.
rainy
snowy
stormy
sunny
today
wet
windy
What's the weather like (today)?

Culture 1
decorations
party games
party items
pool
sing

Unit 3
boots
cotton
hat
How about a sweater?
I'm (cold).
It's (hot).
jacket
pants
plant
Put on your (hat)!
sheep
shoes
shorts
skirt
socks
sweater
Take off your (jacket)!
Thank you.
T-shirt
wool

Unit 4
bathroom
bathtub
bed
bedroom
dining room
Don't worry.
he
(He)'s in the (yard).
I'm scared!
It's my turn!
kitchen
living room
new
old
she
(She)'s in the kitchen.
sofa
table
yard
Where's (Uncle Alex)?

Culture 2
boat
clothes
hotel

motor home
tent

Unit 5
catch
climb
cook
dance
dangerous
dive
flag
fly
I can (swim).
I can't (cook).
jump
lifeguard
run
safe
sign
sing
swim
Quick!

Unit 6
(A duck) can swim.
A horse.
asleep
awake
bat
Can (a cow) swim?
Can it fly?
chicken
cow
day time
duck
fox
frog
goat
horse
night time
No, it can't.
pig
squirrel
What's your favorite animal?
Yes, it can.

Culture 3
butterfly
chipmunk
rabbit
snail

Unit 7
candy
cheese

chicken
fries
grass
I don't like (cheese).
I feel sick!
I like (salad).
ice cream
milk
pasta
rice
salad
store
water
What's wrong?

Unit 8
block
eighteen
eleven
fifteen
fourteen
graph
How many … ?
hula hoop
I don't have (eleven) (shoes).
I have (eleven) (shoes).
jump rope
nineteen
seventeen
sixteen
skateboard
students
thirteen
trampoline
twelve
twenty
You can do it!

Culture 4
banana
packed lunch
sandwich
school lunch

Mother's Day
breakfast
cookies
flowers
hug

Halloween
ghost
mask
pumpkin
skeleton

I can ...

Unit 1 Happy Birthday!

		☹	😐	🙂
A-Z	I can say 10 words about parties in English.	☹	😐	🙂
💬	I can use *"There is"* and *"There are"* in English.	☹	😐	🙂
🎵	I can sing a song about a party in English.	☹	😐	🙂
📖	I can understand a story in English.	☹	😐	🙂

Unit 2 What Weather!

		☹	😐	🙂
A-Z	I can say 10 words about the weather in English.	☹	😐	🙂
💬	I can describe the weather in English.	☹	😐	🙂
🎵	I can sing a song about the weather in English.	☹	😐	🙂
📖	I can understand a story in English.	☹	😐	🙂

Unit 3 My Clothes!

		☹	😐	🙂
A-Z	I can say 10 clothes words in English.	☹	😐	🙂
💬	I can talk about putting on and taking off clothes in English.	☹	😐	🙂
🎵	I can sing a song about clothes in English.	☹	😐	🙂
📖	I can understand a story in English.	☹	😐	🙂

Unit 4 Home, Sweet Home

		☹	😐	🙂
A-Z	I can say 10 words about the home in English.	☹	😐	🙂
💬	I can ask and answer about where someone is in the home in English.	☹	😐	🙂
🎵	I can sing a song about a house in English.	☹	😐	🙂
📖	I can understand a story in English.	☹	😐	🙂

Unit 5 At the Beach

		😞	😐	🙂
A-Z	I can say 10 action words in English.	😞	😐	🙂
💬	I can talk about what I can and can't do in English.	😞	😐	🙂
🎵	I can sing a song about actions in English.	😞	😐	🙂
📖	I can understand a story in English.	😞	😐	🙂

Unit 6 Animal Fun!

		😞	😐	🙂
A-Z	I can say 10 animal words in English.	😞	😐	🙂
💬	I can talk about what animals can and can't do in English.	😞	😐	🙂
🎵	I can sing a song about animals in English.	😞	😐	🙂
📖	I can understand a story in English.	😞	😐	🙂

Unit 7 Picnic Time!

		😞	😐	🙂
A-Z	I can say 10 food words in English.	😞	😐	🙂
💬	I can talk about foods I like and don't like in English.	😞	😐	🙂
🎵	I can sing a song about food in English.	😞	😐	🙂
📖	I can understand a story in English.	😞	😐	🙂

Unit 8 Numbers Everywhere!

		😞	😐	🙂
A-Z	I can say 10 new numbers and 4 new toy words in English.	😞	😐	🙂
💬	I can talk about things I have and don't have in English.	😞	😐	🙂
🎵	I can sing a song about numbers in English.	😞	😐	🙂
📖	I can understand a story in English.	😞	😐	🙂

Workbook Answer Key

STARTER UNIT

Lessons 1 and 2

1 Look, read, and write.
1 one, 3 three, 5 five, 6 six, 9 nine

2 Look, read, and match. Say the letters.
1 dog   2 bike   3 scooter
4 ball,   5 kite
Children spell out the words using the English alphabet letter names.

Lesson 3

1 Look, read, and match.
1 hello   2 sad   3 happy
4 goodbye

UNIT 1

Lesson 1

1 Look, read, and make a ✓ or an X.
1 clown ✓ balloon X
2 candle X present ✓
3 cake X card ✓
4 balloon ✓ card X
5 cake ✓ present X
6 candle ✓ clown X

Lesson 2

1 Count, read, and match.
1 1 cake
2 6 clowns
3 7 candles
4 2 presents
5 5 balloons
6 4 cards

Lesson 3

1 What's missing? Match.
1 balloon   2 basketball   3 cake
4 Megabyte

2 Read, look, and circle.
1 second picture   2 first picture
3 first picture   4 second picture

3 Look, read, and match.
1 I'm three.
2 I'm eight.
3 I'm six. / Me, too!

Lesson 4

1 Are the sides the same or different? Look and circle.
1 the same   2 different
3 different   4 the same

2 Draw. Make the sides the same.
Children's own drawings.

Review

1 Look, read, and count. Write.
6 cars, 1 cake, 3 presents,
4 balloons, 5 cards, 1 robot

UNIT 2

Lesson 1

1 Read and draw.
Children's own drawings.

Lesson 2

1 Look, read, and write.
1 It's cloudy.
2 It's stormy.
3 It's sunny.
4 It's rainy.
5 It's windy.
6 It's snowy.

Lesson 3

1 Read, circle, and write.
1 stormy   2 dry   3 rainy,
4 snowy

2 Look, read, and circle.
1 It's dry.
2 It's wet.
3 It's cold.
4 It's hot.

3 Look, read, and write.
1 I don't understand! Let's check.
2 How old are you? I'm nine. Me, too!

Lesson 4

1 Read, look, and number.
3, 2, 4, 1

2 Draw the weather today. Read and write.
Children's own drawings.
Example: Today it's cold and windy.

Review

1 Look, read, and make a ✓ or an X.
1 It's sunny.   ✓
  It's rainy.   X
  It's dry.   ✓
2 It's snowy.   X
  It's rainy.   ✓
  It's windy.   ✓
3 It's hot.   ✓
  It's cold.   X
  It's wet.   ✓

2 Read and draw.
Children's own drawings.

REVISION 1

1 Look, write, and match.
1 basketball   2 card   3 puzzle
4 cake   5 candle   6 robot

2 Look, read, and write.
Across: 2 sunny, 4 snowy, 6 stormy
Down: 1 windy, 3 cloudy, 5 hot

3 Look, read, and count. Write.
1 candle
2 presents
3 clown
4 balloons
5 cards
6 cakes

4 Read, look, and number.
4, 3, 5, 2, 6, 1

UNIT 3

Lesson 1

1 Read, find, and color.
Children color the clothes in the picture.
● gray socks, ★ blue jacket,
■ yellow hat, ♦ green pants,
▲ black boots, ♣ brown shoes

Lesson 2

1 Look, read, and circle.
1 Take off your hat!
2 Put on your boots!
3 Take off your jacket!
4 Put on your sweater!
5 Put on your hat!

Lesson 3

1 Who's missing? Match. Then read and circle.
1 I'm cold.
2 A sweater!
3 A T-shirt and shorts!
4 I'm hot.

2 Look, read, and match.
1 shorts, T-shirt
2 skirt, sweater

3 Look, read, and write.
1 hat
2 T-shirt / you
3 jacket / Thanks

Lesson 4

1 Follow, read, and circle.
1 plant, cotton
2 sheep, wool
3 sheep, wool
4 plant, cotton

2 Look at some clothes. Draw.
Children's own drawings.

Review

1 Look, read, and write.
1 Put on your hat!
2 Take off your sweater!
3 Put on your jacket!
4 Put on your shoes!
5 Take off your boots!
6 Take off your T-shirt!

UNIT 4

Lesson 1

1 Look, read, and write. Match.
1 kitchen   2 dining room
3 bathroom   4 bedroom
5 yard   6 living room

Lesson 2

1 Look and read. Write *He's* or *She's*. Then match.
1 She's in the bathroom.
2 He's in the bedroom.
3 She's in the dining room.
4 She's in the living room.
5 He's in the kitchen.

Lesson 3

1 Order the story. Choose and write.
3, 2 sofa, 5, 1 bed, 6 bathtub, 4

2 Look, read, and number.
2, 4, 3, 1

3 Look, read, and write.
1 How about a hat? Thank you.
2 I'm scared! Don't worry.

Lesson 4

1 Look, read, and match.
1 old   2 new,   3 new   4 new
5 old   6 old

2 Look, read, and write.
1 old   2 new

Review

1 Look, read, and circle.
1 dining room   2 yard
3 kitchen   4 living room

REVISION 2

1 Find, circle, and write.

n	f	s	p	a	p	t	d
b	y	w	m	n	a	s	r
s	i	e	g	o	n	a	j
l	b	a	t	h	t	u	b
e	t	t	o	w	s	u	w
b	u	e	r	s	y	c	a
o	q	r	k	o	p	e	l
o	e	t	z	f	m	s	o
t	x	i	t	a	b	l	e
s	n	a	v	h	g	c	r

1 pants   2 sweater   3 sofa
4 table   5 boots   6 bathtub

2 Look, write, and match.
1 yard   2 jacket   3 bathroom
4 shoes   5 bed

3 Look, read, and number.
4, 2, 3, 1

4 Find, read, and write.
1 bedroom.
2 kitchen.
3 living room.
4 yard.

UNIT 5

Lesson 1

1 Look, read, and write.
1 sing   2 run   3 dive   4 cook
5 swim   6 climb

Lesson 2

1 Read, look, and number.
1 Girl diving into pool.
2 Man in chef's hat.
3 Boy swimming in pool.
4 Girl at the top of the rocks.
5 Boy on diving board looking scared.
6 Woman by barbecue.
7 Little girl in small pool.
8 Girl at bottom of the rocks looking nervous.

Lesson 3

1 Read, circle, and write.
1 dance   2 jump   3 climb
4 fly

2 Look, match, and write.
1 j – ump – jump
2 c – atch – catch
3 d – ance – dance
4 f – ly – fly

3 Look, read, and match.
1 I don't understand! Let's check.
2 Oh no! Quick!

Lesson 4

1 Look, read, and circle. Color the flags green or red.
1 dangerous   2 safe
3 dangerous   4 safe
Safe – green flag, dangerous – red flag

2 Look, read, and write.
1 dangerous
2 safe
3 dangerous
4 safe

Review

1 Write *can* or *can't* for you. Look and match.
1 third picture   2 fourth picture
3 second picture   4 sixth picture
5 first picture   6 fifth picture
Children's own answers.
Example answers:
1 I can swim.
2 I can jump.
3 I can't dance.
4 I can run.
5 I can't fly.
6 I can sing.

UNIT 6

Lesson 1

1 Find, circle, and match.
goat 3, pig 4, chicken 6, horse 2, duck 1, cow 5

Lesson 2

1 Read and match. Write *Yes, it can.* or *No, it can't.*
1 Can a horse jump?
   fourth picture – Yes, it can.
   Can it fly? No, it can't.
2 Can a pig sing?
   second picture – No, it can't.
   Can it run? Yes, it can.
3 Can a goat climb
   first picture – Yes, it can.
   Can it dance? No, it can't.
4 Can a bird cook?
   fifth picture – No, it can't.
   Can it fly? Yes, it can.
5 Can a duck swim?
   third picture – Yes, it can.
   Can it jump? No, it can't.

Lesson 3

1 Read, choose, and write.
1 squirrel   2 bat   3 frog   4 fox
5 animal

2 Look, read, and color. Write.
1 squirrel   2 bat   3 fox   4 frog
Children color the squirrel gray,
the bat black, the fox brown, and
the frog green.

3 Look, read, and write. Draw.
animal, scared, worry, favorite,
squirrel
Children draw a picture of
a squirrel.

Lesson 4

1 Look, read, and circle.
1 day, asleep
2 night, awake
3 day, awake
4 night, asleep

2 Read and draw. Write.
Children's own answers and
drawings.
Example: It's day time. I'm awake. /
It's night time. I'm asleep.

Review

1 Read, write, and circle.
1 fox, No, it can't.
2 frog, Yes, it can.
3 bird, No, it can't.
4 goat, Yes, it can.
5 bat, Yes, it can.
6 squirrel, No, it can't.

REVISION 3

1 Unscramble and write.
1 fox   2 frog   3 dog   4 goat

**2 Look, read, and write. Find the
mystery animal.**
1 imb   2 catch   3 squirrel
4 cow   5 duck   6 dive   7 dance
The mystery animal is a chicken.

3 Look, read, and write.
1 I can't cook.
2 I can swim.
3 I can climb.
4 I can't dive.

4 Look, read, and match.
1 Yes, it can.
2 No, it can't.
3 Yes, it can.
4 No, it can't.
5 No, it can't.
6 Yes, it can.

UNIT 7

Lesson 1

1 What's next? Look, read, and write.
1 salad   2 pasta   3 milk
4 cheese   5 rice   6 chicken

Lesson 2

**1 Read and draw ☺ or ☹. Write *like*
or *don't like*.**
1 ☺, like
2 ☺, like
3 ☹, don't like
4 ☹, don't like
5 ☺, like
6 ☺, like

Lesson 3

1 Look, read, and match. Write.
1 third picture, candy
2 fourth picture, water
3 first picture, fries
4 second picture, ice cream

**2 Look, read, and unscramble.
Match.**
1 I like ice cream. – second picture
2 I like candy. – fourth picture
3 I like water. – first picture
4 I like fries. – third picture

3 Look, read, and number.
first picture 2, 1
second picture 4, 3

Lesson 4

**1 Look and number in order. Read
and write.**
5 cheese store, 3 milk, 1 cow, grass,
4, 2

2 Look, read, and write.
1 store   2 grass

Review

1 Follow, write, and draw ☺ or ☹.
1 I don't like pasta. – fifth picture –
pasta – ☹
2 I like ice cream. – third picture –
ice cream – ☺
3 I don't like fries. – first picture –
fries – ☹
4 I like cheese. – sixth picture –
cheese – ☺
5 I don't like milk. – second
picture – milk – ☹
6 I like candy. – fourth picture –
candy – ☺

UNIT 8

Lesson 1

**1 Count and write the number. Read
and circle.**
1 17, seventeen balloons
2 12, twelve boats
3 18, eighteen books
4 11, eleven balls
5 14, fourteen presents
6 19, nineteen chairs

Lesson 2

**1 Count and write the number. Write
have or *don't have*.**
1 16, I don't have nineteen
pencils.
2 15, I don't have seventeen
books.
3 12, I have twelve hats.
4 11, I don't have fifteen rulers.
5 20, I have twenty socks.
6 13, I don't have fourteen shoes.

Lesson 3

1 Order the story. Choose and write.
4, 6 fourteen, 1 trampoline, 3, 2
I have, jump rope, 5 twelve, I don't
have

2 Follow, read, and write.
1 first child, skateboard
2 fourth child, hula hoop
3 second child, jump rope
4 third child, trampoline

3 Look, read, and number.
Girl: 3, 2, Boy: 1

Lesson 4

**1 Count and write the numbers.
Color the blocks.**
skateboard 6, scooter 8,
hula hoop 11, kite 5

2 Look, read, and match.
1 second speech bubble
2 first speech bubble

Review

1 Match and write.
14 fourteen, 13 thirteen,
18 eighteen, 11 eleven,
17 seventeen

2 Look, read, and number.
4, 2, 1, 3

REVISION 4

1 Look, match, and write.
   1 s – alad – salad
   2 w – ater – water
   3 r – ice – rice
   4 c – andy – candy
   5 p – asta – pasta
   6 m – ilk – milk

2 Find, circle, and match. Write.
sixteen 16, twelve 12, nineteen 19, twenty 20, fifteen 15, eleven 11

3 Look and write *like* or *don't like*.
I don't like cheese. I like rice.
I like salad. I don't like chicken.
I don't like fries. I like ice cream.

4 Look, read, and make a ✓ or an ✗.
chicken ✓, duck ✗, trampoline ✗, skateboard ✓, T-shirt ✓, sweater ✗

HOLIDAYS

Mother's Day

1 Write the words. Find and number.
   1 present **2** flowers **3** hug
   4 breakfast **5** card **6** cookies
first picture – 6
second picture – 3
third picture – 1
fourth picture – 2, 4
fifth picture – 5

2 Design a Mother's Day breakfast. Draw or write.
Children's own drawings or answers.

Halloween

1 Look, read, and write.
Across: 1 cat, 3 candle, 4 skeleton, 5 pumpkin, 7 ghost
Down: 1 cake, 2 balloons, 6 mask

2 Design two pumpkin faces. Draw and color.
Children's own drawings.

Notes

Notes